WORDWORKS

Exploring Language Play

Bonnie von Hoff Johnson

fulcrum resources
Golden, Colorado

For Tyke,
who is number one in my book

Library of Congress Cataloging-in-Publication Data

Von Hoff Johnson, Bonnie.
    Wordwords : exploring language play / Bonnie von Hoff Johnson.
        p.   cm.
    Includes bibliographical references (p.   ) and index.
    ISBN 1-55591-402-0 (paperback)
    1. Language and languages—Study and teaching. I. Title.
P51.V66   1999
418'.007—dc21   99–29507
                                                                      CIP

Printed in the United States of America
0 9 8 7 6 5 4 3 2 1

Cover illustration: © 1999 Lauren McAdam
Cover design: Alyssa Pumphrey
Interior illustrations: Insight Creative Services

Fulcrum Publishing
350 Indiana Street, Suite 350
Golden, Colorado 80401-5093
(800) 992-2908 • (303) 277-1623
www.fulcrum-resources.com

Contents

A Potpourri of Language Play · 185

Foreword

Serious scholarship, serious fun. These four words capture the essence, spirit, and originality of *Wordworks: Exploring Language Play.* After reading just the first sentence in the first chapter, the reader knows that this book was written by an experienced professional—one who has taught, one who knows children and adolescents, and one who knows language. She writes with clarity, beauty, and a teasing wit.

Word and language play largely has been shortchanged in the schools, and that is a pity, because play with words comes naturally. Herbert Kohl observed, "Throughout the world people play word games, invent or repeat riddles and jokes, solve puzzles, sing and chant. ... Through this play with words, as well as through poetry and stories, people discover themselves as speakers and learn to develop their own personal voices" (*A Book of Puzzlements,* Schocken Books 1981, p. x).

Each of the ten chapters in Bonnie von Hoff Johnson's refreshing volume presents engaging, well-researched facts and stories about dimensions of word play. Each chapter also sets forth descriptions of creative teaching activities and recommends books for children and teachers. The author has taken complicated or standard topics under the vocabulary tent and has brought them to life. Her chapters on names, idioms, proverbs, and established slang are enlightening, imbuing the reader with "I never knew that" wonder. Fans of the enduring hink hink riddles will delight in meeting new hink hink and pink pink cousins of their old friends. Each chapter holds pearls from the author's research that are destined to be cited from the teachers' lounge to the cocktail lounge. Did you know, for example, that hairdressers coin more creative names for their businesses (e.g., Curl Up and Dye) than perhaps any other type of business owner, or that the slang term *clink* has been around since 1785 and *geek* since 1876?

Dr. von Hoff Johnson has been a professional educator for more than 25 years, having taught learners from preschool through graduate school. She is widely published, having written articles, chapters, instructional books, and even an instructional game on word play. Her extensive background, scholarly interest in language, and keen intellect permeate this volume. The book was written for teachers, who will find it an invaluable reference in their work. Additionally, *Wordworks: Exploring Language Play* will be discovered and cherished by language buffs of every stripe. This book is serious scholarship, serious fun!

—Dale D. Johnson, Professor of Education
Past President, International Reading Association

Preface

Not to know is bad; not to wish to know is worse.

I wasn't born yesterday, and I know that something is rotten in Denmark when language play is given the brush-off in education. Finding a reference work that combines research with down-to-earth teaching suggestions is like looking for a needle in a haystack. People who live in glass houses shouldn't throw stones, and that is why I wrote this book. Although the work's primary audience is classroom teachers, it should be just what the doctor ordered for word hounds, too.

The book is divided into ten chapters. Chapter 1, "Names," introduces the reader to O. O. Oops, a surgeon; Eek, Alaska; and Smooth Operators, hairdressers. The hink pink family is discussed in Chapter 2. Question: What could you call a person who is snotty about a piece of corn? Answer: a cob snob. The reader hops on the bandwagon of idioms in Chapter 3 and learns some history to boot. Chapter 4, "Established Slang," investigates handy-dandy words that would bring a smile to the most dyed-in-the-wool, hoity-toity fuddy-duddy. Multiple-meaning words are the topic of Chapter 5. Did you know that a *dense* population can cause traffic problems? Chapter 6, "Proverbs," reminds us that "Half a loaf is better than none," but "People do not live by bread alone." Mother Murphy's Moo Burger restaurant is the scene for an alike-and-different activity in Chapter 7. At this dining establishment, one critic refers to the meat as "well-cooked"; another describes it as "heat-tortured." Chapter 8, "Word Formation," examines affixes (not so yawnsville), abbreviations (e.g., AP, UV), and so on. In Chapter 9, the reader is taken back to the 1800s, when fried hotcakes (i.e., cornmeal fried in bear grease) were so wildly popular that the simile "to sell like hotcakes" was born. "A Potpourri of Language Play," Chapter 10, points out how euphemisms can comfort or con. Through anagrams, "aside" becomes "ideas." The reader meets a *gang* of outlaws and a *gang* of elks. Finally, slogans, mottoes, and catchphrases that have helped to shape American history are presented.

When eating a fruit, think of the person who planted the tree.
I am grateful to:
Dale, who daily shows me that *in the eyes of one who loves, pockmarks are dimples.*
Suzanne Barchers, Fulcrum Publishing, who is wise enough to know that *one should not be afraid to go out on a limb, because that's where the fruit is,* and that *humor is the hole that lets the sawdust out of a stuffed shirt.*

Susan Hill, Fulcrum Publishing, who understands that *a pat on the back,* though only a few vertebrae removed from *a kick in the pants, is miles ahead in results.*

Mary Anna and Stanley von Hoff. *The apple doesn't fall far from the tree.*

Deb Gallagher, John Smith, Jenny Cai, and Mingshui Cai. *It is only when the cold season comes that we know the pine and cypress to be evergreens.*

Lucille Lettow, who knows that *if you drop gold and books, pick up the books first, then the gold.*

CHAPTER 1

Names

You name it; if it exists, the name of the game is to give it a name. Humans seem to have a need to name everyone and nearly everything. They name pets, boats, homes, and cars. Names are necessary to eliminate referent confusion (e.g., that is a petunia, this is a sunflower). When we want to honor a person, we name someone or something after that person. If we try to impress others, we "drop names" ("When I had lunch with Superintendent Wilmar ..."). We have names for people and things when we can't remember their names. There are What's-her-name and What-cha-ma-call-him. There are gizmos, doohickeys, thingamabobs, and thingamajigs. We make up names for people and things when an existing word does not fit our lexical needs. The concept of "bagonizing" (i.e., nervously waiting for checked luggage at an airport) recently was coined because no other name quite filled the bill (Crystal 1995).

We give nicknames to people we love (Sweetie, Little Tykie), despise (Creepo), or want to demean (Birdbrain). Places and things have nicknames, too. Boston is Beantown and the Athens of America; the USS *Constitution* is Old Ironsides. It probably comes as no surprise that there is a name for the study of names: onomastics. Onomasticians have their own organization and journal. Birds of a feather flock together.

This chapter is divided into three sections: names of people, names of places, and names of things. Activities that you can use with your students are recommended throughout each section.

People

Keeping Up with the Joneses:
Real and Imaginary Characters

Americans have invented a motley crew of sister and fellow denizens. Some are imaginary; others are based on actual people. Yes sirree, Bob, there are Mr. Big and Mr. Nice Guy, Big Brother, Casper Milquetoast, Good-time Charlie, Gloomy Gus, Joe Blow, Joe College, Joe Schmoe, Johnny-on-the-Spot, and Johnny-Come-Lately. But hold it, Buster! Where in Sam Hill are the women? They usually come as part of a pair: Jane Doe, John Doe; a Barbie doll, a Ken doll; Jane Q. Public, John Q. Public. Why isn't the representation even-Steven? Women should raise Cain, for Pete's sake.

A Goody-Two-Shoes, one who could not be classified as a party animal, can be either gender. Ammer (1992) stated that the name came from a female character in a 1765 nursery tale who happily received and displayed a pair of shoes after owning just one shoe.

If you look at photographs from World War II, you might spot the words "Kilroy was here." According to Smith (1969), James I. Kilroy, an inspector in a shipyard, wrote the sentence with chalk on parts of war vehicles and vessels. American GIs saw the sentence in many locations overseas. The soldiers themselves began writing "Kilroy was here" in various places. Although Kilroy died in 1962, Americans occasionally spot his surname in this country and others.

Activity ....

Your younger students might have heard of John Henry and Paul Bunyan, but have they heard of Angelica "Swamp Angel" Longrider? Read the book *Swamp Angel* by Anne Isaacs (1994) to your class. It is a tall tale about a gigantic baby who grows up to be a fearless, persistent woman. When you have finished the story, ask the children to think of words or groups of words that describe Angelica (e.g., brave, doesn't give up). Ask the children if they know other people who are like Angelica in these ways. A helpful resource for this type of activity is *Picture Books to Enhance the Curriculum* by Jeanne McLain Harms and Lucille Lettow (1996). The reference organizes picture books by theme. The theme "Behavior," for example, lists books that contain characters who are bored, bossy, cooperative, greedy, lazy, patient, and so on.

Have older students keep a list of first names and surnames used to refer to a type of individual (e.g., a Rambo, a Scrooge, a Scarlett O'Hara, a Barney Fife, a Brutus, a Napoleon, a Picasso), an inclusive group (e.g., every Tom, Dick, and Harry), a company (e.g., Ma Bell, Baby Bell), or a name used to mean something else (e.g., a John Hancock). Ask students to present their lists at designated times and have them explain any entries that are unfamiliar to classmates. Here are some suggested resources and categories.

Newspapers
Cartoon characters (e.g., Garfield, Dilbert)
Local ads (e.g., car dealers, appliance store owners)
Business section (e.g., "The Blues" for Blue Cross/Blue Shield, names of moguls such as Bill Gates)

Television
Characters in classic series (e.g., Archie Bunker, Carol Brady, Eddie Haskell)
Current TV characters and broadcasters

Books
Children's book authors (e.g., Dr. Seuss, Judy Blume)
Other authors and their characters (e.g., Charles Dickens and Fagin, Arthur Conan Doyle and
    Sherlock Holmes, Mark Twain and Tom Sawyer)

Film
Characters from well-known films (e.g., Dorothy, Indiana Jones, Darth Vader)
Characters and stars from current hit movies

Additional Categories
Music (e.g., Mozart, Bob Dylan, current rock and country stars)
Scientists (e.g., Marie Curie, Einstein)
Inventors (e.g., Ford, Edison)
Artists (e.g., Rembrandt, Warhol)

Was There Really a Mr. Silhouette?
Eponyms

Yes, there was a Mr. Silhouette, although he probably was addressed as "Monsieur Silhouette." The word "silhouette" is an eponym, that is, a word named after a person. Etienne de Silhouette was a controller-general in eighteenth-century France. Various authors have suggested different reasons that the dark outlines, usually human profiles, were named after Silhouette. Louis (1983) stated that Silhouette "was highly skilled at the art of cutting profiles out of paper" (p. 116). Almond (1985) pointed out that on the job, Silhouette was known for his economic cutbacks and downsizing; therefore, "in this spirit of economy, portraits in black-and-white outline were named 'silhouettes' in honor of the financier whose economy had suggested them" (p. 220). *The American Heritage Dictionary of the English Language* (1975) stated that the origin is "French, short for *portrait à la silhouette*, from *silhouette*, object intentionally marred or made incomplete, something of ephemeral value, after Etienne de Silhouette (1709–1717), with reference to his evanescent career (March–Nov. 1759) as a French controller-general" (p. 1205). Room (1994) believed the penny-pinching theory to be the most plausible, "since this would have been the most widely known" (p. 160).

Activity..

All of the following words in italics are eponyms, words named after people. The brief information about each eponym is true. The words that are not in italics (i.e., diamond, dresser, zakoo, and soon) are not eponyms, and the information about each of these words is false. Have older students guess which words are eponyms. Then have them check their guesses by looking up the words in an unabridged dictionary. The origins of the words will tell students if their guesses are correct. If your students would like to replicate this activity using different words, J.L.H. Strouf's *The Literature Teacher's Book of Lists* (1993) contains a lengthy list of eponyms you can share with them.

ampere—The name of André Marie Ampère (1775–1836) was given to a unit of electric current. Ampère was a French mathematician and physicist.

bloomers—Amelia Bloomer (1818–1894), fed up with the unwieldy attire of her day, began sporting pants, or bloomers, in 1851.

boycott—Captain Charles Boycott (1832–1897) was shunned in 1880 when he tried to collect exorbitant rents from Irish tenants.

braille—Louis Braille (1809–1852) was blind himself. As a teacher of the blind in France, he developed the braille system for reading and writing.

Bunsen burner—This fixture in nearly every high school science lab is named after Robert Wilhelm Bunsen (1811–1899), a German professor of chemistry.

cardigan—During the charge of the Light Brigade in the Crimean War, British general James Thomas Brudenell, the 7th Earl of Cardigan (1797–1868), is said to have worn a warm piece of clothing that bears his name today.

diamond—This hard, precious gem is named for Jean-Claude Diamonde (1716–1762), a French miner who discovered the rough stones in an African mine.

diesel—Rudolf Diesel, a German engineer, lent his name to this type of fuel. He lived from 1858 to 1913.

dresser—Sylvia Dresser (1720–1780), from Birmingham, England, introduced this piece of furniture to the British upper class.

Fahrenheit—German physicist Gabriel Daniel Fahrenheit (1686–1736) invented the mercury thermometer.

Ferris wheel—American George W.G. Ferris designed the first Ferris wheel for an exhibition in Chicago in 1893.

kazoo—Bashpinall Kazoo (1820–1870), a Turkish musician, introduced this instrument that nearly everyone can play.

leotard—Jules Leotard (1842–1870) was a circus performer who wore the snug piece of clothing during shows.

maverick—Samuel Augustus Maverick (1803–1870) was a Texas resident who wouldn't brand his livestock.

mesmerize—The verb "mesmerize" comes from the practice of "mesmerism," which is similar to hypnotism. Mesmerism was named for Franz Anton Mesmer (1734–1815), an Austrian physician.

Oscar—The coveted statuette in the American film industry, awarded by the Academy of Motion Picture Arts and Sciences, was named in 1931. An employee of the Academy said that the statuette resembled her uncle, Oscar Pierce.

saxophone—Adolphe Sax (1814–1894) patented his musical instrument in France in 1843.

scissors—The ancient Greek, Herodotus Scissorus, is credited with inventing the first pair of scissors in 456 B.C.

teddy bear—The popular toy has been called "Teddy" in America since President Teddy Roosevelt (1858–1919) spared the life of a young bear while he was hunting. A cartoonist captured the event, and toy bears soon were referred to as teddy bears.

tent—Although types of tents have been used for centuries, the modern tent, as we know it, takes its name from the Hosiah Tentum family of Philadelphia. The Tentums hand-stitched durable tents from 1780 to 1816.

volt—The voltage referred to in "DANGER: HIGH VOLTAGE" signs was derived from the name of Italian physicist Count Alessandro Volta (1745–1827).

watt—Watts (in a 100-watt lightbulb, for instance) are named after British inventor James Watt (1736–1819).

What's for Dinner?
Food Eponyms

Caesar salad is an eponym. The name and ingredients (Parmesan cheese, olive oil) suggest that its origin lies in a highbrow Roman restaurant or a villa in ancient Rome. Baloney! According to Shook (1994), Tijuana, Mexico, restaurateur Caesar Cardini first concocted the salad (circa 1920–1930).

Here are some other food eponyms: oysters Rockefeller (named after John D. Rockefeller (1839–1937)), peach melba and melba toast (named after the opera singer Nellie Melba (1861–1931)), eggs Benedict (named after New Yorker Samuel Benedict; created at the Waldorf-Astoria Hotel in 1894), and graham crackers (named after Sylvester Graham (1794–1851), a nutrition advocate).

Activity

In small groups or as a class, have students design a food-eponym menu using their names. All courses and beverages should be represented. For example, Cai Ming is a student in your class. Here is his appetizer.

Mushrooms Ming
a memorable, mouthwatering blend of garlic, onion,
and herbs marinated to magnificence—$3.95

Menus from actual restaurants will help students with format and expectations of diners (e.g., "a 15% gratuity will be added for parties over 6"). Don't forget to add up what a meal would cost from the class's menu. For menus from restaurants in big cities, check an Internet resource such as *World Wide Web Yellow Pages,* available in the reference section of bookstores and libraries.

His Rotundity or
Father of American Independence?
Nicknames for People

It must be the indomitable creative human mind that insists on giving people nicknames. Even the ancient Egyptians had nicknames for each other. Dickson (1996) commented, "Losing seemingly little in translation, common nicknames in the Egypt of yore included Red, Buddy, Tiny, Lazy, Ape, Frog, Donkey, and Big Head." (p. 155).

Some nicknames are based on romance. These rear their saccharine heads in the local newspaper close to every Valentine's Day (e.g., "To my Pookie ... Your Bun Bun"). Cruel nicknames are used for body size (Shrimp, Lardo), intelligence (Brain, Dummy), and personality traits (Blabbermouth, Tightwad, Wimp). Nicknames commonly are short-ened forms of first names (Lar for Larry, Lor for Lorraine).

World leaders have been given nicknames: Bloody Mary (Queen Mary I of England), the Iron Chancellor (Otto von Bismarck), and the Iron Lady (Margaret Thatcher). Many think we are too hard on our presidents these days. Nicknames for recent presidents include Tricky Dick for Richard M. Nixon, the Teflon President for Ronald Reagan, George "No New Taxes" and "Read My Lips" Bush, and Slick Willie for Bill Clinton. Now, get a load of these nicknames for presidents of "the good old days." John Adams was called His Rotundity, James Buchanan was referred to as the Do-Nothing President, William Henry Harrison was known as Old Granny, Ulysses S. Grant's nickname was Useless Grant, Rutherford B. Hayes was called His Fraudulency, and William McKinley was known as Wobbly Willie (Shook 1994; Partin 1992). The nicknames for presidents of long ago remind one of what two other former world leaders had to say about history. Winston Churchill said, "The further backward you look, the further forward you are likely to see." Harry S. Truman commented, "The only thing new in the world is the history you don't know."

Not all presidential nicknames, however, have been unflattering. John Adams, in addition to His Rotundity, also was called the Father of American Independence. Other complimentary nicknames include Father of the Declaration of Independence (Thomas Jefferson), Father of the Constitution (James Madison), Handsome Frank (Franklin

Pierce), the well-known Honest Abe (Abraham Lincoln), Grover the Good (Grover Cleveland), and, more recently, the Great Communicator (Ronald Reagan). Here are two helpful resources for those who want to pursue the study of presidential nicknames: *The Social Studies Teacher's Book of Lists* by Ronald L. Partin (1992), and *By Any Other Name* by Michael D. Shook (1994). Shook's book gives brief explanations about how each nickname was acquired.

Other well-known Americans have had nicknames, too. Some nicknames reflect courage and compassion (Harriet Tubman: Moses; Clara Barton: Angel of the Battlefield). Some speak of military capabilities (General George Patton: Old Blood and Guts; General Norman Schwarzkopf: Stormin' Norman). Nicknames for those in the entertainment field include the Greatest Showman on Earth (P. T. Barnum), the Little Sparrow (Edith Piaf), the Father of Rock and Roll (Chuck Berry), the King (Elvis Presley), and the Fab Four (the Beatles).

The Wizard of Menlo Park, Thomas Edison, was the only familiar nickname I could find among famous scientists and inventors. I did not, however, have difficulty in locating nicknames for outlaws. Dickson (1996) reported that as early as 1936, more than 100,000 nicknames of criminals were in the FBI's files. Dickson noted, "As J. Edgar Hoover later explained, aliases changed all the time but nicknames stuck. Because the nicknames were often based on appearance, mannerism, or attitude, they were considered valuable clues" (p. 156).

Nicknames of well-known criminals include Billy the Kid (William H. Bonney), Butch Cassidy (Robert LeRoy Parker), the Sundance Kid (Harry Longbaugh), Pretty Boy (Charles) Floyd, Machine Gun (George) Kelly, Baby Face (Lester) Nelson, Bugsy (Benjamin) Siegel. Concentration camp survivors from World War II gave nicknames to the murderers in charge of the camps. Those who survived the horrific cruelty of Auschwitz-Birkenau remember Dr. Josef Mengele as the Angel of Death. We have a tendency to give serial killers nicknames (the Zodiac Killer, the Boston Strangler).

The sports arena is a gold mine of nicknames. In addition to team nicknames (e.g., the University of Wisconsin–Madison Badgers, the University of Virginia Cavaliers), individual athletes have nicknames. Some of the best known are basketball players Dr. J (Julius Erving) and Magic (Earwin) Johnson; football players The Fridge (William Perry), Crazy Legs (Elroy) Hirsch, and Broadway Joe Namath; and baseball players Yogi (Lawrence) Berra, the Iron Horse (Lou Gehrig), Babe (George Herman) Ruth, and Pee Wee (Harold) Reese.

■■...**Activity**

Survey the class and have students survey their parents, friends, and well-known locals to create four lists: "Nicknames of Class Members," "Nicknames of Parents," "Nicknames of Friends," "Nicknames of Well-Known Local People." Within each list, discuss the meaning of each nickname. For example, some nicknames are shortened forms of names (e.g., Pat for Patricia, Rog for Roger). Others refer to physical characteristics (e.g., Slim, Red). Some refer to personality traits or reputation (e.g., Pig Man, Lucky).

Ask younger children if they have heard unflattering nicknames, and discuss how these nicknames can be hurtful. Then read the story *The Hallo-Wiener* by Dav Pilkey (1995). It is a tale about how several dogs make fun of the dachshund Oscar's appearance. Oscar's heroic deed one Halloween night, however, convinces the other dogs to change Oscar's nickname from Wiener Dog to Hero Sandwich.

Have older students find nicknames of entertainers, sports figures, and world leaders in newspapers and magazines. Ask students to select a well-known entertainer, sports figure, or world leader and create a nickname for that person. Have students tell the reasons for the nicknames they have created.

If your older students frequently use a computer, ask them to choose a computer term for their nicknames (e.g., Byte, The Disk). You will find a list of words commonly associated with computers in *The Reading Teacher's Book of Lists, 3rd Edition* by Fry, Kress, and Fountoukidis (1993). *Kidstuff on the Internet* by Sara Armstrong, Ph.D. (1996), contains a glossary of terms especially related to Internet use.

On a First-Name Basis:
Popular First Names

Popular first names, just like car colors, fashions, and other fads, come and go with the times. In 1875, Mary was the most popular girl's name in America. By 1970 the name had disappeared from the top ten girls' names. The names Emma, Edith, and Florence appear on the 1875 top ten but are missing on the top ten by 1900, when Dorothy, Mildred, and Frances appear.

William was the most popular boy's name in 1875. It also appears on the top ten lists from 1900 (number 2), 1925 (number 3), 1950 (number 6), and 1960 (number 9). By 1970, though, William is no longer among the top ten.

More recent top ten girls' names include Brittany, Ashley, Jessica, and Amanda; boys' names include Justin, Joshua, Nicholas, and Andrew (Ash 1996; Crystal 1995; Shook, 1994). Certainly, the most popular first names will vary according to ethnic groups; often top ten name lists look suspiciously Anglo-Saxon.

Perhaps prospective parents should conduct research on first names before deciding what to call their newborns. According to Dickson (1996), a research study found that "first-graders would much rather have a substitute teacher named Stephanie than one named Bertha. Among other things, it was felt that Bertha would make the kids work harder" (p. 175). Dickson also noted that teachers gave lower grades on "essays from hypothetical children ... when they bore unpopular names" (p. 177).

Activity

Collect books such as old basal textbooks that remain in a closet or storeroom, old storybooks from your classroom or school library, and other old children's books that you or your colleagues have at home. Individual students can peruse the books and make a list of first names of characters in the stories. Have older students note the copyright dates of the books. Consolidate the lists and determine the most and least popular names. Then compile a list of your students' names and their friends' names. The class can compare the two lists of "then and now" names and can note the names that overlap and those that don't. You might want to compare the "now" names with those found in current "names for your baby" books found in libraries, bookstores, and supermarkets.

I Didn't Catch the Name:
Last Names

You and your students can have a lot of fun—and learn something, too—by collecting and examining last names or surnames. The author personally knows of T. Wheat, S. Straw, and M. Oats; recently came in contact with P. Hay; and spotted a Barley in a large northeastern city's phone book. In the same phone book were the last names of Salt, Pepper, Dill, Pickle, Ham (but no Eggs), Bun, Wieners, Burgers, French, and Fries. A Handy and a Klutz also are listed. In a small midwestern town live D. Pike, G. Bass, and N. Marlin; G. Lake, D. Rivers, B. Strait, and B. Pond live there, too. Smith (1969) pointed out the difficulty cartoonists have when they are giving names to their characters: "A man named Woodruff Woodpecker complained to Walter Lanz, creator of the animated cartoon series starring Woody Woodpecker, because people laughed at him upon observing the similarity of the name" (p. xii). Unusual surnames are not strictly an American phenomenon. A *U.S. News & World Report* article (February 10, 1997) noted the following names in a German phone book: "Faul (lazy), ... Dreckmann (filth man), ... Brathuhn (roast chicken), Schwein (pig), and Kotz (vomit)" (p. 14).

Activity

Create a semantic map of known surnames within categories. Here is an example:

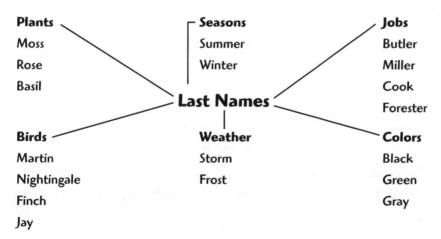

Add other categories and members such as "Three-Letter Names" (e.g., Eck, Eng) and Body Parts (e.g., Foot, Back). After you complete the map, engage students in a discussion about how the names could have originated.

Activity..

According to Ash (1996, p. 53), these are the most common surnames in the United States:

1. Smith
2. Johnson
3. Williams/Williamson
4. Brown
5. Jones

6. Miller
7. Davis
8. Martin/Martinez/Martinson
9. Anderson/Andersen
10. Wilson

Have students peruse the local telephone book. Ask them how common the names on Ash's list are in your area. Is the rank order the same? Which surnames appear as often as or more frequently than those listed by Ash? Discuss why. Now compare common surnames in your area with those from a larger city or smaller town. For this activity you might ask phone companies or friends in other locations to obtain phone books for you.

An invaluable resource for surname information is *American Surnames* by Elsdon C. Smith (1969). Of particular interest is the section listing the 2,000 most common surnames in the United States.

A. Plant, Botanist:
Aptronyms

The term "aptronym" is used when a person's name and the person's occupation are particularly well suited to one another. Smith (1969) reported, "A Memphis, Tennessee, plastering company's truck carried the sign: 'Expert Plastering, Will Crumble & Son'" (p. 141). Smith also found that a "C. W. Buggs was a professor of bacteriology at Wayne University in Detroit, Michigan. Rodney Prior Lien became a vice-president of the Cleveland Trust Co. Forest Burns was hired in Marquette, Michigan ... to man a forest fire lookout tower" (p. 141).

Dickson (1996) has collected many aptronyms. Among them are "John Buckmaster, bank manager, Maryland; Walter Candy, wholesale confectioner; Marvin Dime, stamp and coin dealer; Roy Holler, Wisconsin auctioneer; Viking Jerk, Swede who worked for the Nazis; Earl Risky, stockbroker; Elizabeth Shelver of the Minneapolis Public Library; Linda Toote, flautist in an orchestra in Florida; M. D. Bonebreak, M.D.; O. O. Fuzzy, optometrist; O. O. Oops, M.D., surgeon" (pp. 27–32). Dickson found some partnership aptronyms, too. Among them are "Buckett and Son, Ltd., Southampton plumbers; Burnham and Overbake, bakers from Newark, New Jersey; and Mush and Sons, fruits and vegetables, Dayton, Ohio" (p. 33).

Names

..........Activity

Using big-city Yellow Pages, have your students locate aptronyms. Then have them create their own aptronyms. Students can make business cards and logos for their original aptronyms. Ask a colleague to select the five most clever business cards in the class.

Surnames can be serious business when one enters the political arena. A Dukakis is likely to win some votes from those of Greek ancestry, a Kennedy should garner some Democratic votes, and a Bush probably will be popular among many Republican voters. Would you vote for B. Sillee, A. Loozer, or I. M. Dumm? Data from telephone directories reveal the ethnicity of American cities. Sullivan, Murphy, and Cohen are common names in Boston, as are Schmidt and Schultz in Milwaukee, Olson and Larson in Minneapolis, Wong in San Francisco, and Rodriguez and Gonzalez in Miami.

Surnames come from a patronym or father's name (e.g., Johnson means son of John), occupation (e.g., Baker), a place (e.g., Wald is German for woods), or physical characteristics (e.g., Longfellow). Tracing the origin of a surname, however, can be dauntingly labor intensive. Past immigration procedures certainly complicate the matter. Often the newly arrived families could not make themselves understood when asked for their surnames, or harried workers might have inadvertently altered the spelling. Some immigrants, eager not to "stand out in the crowd," willingly had their surnames Americanized. Others, as Bryson (1990) pointed out, might have wanted to shed their somewhat embarrassing last names.

To further confound investigators, a deceptively simple surname can have a myriad of origins. Smith (1969) said, "Even the ubiquitous SMITH derives from words designating other than the worker in metals. SMITH sometimes comes from smethe, 'smooth,' as in Smithfield, 'the smooth field in London'" (p. 11).

You and your students do not have to be surname researchers to appreciate the wildly varied last names in our country. To recognize the living American family of surnames, with new additions as immigrant groups arrive, is to give your students a lesson in our ever-changing American composite.

..........Activity

Read *American Too* by Elisa Bartone (1996) to older students. It is a true story about Rosina, a young Italian immigrant, who wants to be like other Americans. She discovers, however, that a mix of "old" and "new" cultures is the best. Discuss the story and how the surnames convey the characters' Italian backgrounds. Tell students that in the past, immigrants sometimes changed their names to become "more American." Ask them to speculate about why this practice is not as common as it used to be. Point out the dangers of developing stereotypes based on surnames.

George Eliot Was a Woman:
Pseudonyms

Pseudonyms are names other than one's given name. A pseudonym might be a media name or a pen name. People use pseudonyms to make their names more memorable or easier to pronounce, or to hide their identity. When we think of name changes, we usually think first of entertainers. Fred Astaire's real name was Frederick Austerlitz, Audrey Hepburn's was Edda Hepburn van Heemstra, Billie Holiday's was Eleanora Fagan, and Bob Dylan's was Robert Zimmerman.

Writers have used pen names to hide their gender or their fame. Shook (1994) noted that "William Sidney Porter ... used the name O. Henry to conceal his jail record" (p. 125). Other authors, better known by their pen names, include Charles Lutwidge Dodgson (Lewis Carroll), Mary Ann Evans (George Eliot), Theodore Seuss Geisel (Dr. Seuss), Samuel Langhorne Clemens (Mark Twain), and Agatha Mary Clarissa Miller (Agatha Christie). Some fictional characters better known by their first names have surnames, too: for example, Dorothy Gale from *The Wizard of Oz;* Rick Blaine, played by Humphrey Bogart in *Casablanca;* and the doll known as Barbie, who has Roberts for a last name (Cosmopulos 1995).

Activity......

Tell older students that Whoopi Goldberg's given name is Caryn Johnson and Ann Landers's is Esther Pauline Friedman. Charles Dickens used the pen name Boz, and Benjamin Franklin wrote under the name Poor Richard. Ask students to think of reasons that people might want to use names other than their given names. Possible responses might include privacy, a fear of public rejection, a fear of celebrity, to avoid discrimination due to gender or ethnicity, or to see if something can be accomplished as an unknown. Two books will be helpful in your discussion of pseudonyms. Judie L.H. Strouf, in *The Literature Teacher's Book of Lists* (1993, pp. 372–373), lists pseudonyms of well-known writers. Michael D. Shook's *By Any Other Name* (1994) lists the given names and stage names of actors and actresses (pp. 125–132), people from the music world (pp. 133–136), and writers' pseudonyms (pp. 136–137). Shook also includes a section on how some popular rock groups were named (p. 134). Perhaps your students would enjoy researching the origin of their favorite musical groups' names. (Many contemporary rock groups have their own Websites.)

Places

To the Ends of the Earth:
Toponyms

Toponyms are words derived from place names. For example, "baloney" is the American version of Bologna, Italy. The word "canary" comes from the Canary Islands. The Rhine River, in Europe, is the geographical feature from which the toponym "rhinestone" is derived. Other toponyms include "paisley" (from Paisley, Scotland), "limousine" (from Limousin, a region of France), and "tangerine" (from Tangier, a city in Morocco).

···**Activity**

▪▪

Have students create a toponym skit. For example, they might perform a vaudeville (from Vau de Vire, France) act using magenta (from Magenta, Italy) duffel (from Duffel, Belgium) bags. Ask students to explain the origins of the toponyms being portrayed. Lynda Graham-Barber's *A Chartreuse Leotard in a Magenta Limousine and Other Words Named After People and Places* (1994) will be a helpful resource for your students' skits. This delightful and informative book explains the origins of toponyms such as "mall," "polka dot," and "magnet" as well as the origins of numerous eponyms.

▪▪

···**Activity**

▪▪

Bring several locally written cookbooks into your classroom. Many religious organizations and groups such as the Junior League periodically produce cookbooks that contain the favorite recipes of their members. Often the names of these recipes include local place names (e.g., Dubuque Dumplings, Cincinnati Cinnamon Chili). Commercially available cookbooks such as *Joy of Cooking* (Rombauer, Becker, and Becker, 1997) also contain foods named after places (e.g., New Orleans shrimp). As a tie-in to social studies, have students locate these place names on a map. If time and budget permit, have a toponyms meal featuring such foods as sardines (from Sardinia) and brussels sprouts (from Brussels, Belgium).

▪▪

···**Activity**

▪▪

Share Marvin Terban's *Guppies in Tuxedos: Funny Eponyms* (1988) with your class. Although Terban does not distinguish between eponyms and toponyms, the book can be used as a springboard for students' posters of fanciful illustrations of eponyms and toponyms. For example, a student might draw a valentine (from Saint Valentine) hamburger (from Hamburg, Germany). Students should include explanations of the origins of the eponyms and toponyms on their posters. Display the posters in a hallway of your school.

▪▪

Location, Location, Location?
The Importance of a Place Name

Perhaps you have driven past a new real estate development in your area and have been uplifted by the calming, tranquil name the developer has selected. It's a sure bet that at the end of a day, most exhausted workers would rather return to Whispering Ridge than to Rat Race Hill, to Quiet Acres rather than to Noisy Knoll, and to Peaceful Valley rather than to Hectic Hollow. Bryson (1994) reported that changing a development's name "can give property values an instant boost of up to 15 percent" (p. 109), and that's not chicken feed.

Activity..

Pick up some real estate brochures and catalogs of listings at a local supermarket or shopping mall. Add to these the real estate sections from Sunday newspapers. Have students examine the materials and make lists of the names of developments, subdivisions, and apartment and condominium complexes. Discuss the feelings these names elicit. Compose class letters to developers and realtors asking about the importance of names of properties and how they go about naming new properties.

Where Is Easy Street?
Street Names

There might not be an Easy Street in your town, but there certainly are some unusual street names in America's rural, suburban, and urban areas. Wallechinsky and Wallace (1993, p. 301) reported the following uncommon names for byways:

Road to Happiness in Vermilion, Ohio

None Such Place in New Castle, Delaware

Almosta Road in Darby, Montana

Ewe Turn in Kaysville, Utah

Family Circle in Sandy, Utah

The Living End in Austin, Texas

According to Ash (1995, p. 207), the most common street names in the United States are:

1. Second Street	8. Seventh Street	15. Ninth Street
2. Park Street	9. Washington Street	16. Pine Street
3. Third Street	10. Maple Street	17. Walnut Street
4. Fourth Street	11. Oak Street	18. Tenth Street
5. Fifth Street	12. Eighth Street	19. Cedar Street
6. First Street	13. Elm Street	
7. Sixth Street	14. Lincoln Street	

Such a list suggests some groupings among the most common street names: some are numerical, two presidents are represented, and others are named for trees. It seems odd that First Street ranks number six, but Ash pointed out that most streets that would otherwise be called First Street are called Main Street. Yet Main Street isn't among Ash's list, so what are "Main Streets" called? Students might be interested in knowing that few new streets are called Elm Street these days because Dutch elm disease has killed most elm trees in the United States.

My Kind of Town:
Town and City Names

These are the most common place names in the United States, according to Ash (1996, p. 96).

1. Midway
2. Fairview
3. Oak Grove
4. Five Points
5. Pleasant Hill

6. Centerville
7. Mount Pleasant
8. Riverside
9. Bethel
10. New Hope

Note that there isn't a Skunk Trail among them. Also note that "Pleasant" is used in two of the names. Dilts (1993) reported, "Pleasant is a common word used in town names. At one time it appeared twenty times in Iowa town names" (p. 135). A quick glance at a U.S. atlas reveals the following:

Pleasant Plains, Illinois	Pleasantdale, New York
Pleasant Lake, Indiana	Pleasantville, New York
Pleasanton, Kansas	Pleasant Run Farms, Ohio
Pleasant Ridge, Kentucky	Pleasant Valley, Ohio
Pleasant View, Kentucky	Pleasantville, Ohio
Pleasant Ridge, Michigan	Pleasant Gap, Pennsylvania
Pleasant Valley, Missouri	Pleasant Unity, Pennsylvania
Pleasantville, New Jersey	Pleasanton, Texas
Point Pleasant, New Jersey	Pleasant Valley, West Virginia
Pleasant Valley, New York	Point Pleasant, West Virginia

Activity

To help younger students understand how some place names came about, read *Roxaboxen* by Alice McLerran (1991). The book is about a "town" created by children out of rocks and scraps as a place to play. Its name, Roxaboxen, reflects features of the "town." Have students create their own Roxaboxens from recyclable materials.

Activity..

Bring in several maps of your state. Groups of older students can examine the index of towns and cities to see if any of the top ten place names are located in your state. Speculate with students about how the places with the most common names got those names.

Many founding mothers and fathers were descriptive in naming towns, or they had a sense of humor. There isn't a state without novel—and often amusing—town names. Some towns have animal names: King Salmon, Alaska; Eagle, Colorado; and Bear, Delaware. There are many Buffalos in addition to the well-known Buffalo, New York:

Buffalo, Iowa	Buffalo, Oklahoma
Buffalo, Kentucky	Buffalo, South Carolina
Buffalo, Minnesota	Buffalo, South Dakota
Buffalo, Missouri	Buffalo, Wisconsin
Buffalo, Ohio	Buffalo, Wyoming

There are at least two towns that have the name Sun City (in Alaska and California), two named Enterprise (in Utah and West Virginia), and two by the name of Price (in Utah and Texas).

Wallechinsky and Wallace (1993, pp. 299–300) list the following places in their "40 Curious Place Names in the United States":

Boring, Maryland	Frankenstein, Missouri	Roachtown, Illinois
Ding Dong, Texas	Muck City, Alabama	Sandwich, Illinois
Disco, Tennesee	Odd, West Virginia	Toad Suck, Arkansas
Dismal, Tennessee	Panic, Pennsylvania	Two Egg, Florida
Eek, Alaska	Porkey, Pennsylvania	Worstville, Ohio
Zap, North Dakota		

Shook (1994, p. 90) includes the following locations among his list of "More Colorful Town Names":

Coolville, Ohio	Rich, Mississippi
Dog Bone, West Virginia	Santa Claus, Indiana
Good Times, South Carolina	Troublesome, Colorado
Luck, Wisconsin	What Cheer, Iowa
Nameless, North Dakota	Why, Arizona
Ordinary, Virginia	Whynot, North Carolina

I found the following unique names:

Brilliant, Alabama	Hazard, Kentucky	Comfort, Texas
Eclectic, Alabama	Quicksand, Kentucky	Early, Texas
College, Alaska	Salt Lick, Kentucky	Earth, Texas
Carefree, Arizona	Staples, Minnesota	Prosper, Texas
Show Low, Arizona	Young America, Minnesota	Rule, Texas
Surprise, Arizona	Belt, Montana	Wink, Texas
Tuba City, Arizona	Circle, Montana	Bountiful, Utah
Smackover, Arkansas	Plentywood, Montana	Plain City, Utah
Cool, California	Superior, Nebraska	Chase City, Virginia
Happy Camp, California	Jackpot, Nevada	Experiment, Virginia
Needles, California	Deposit, New York	Hurt, Virginia
Brush, Colorado	Gang Mills, New York	Iron Gate, Virginia
Divide, Colorado	Apex, North Carolina	Electric City, Washington
Dinosaur, Colorado	Cannon Ball, North Dakota	Forks, Washington
Fairplay, Colorado	Defiance, Ohio	Ritzville, Washington
Gardens, Delaware	Dry Run, Ohio	Prosperity, West Virginia
Ideal, Georgia	Economy, Pennsylvania	Bar Nunn, Wyoming
Volcano, Hawaii	Eighty-Four, Pennsylvania	Ten Sleep, Wyoming
Beauty, Kentucky	Bangs, Texas	

Even more fascinating than the names themselves are the stories behind the origins of the names. Shook (1994) reported that Peculiar, Missouri, got its unusual name because the citizens had tried every common name under the sun for their town, only to have the names turned down because they already were in use in Missouri. Most likely, "Pleasant" something was suggested. Eventually the inhabitants told the post office to call the town any peculiar name they wanted. The name stuck.

Activity

Using your state maps, have students locate and list peculiar town names. Discuss the names and create questions about the origins of the names. Write class letters to town historical societies, libraries, or mayors to collect information about the towns and their origins.

Place names do not have to be unique for your students to learn things about history, geography, and human nature. Students might speculate about why there is a Belgium, Wisconsin; a Canada, Kentucky; a Norway, Indiana; and a Mexico, New York. City names from other countries appear frequently in our states:

Amsterdam, New York	Berlin, Wisconsin	Genoa, Illinois
Athens, New York	Dublin, California	Genoa, Nebraska
Athens, Ohio	Dublin, Georgia	Glasgow, Kentucky
Athens, Texas	Dublin, Ohio	Glasgow, Montana
Belfast, New York	Dublin, Texas	London, California
Berlin, Georgia	Dublin, Virginia	Munich, North Dakota
Berlin, New Hampshire	Geneva, Alabama	Rotterdam, New York
Berlin, New York	Geneva, Illinois	
Berlin, Ohio	Geneva, Nebraska	

State names appear in various city names: Iowa, Wisconsin; Michigan, North Dakota; Wyoming, Pennsylvania; Wyoming, Rhode Island; Vermont, Illinois; Ohio, Indiana; Delaware, Indiana; Florida, Delaware; and Maine, New York. You might wonder why "Wyoming" appears in areas where Europeans were living before they moved west. The Algonquian Indians, who lived in Pennsylvania and New York, used the word "Wyoming" for places that were large and flat (Scholes 1996). Familiar U.S. city names reappear in various states. There is a Boston, Georgia; a Boston, Kentucky; and a Des Moines, Washington.

There are many "New _____." In Connecticut are towns called New Britain, New Canaan, New Fairfield, New Hartford, New Haven, New London, New Milford, and New Preston. In Ohio are New Athens, New Boston, New Bremen, New Concord, New Holland, New Lebanon, New Lexington, New Paris, New Philadelphia, New Richmond, New Vienna, and New Washington. In North Dakota are New England, New Leipzig, New Rockford, and New Salem.

Some place names acknowledge the people who inhabited the land before immigration: Apache, Arizona; Iroquois, South Dakota; Mohawk, New York; and Cherokee, Cheyenne, Comanche, Kiowa, Osage, and Pawnee, Kansas. Some place names reflect the nationalities of explorers and other newcomers to the country. Mer Rouge, Louisiana; Meraux, Louisiana; Eau Claire, Wisconsin; and De Pere, Wisconsin, reflect French explorers or settlers. Los Alamos and Los Lunas, New Mexico, reflect Hispanic influence.

Names

Using your state maps, ask students to locate all of the towns and cities in your state that either begin with "New" (e.g., New Berlin, Wisconsin) or have the same name as a foreign city (e.g., Rome, Georgia). Next, the students should examine atlases, especially maps of Europe, to find the "old," or original, places with the same names. Which foreign locations are most often found in your state? What areas or countries are represented least or not at all? Discussion might begin to focus on immigration patterns to North America.

Do People Grow on Family Trees? Genealogy for Kids and Other Beginners: The Official Ellis Island Handbook by Ira Wolfman (1991) will help you introduce American immigration to your older students. It includes information about why immigrants left their homelands and where they settled in America, and a section on the Africans who were kidnapped and brought to America against their will. The book also gives children manageable advice about how to trace their ancestral roots.

Place names often tell us a lot about U.S. history. For example, several towns west of the Mississippi were named after railroad builders and railroad officials. Dilts (1993) tells about John Blair, a railroad builder from Blairstown, New Jersey, who had completed a stretch of track during the 1800s originating in Sioux City, Iowa. At the other end of the track was an unnamed station. Among the first riders on the new stretch of track was a group of women who, after inquiring about the station's name, were invited by Blair to devise a name. The first letter of each of their first names was selected (i.e., "L" for Laura and Lucy; "e" for Elizabeth and Ellen; "M" for Martha and Mary; "a" for Adeline; "r" for Rebecca; "s" for Sarah), and LeMars, Iowa, was born.

Many towns and cities have the same names as well-known presidents. There is a "Lincoln" in Arkansas, California, Illinois, Maine, Montana, Nebraska, and North Dakota. There is a "Madison" in Connecticut, Illinois, Maine, Minnesota, Nebraska, West Virginia, and Wisconsin. Some of our largest cities are named after royalty. Albany is named after the Duke of York and Albany, Baltimore after Lord Baltimore, Charleston for Charles II, Charlottesville for Queen Charlotte, Louisville after King Louis XVI, and New Orleans after the Duke of Orleans. Other cities and towns are named after military leaders (Fort Worth, Houston, Nashville, Reno, Stockton), and many are derived from Native American words (Chicago, Flint, Kalamazoo, Milwaukee, Omaha, Savannah, Tampa).

One well-known place has a name with a particularly charming origin. The name of Ann Arbor, Michigan, came from two women named Ann who settled in the shaded, arborlike area (Shook 1994). Names of some lesser-known places also have charming histories. A music teacher, Mrs. Scofield, named a town in Iowa "Ladora" by combining a few syllables from do-re-mi-fa-so-la-ti-do (Dilts 1993).

Activity......................................

As a group activity, assist younger students in finding out why parks and schools in their community have the names that they do. This will require some information from your town or city hall. Using reference materials, electronic sources, or local or state historical societies, have older students research the origins of place names of their choice. Results of their investigations can be categorized into "Best Stories," "Famous People," "Native American Names," and so on. Conduct a class competition to determine who uncovered the best story.

As vast as the United States is, you probably will find that even if you are in a remote area, everything has already been named. The names might come from earlier inhabitants of a place or from its physical features (e.g., Mount Tom, Half Moon Lake). As noted by Louis (1983), an ordinary citizen can name an unnamed hill or a mountain as long as the person doesn't name the landform after herself or himself. There is, of course, a formal procedure for naming unnamed places, beginning with the county clerk. At the time Louis's book was printed, about a thousand new names were being added each year.

Activity......................................

Have your students name an unnamed physical feature (e.g., a hill or a stream) in your area. The procedure will vary from county to county, but the best places to begin are often the county assessor's office and the county recorder's office. When your name has been "cleared" by local authorities, you will have to contact the U.S. Board on Geographic Names. Their website (www.nmd.usgs.gov/www/gnis/bgn.html) states, "Any person or organization, public or private, may make inquiries or request the Board to render formal decisions on proposed new names, proposed name changes, or names that are in conflict." The address of the board is U.S. Board on Geographic Names, 523 National Center, Reston, VA 20192.

Perhaps you have a nature preserve nearby. If you do, naming a grove of trees or a bridge within the preserve should not be as complicated as naming a more prominent physical feature in your area. It might simply require approval of the preserve staff.

Regardless of what you choose to name, your students will get a firsthand look at how agencies of local, state, and federal government operate. Students also will realize that making a change, such as giving a feature a name, can have many ramifications. For example, a new name may necessitate new maps, perhaps new ads in the Yellow Pages (e.g., "next to Purple Creek"), and so on.

Where Is the Big Easy?
Place Nicknames

All fifty states in the United States have at least one nickname; some have three. New Mexico is the Land of Enchantment and the Cactus State, Nebraska is known as the Cornhusker State and the Tree Planter State, and the Last Frontier and the Land of the Midnight Sun are nicknames for Alaska. Michigan is the Great Lakes State, the Auto State, and the Wolverine State. North Dakota is the Sioux State, the Peach Garden State, and the Flickertail State. South Carolina is the Iodine State, the Swamp State, and the Rice State (Partin 1992).

Many big cities in America have one or more nicknames. Although some origins of nicknames are obvious (e.g., Nashville is Music City, USA), other origins can be foolers. Most people think that Chicago is called the Windy City because of the rather stiff breezes associated with Lake Michigan, but as Shook (1994) pointed out, wind speed had nothing to do with it. The city's nickname came from "proverbially long-winded politicians, not its weather" (p. 81).

....**Activity**

Engage older students in a discussion of community and state nicknames by asking if anyone knows the nicknames of your city and state. Do they know the nicknames of any other cities or states? Then, as a class, try to match the cities with the correct nicknames in the box below. Tell students that some cities have more than one nickname (e.g., Chicago is the Hog Butcher to the World and the City of Big Shoulders).

1. Philadelphia	A. Golden Gate City
2. Dallas	B. Motor City
3. Los Angeles	C. The Big Apple
4. New York City	D. The Big Easy
5. Detroit	E. Mile-High City
6. San Francisco	F. Gateway to the West
7. St. Louis	G. City of Angels
8. Denver	H. Big D
9. New Orleans	I. City of Brotherly Love

(Answers: 1-I, 2-H, 3-G, 4-C, 5-B, 6-A, 7-F, 8-E, 9-D)

Have your students consult almanacs, encyclopedias, and various city and state home pages on the World Wide Web to answer the following questions: How were nicknames selected? Are the nicknames still appropriate for the city or state? If not, why not?

Things
Does Your Pencil Have a Ferrule?
Unusual Names for Familiar Things

Most likely, the doodads, geegaws, and gizmos you encounter have names. A "tilt cord" is the doohickey that controls the amount of light the slats on venetian blinds allow to filter into a room. The "equalizing buckle" is the small metal piece that ensures the blinds will be straight at the sill. A "bill file" is one of those thingamajigs that sits on desks. It has a pointed piece of metal coming from the center of a circular ring. People stick "While You Were Out"–type notes on it. The whatchamacallit on the end of a shoelace has two names: "tag" and "aglet." A "chuck" is the opening into which a pencil is placed to be sharpened, and a "stator" is the visible stationary part next to the keyhole in a cylinder lock. A "breve" is the mark used above a vowel to indicate a short sound, and a "macron" indicates a long vowel sound. "Foxing" refers to dark stains in old books, "dragées" are the tiny silver particles used for decoration of cookies and cakes, and "rasceta" are the lines on the back of a wrist.

Activity

Show students a pencil, a table knife, a paintbrush, a golf club, and an umbrella. Tell the students that each object has a "ferrule." Have students infer that a "ferrule" is a metal ring used for reinforcement. Follow the same procedure with belts that do and do not have a "keeper" (a loop that holds the belt in place), "tubers" (plants, such as potatoes, that have "eyes"), and "colophons" (logos that a publisher uses).

Charles Harrington Elster's *There's a Word for It!* (1996) is a Golconda of unusual words for everyday things. (He also includes uncommon words related to food, phobias, politics, and so on). Choose unusual words for several everyday objects, and then send your students on a dictionary search to discover what the objects are. Have older students find the "oddest" words they can for several everyday objects, and then write letters to their parents that contain hints about where these objects are in their homes.

The occupation-specific vocabulary used by workers in any job is always impressive. A "union nut" is not a card-carrying cashew but rather a term used by plumbers for connecting pipes. A "slip joint" is not a dumpy nightclub where people fall but a term used by carpenters for a part on a pair of pliers (technically speaking, that little round piece with the opening that the round piece slides into). A "spring wing" is not a part of a newly hatched bird but a carpentry term for a piece that fits over a toggle bolt.

▪▪▪

To introduce the notion of occupation-specific vocabulary to younger students, read selections from the *I Can Be ...* series published by Children's Press. Each book contains a glossary of occupation-specific "Words You Should Know." For example, *I Can Be an Oceanographer* by Paul P. Sipiera (1987) explains words such as "plankton" and "sounding." Some of the professionals in the series include an astronaut, a lawyer, a zookeeper, an architect, a teacher, a baseball player, and a forest ranger.

Have older students, in cooperative groups, interview their parents about any occupation-specific vocabulary, and tell the students to make a list of these words. Then have students read their lists and have classmates try to guess the occupations. Tell students to listen for any words among the lists that have multiple meanings (e.g., "scoop" will mean different things to a newspaper reporter, a clothing designer, a casino worker, a movie or TV lighting expert, a musician, a road construction worker, and an ice cream shop worker). Discussion of occupation-specific vocabulary will show the students the importance of vocabulary development in any job, and it certainly will instill respect for any occupation.

▪▪▪

Smooth Operators:
Names for Businesses

Businesspeople know the advantages of selecting the appropriate names for their enterprises. Perusal of the Yellow Pages for a midwestern area with a population of about 100,000 turns up several clever names under certain categories.

Many hairdressers appear to have a sense of humor and a creative spirit. Some of the names: Hair Looms, Country Short Cuts, Cut Hut, The Hair Port, The Head Shed, Headliner, Headquarters, Mane Attraction, Mane Street, Mane Stop, Mane Station, Scissors Shack, Shear Magic, Shear Pleasure, Cut Loose, and Smooth Operators.

Restaurant owners also seem to think that their establishment's name alone can attract customers. Many try to associate their fare with comfort and home cooking. There are several Gramma _____ , and Mom's _____ in this midwestern area; however, there are no Grampa _____ , or Dad's _____ .

A business name can try to reassure prospective consumers. Wee Care, a child care facility, uses a homophone to reassure. Jail Busters Bail Bonds and Speedy Release Bail Bonds sound like helpful establishments. Speedy Release Bail Bonds even has a snappy motto: "We'll put your feet back on the street."

Some businesses seem to insist on using misspellings (e.g., EZ Stop, Serv-U-Kwik). This can be carried a bit far, however, when a day care center is named Kuddles-N-Kids. Even proponents of "invented spelling" probably wouldn't think this is an appropriate spelling for such a business.

Airlines, attorneys, banks, and physicians do not seem to find value in witty business names. Even businesses that could be a little more adventuresome seem to stick mainly to family names. I found a Davis Photography, a Cole Photography, and a Mowatt Photography, but no Say Cheese. Furniture stores also seemed to be surname bound—not a Sitting Pretty or Take a Seat among them.

Activity ·····································

Have younger students, alone or in groups, design a town with a clever name for each business. Then, perhaps using shoeboxes, they can construct, decorate, and label the businesses. Your box of scraps, colored paper, yarn, and paints will come in handy. Older students will enjoy scanning the Yellow Pages in search of clever business names. Use local and out-of-town phone books, which are often available in local libraries. What discoveries can the students make about the businesses and the appropriateness of witty or whimsical names? Why do some types of businesses use clever names? Why don't other types (e.g., dentists, pharmacies, funeral homes)? A class project could involve writing a letter to local businesses with clever names to ask who selected the names and why they were selected. Have the names increased business?

Shells and Buck Shots:
Unusual Names Under Familiar Categories

Members of particular categories of food have individual names even though they are often lumped under the category name. For example, the category "Pasta" is made up of noodles, lasagna, spaghetti, vermicelli, macaroni, lumache, cannelloni, mafaldine, ditali, ziti, mezzani, shells (baby and regular), manicotti, pennine, turrets, ravioli, tortellini, seeds, elbows, bows, buck shots, wheels, stars, alphabets, gemelli, agnolotti, and others. Cheese is another category with numerous members: Colby, cheddar, Monterey Jack, mozzarella, Muenster, Swiss, Asiago, Bel Paese, brick, Brie, Camembert, cottage, cream, Edam, feta, fontina, Parmesan, Gouda, Limburger, Neufchâtel, provolone, Port du Salut, ricotta, Romano, string, blue, and others.

Activity ·····································

Using a reference book such as *The Great Food Almanac* by Irena Chalmers (1994) or, better yet, on a field trip to a local supermarket, have students list and describe unusual or unfamiliar members of such common categories as breads, grains, salad greens, fish, herbs, and snack foods. With the lists and descriptions, have small teams create word grids (semantic feature grids) for the categories. Such grids clearly show how the different members of a category are alike and different. Here is a partial word grid for the category "Pasta."

PASTA						
	long	flat	hollow	thin	wide	curved
spaghetti	+	-	-	+	-	-
lasagna	+	+	-	-	+	-
macaroni	-	-	+	-	-	+
ziti						
vermicelli						
tortellini						

To make a word grid, follow these steps:

1. Put the category name at the top of the grid.
2. List category members in a column on the left.
3. List the descriptive features in a row along the top.
4. Use a "+" if a category member usually has that feature.
5. Use a "-" if a category member usually does not have that feature.
6. Use a "?" if you are unsure or if it isn't clear-cut.
7. Add more category members and descriptive features as you think of them.
8. Use the completed word grid as the basis for a discussion of how category members are alike and different.

Completed word grids also can be used to create analogies. For example: Spaghetti is to straight as macaroni is to curved. Ziti is to short as lasagna is to long.

Activity

Younger students will enjoy food poems from *What's on the Menu?* by Bobbye S. Goldstein (1992). After reading several of the poems, have students write a poem about their favorite food and then create the food out of art materials from your scrap box. When the students are finished with the poem and the "food," put a tablecloth over a group of desks. Place completed food poems and food on the "table" and share them with other classes. The "table" also is a good icebreaker when parents arrive for their parent-teacher conferences.

A Final Word

This has been a chapter about names: names of people, places, and things, nicknames, unusual names, and common names. My intent has been to show how much is to be learned through the study of names. For example, tornadoes are not named Cesar or Cindy; hurricanes are. According to the National Weather Service (www.thematrix.com/nws/aware/hrcnname.html), hurricanes have short, easy-to-remember names because the names eliminate confusion that would be caused if only coordinates of latitude and longitude were used. Also, sometimes one hurricane follows another, and the names help forecasters and the public keep the storms straight. Members of the World Meteorological Organization determine the names at their meetings. Female names for hurricanes began being used in the United States in 1953; male names were added in 1978–1979. The names of hurricanes that caused a great deal of damage are not used again. There is a set of names for Atlantic hurricanes and a different set of names for Pacific storms. By checking the website listed above, you will be able to find out if a hurricane will have your name within the next six years.

My intent in this chapter also has been to show how much fun is to be had through the study of names. For example, the world of colors is filled with names we rarely hear or see in print: chartreuse, celadon, griege, ocher, and umber are but a few. A trip to the cosmetics counter reveals imaginative names for colors of foundations, lipsticks, blushes, eye shadows, and other "beauty enhancing" products. Marketing specialists must know that a color name such as "apple delight" is more appealing to the consumer than "red." Readily available resources such as telephone directories, atlases, and dictionaries take on a new life when they are used to learn about names.

The next chapter moves from names to special riddles as mechanisms for generating an interest in language. Specifically, Chapter 2 shows the many nuances of the ever-popular hink pink riddles.

References

Almond, J. *Dictionary of Word Origins: A History of the Words, Expressions, and Clichés We Use.* New York: Carol Publishing Group, 1985.

The American Heritage Dictionary of the English Language. Boston: Houghton Mifflin, 1992.

Ammer, C. *Have a Nice Day—No Problem!: A Dictionary of Clichés.* New York: Plume Books, 1992.

Ash, R. *The Top 10 of Everything 1996.* London: Dorling Kindersley, 1995.

———. *The Top 10 of Everything 1997.* London: Dorling Kindersley, 1996.

Bryson, B. *Made in America: An Informal History of the English Language in the United States.* New York: William Morrow, 1994.

———. *The Mother Tongue: English and How It Got That Way.* New York: Avon Books, 1990.

Chalmers, I. *The Great Food Almanac: A Feast of Facts from A to Z.* San Francisco: CollinsPublishers, 1994.

Corbeil, J. C. *The Facts on File Visual Dictionary.* New York: Facts on File Publications, 1986.

Cosmopulos, S. *The Book of Lasts.* New York: Penguin Books, 1995.

Crystal, D. *The Cambridge Encyclopedia of the English Language.* Cambridge: Cambridge University Press, 1995.

Dickson, P. *What's In a Name? Reflections of an Irrepressible Name Collector.* Springfield, Mass.: Merriam-Webster, 1996.

Dilts, H. E. *From Ackley to Zwingle: The Origins of Iowa Place Names,* 2d ed. Ames: Iowa State University Press, 1993.

Elster, C. H. *There's a Word for It!* New York: Scribner, 1996.

Fry, E. B., J. E. Kress, and D. L. Fountoukidis. *The Reading Teacher's Book of Lists,* 3rd ed. Englewood Cliffs, N.J.: Prentice Hall, 1993.

Harms, J. M., and L. Lettow. *Picture Books to Enhance the Curriculum.* New York: H. W. Wilson, 1996.

Louis, D. *2201 Fascinating Facts.* New York: Wings Books, 1983.

Partin, R. L. *The Social Studies Teacher's Book of Lists.* Englewood Cliffs, N.J.: Prentice Hall, 1992.

Rand McNally Road Atlas. Skokie, IL: Rand McNally, 1996.

Rombauer, I. S., M. R. Becker, and E. Becker. *Joy of Cooking.* New York: Scribner, 1997.

Room, A. *NTC's Dictionary of Word Origins.* Lincolnwood, Ill.: National Textbook Company, 1994.

Scholes, I. "Review's Big 4: License to Fishkill." *The Waterloo Courier Review,* 18 September 1996, p. 1.

Shook, M. D. *By Any Other Name: An Informative and Entertaining Look at How Hundreds of People, Places, and Things Got Their Names.* New York: Prentice Hall, 1994.

Smith, E. C. *American Surnames.* Baltimore, Md.: Genealogical Publishing, 1969.

Strouf, J.L.H. *The Literature Teacher's Book of Lists.* West Nyack, N.Y.: The Center for Applied Research in Education, 1993.

Wallace, A., D. Wallechinsky, and I. Wallace. *The Book of Lists #3.* New York: Bantam Books, 1983.

Wallechinsky, D., and A. Wallace. *The Book of Lists: The '90s Edition.* Boston: Little Brown, 1993.

"What's in a Name?" *U.S. News and World Report,* 10 February 1997, p. 14.

World Wide Web Yellow Pages. Indianapolis, Ind: New Riders Publishing.

References:
Children's Books

Armstrong, S. *Kidstuff on the Internet.* San Francisco: Sybex, 1996.

Bartone, E. *American Too.* New York: Lothrop, Lee & Shepard, 1996.

Goldstein, B. S. *What's on the Menu?* New York: Viking, 1992.

Graham-Barber, L. *A Chartreuse Leotard in a Magenta Limousine and Other Words Named After People and Places.* New York: Hyperion Books for Children, 1994.

Isaacs, A. *Swamp Angel.* New York: Dutton, 1994.

McLerran, A. *Roxaboxen.* New York: Lothrop, Lee & Shepard, 1991.

Pilkey, D. *The Hallo-Wiener.* New York: Blue Sky, 1995.

Sipiera, P. *I Can Be an Oceanographer.* Chicago: Children's Press, 1987.

Terban, M. *Guppies in Tuxedos: Funny Eponyms.* New York: Clarion Books, 1988.

Wolfman, I. *Do People Grow on Family Trees? Genealogy for Kids and Other Beginners: The Official Ellis Island Handbook.* New York: Workman, 1991.

CHAPTER 2

Hink Pinks

Hog Jog

Swift Gift

What do "skunk junk," "an ill drill," "a quacker cracker," and "a great grate" have in common? They all are potential answers to questions posed by a hink pink family aficionado. Hink pinks and their relatives (i.e, hinky pinkies, hinkety pinketies, hink hinks, hinky hinkies, hinkety hinketies, pink pinks, pinky pinkies, pinkety pinketies) are answers to descriptive questions. The answers, however, must have a specific number of syllables and must be a member of the specified category within the hink pink family. For example, what is a hink pink (a pair of one-syllable rhyming words) for someone who is snooty about a piece of corn? The answer is "a cob snob." What is a hinky pinky (a pair of two-syllable rhyming words) for a snooty pastime? The answer is "a snobby hobby."

A School Tool:
The Importance of Hink Pinks in the Classroom

Wordplay with hink pinks is more than simply passing time before the dismissal bell rings. It is more than an attempt by teachers to be what education critics refer to as "cutesy." Geller (1985) stated that work with hink pink riddle constructions "represent(s) an exercise in the descriptive use of language" (p. 77). Geller also pointed out that "the requirement that the answer be in rhyme and meter stretches the student's linguistic creativity and originality" (p. 77).

An additional benefit of working with the hink pink family is vocabulary development. Golick (1987) recollected,

"The example that comes immediately to mind from my childhood games is this one:

"Player A: obese feline animal

"Player B: fat cat

"I actually remember, at the age of seven or eight, learning the meaning of the words 'obese' and 'feline' in this context" (p. 27).

Geller (1985) found that even when students were studying a topic such as medieval history, they devised hink pinks in lieu of their traditional sentence writing to incorporate new vocabulary words. Geller gave the following examples (the new vocabulary words are italicized):

"What do you call a sad *gargoyle*? (a pout spout)" (p. 78).

"When two people sign a peace treaty and they drink to it, what do they drink? (*truce* juice)" (p. 79).

Children in the elementary grades have enjoyed solving hink pink riddles, but the activity also has been popular with students in middle school and high school. Adults, too, like to try to stump one another with a particularly obscure or innovative hink pink. Solving and generating hink pink riddles can add some excitement and interest to your language arts classes. It has long been sad but true that many American students do not enjoy the study of their own language. Playing with hink pinks is a time-honored way to spark some language enthusiasm in your students.

Hink pinks probably have been around as long as language. In this chapter, the recent history of the hink pink family is discussed. Then examples from the nine categories of the hink pink family are presented. Ideas for grouping hink pinks according to topics you are teaching are discussed, and, finally, some frequently used formats for introducing hink pinks are given.

Old Gold:
A Brief, Recent History of Hink Pinks

In the late 1950s, Lucky Strike cigarettes sponsored a competition in college and university newspapers across the United States. Undergraduate and graduate students were challenged to create "Sticklers," which were defined as simple riddles with two-word rhyming answers. What was sticky about the sticklers was that both words had to have the same number of syllables. The Sticklers were to be sent to "Happy-Joe-Lucky" in Mount Vernon, New York. There they were judged, and the winners were awarded free cigarettes and other prizes. Many college students, probably when they should have been doing some textbook reading, mustered creative brain power to generate such Sticklers as "What is a disagreement between insects?" (answer: "a gnat spat"). Here is a winner from the 1958 Stickler contest: "What is a phony shellfish?" (answer: "a sham clam"). Some things have changed since the winners received their prizes. University newspapers no longer run ads for cigarettes, and some of the Sticklers that were submitted would be considered insensitive to particular members of our society.

Espy (1980) referred to hink pinks as "Stinky Pinkies." Pearson and Johnson (1978) asked, "Remember the old hink pink game? One person gives a definition, the other person supplies the answer, which is a pair of words that rhyme. For example, a fruit thief is a melon felon, or a sign for a horse ranch might be a stable label" (p. 76). Brandreth (1980) labeled the riddles Stinkety Pinketies: "In Stinkety Pinkety the first player offers a definition ... and the other must translate it into a noun modified by a rhyming adjective" (p. 172). Brandreth added that stink pinks required monosyllabic answers (e.g., a thin twin), stinky pinkies called for two-syllable rhyming responses (e.g., funny money), and stinkety pinketies elicited trisyllabic nouns and adjectives (e.g., a defective detective).

In 1981, Burns and Weston published a small picture book containing hink pinks (sad dad), hinky pinkies (cooler ruler), and hinkety pinketies (delaying decaying). Augarde (1984), in *The Oxford Guide to Word Games*, defined hinky pinkies and gave them the synonymous terms "stinky pinky" and "hanky panky" (p. 199). Golick (1987) wrote about Stinky Pinky and said, "This game has acquired more elegant names since I first played it as a child, but this is the name I knew and the name by which I have introduced it to hundreds of children and teachers whose mother didn't play it with them" (p. 27). Lederer (1988) also called attention to the fun to be had with hink pinks and their more troublesome relatives. Johnson and Johnson (1986) included several pages of hink pinks and hinky pinkies in each book of their vocabulary development series, continued to develop hink pink activities in their language play series (1990), and created an instructional game (*The Brain Train*, 1994) based on the hink pink families.

In the next section, nine categories of hink pinks are defined, and samples are given within each of the nine categories. Often the answer to a hink pink riddle is plausible (a happy pappy), but at other times the answer is absurd (a smart cart). That's part of the fun. The answers to the Fine Nine are given at the end of this section.

The Fine Nine:
The Nine Categories of Hink Pinks

Category I: Hink Pinks

Hink pinks are one-syllable rhyming words.

Examples

Question: What is an aircraft for a particular shellfish called?
Answer: a shrimp blimp

Question: What could you call celery chat?
Answer: stalk talk

Here are some more hink pinks with which you can test your skill. Try to not take "a sneak peek" at the answers.

1. What is a distant twinkler called?
2. What would you call a nice glow?
3. What would you call a quick explosion?
4. What are weak letters and packages called?
5. What is a big dance held in autumn called?
6. How would you label tidy warmth?
7. What could you call disappointed soil?
8. What could you call a high-pitched, screeching medicine tablet?
9. What could you call a fast present?
10. What is a mild fire called?
11. What could you call a smart flying toy?
12. What is it called when everyone runs after a flower container?
13. What is a grumpy person's sofa called?
14. What could you call a tardy saucer?
15. What is a very tiny honey-maker called?
16. What could you call a street for frog relatives?
17. What do you do when you talk back without respect to a lawn?
18. What do you call a heap of ducks?
19. What do you call a poem about a particular green fruit?
20. What could you call a type of business clothing for an owl?

Category II: Hinky Pinkies

Hinky pinkies are two-syllable rhyming words.

Examples

Question: What could you call a tiny bird from New Zealand?
Answer: a peewee kiwi

Question: What could you call a mean gem?
Answer: a cruel jewel

Now test yourself on these hinky pinkies.

1. Who was the tardier crocodile relative?
2. What would you call a soap opera about pack animals?
3. What could you call someone who brags about a particular kitchen appliance?

4. How could you refer to a particular stuffed animal that is prepared?
5. What is a song for vegetables and dressing called?
6. What could you call the violin in the center?
7. What would you call a person who blocks the passage of a kangaroo?
8. What is a very large customer of a lawyer called?
9. What could you call a changeable dill?
10. What could you call a small, burrowing animal that drives others?
11. What might you call a grumpy taxi driver?
12. What might a chillier paper holder be called?
13. What could you call carpeting that is not interesting?
14. What could you call a serving spoon's baby bed?
15. What could you call a dark red floater?
16. What might a happy currant be called?
17. What could you call an odd-behaving Thanksgiving bird?
18. What might you call a particular flower that is goofy?
19. What could you call a directional signal attached to a skunk?
20. What could you call a humorous large town?

Category III: Hinkety Pinketies

Hinkety pinketies are three-syllable rhyming words.

Examples

Question: What do you call a "how-to" book that is published every year?
Answer: an annual manual

Question: What might you call just average boredom?
Answer: medium tedium

Hinkety pinketies are a bit trickier to create. Here are ten rather difficult hinkety pinketies.

1. What might you call a talk about a drum and chimes?
2. What would you call something to eat that is believable?
3. What might you call a yellow fruit's bright, large handkerchief?
4. What could you call the money given to send someone away for two weeks of relaxation?
5. What are you doing when you stop breathing in air?
6. What do you call a singing bird that is antagonistic?
7. What is it called when something without blemishes is held up to a mirror?
8. What could you call a place where everything revolves?
9. What might you call the answer to cleaning up dirty air?
10. What is it called when someone says you may take something away?

Activity...

Assist younger students in compiling one-syllable and two-syllable rhyming word pairs. As a large group or in small groups, write hink pink or hinky pinky questions for the pairs. Introduce older students to a rhyming dictionary. Have them create hink pinks, hinky pinkies, and hinkety pinketies from rhyming word pairs.

There are rhyming riddles with four syllables (hahinkety papinketies); however, these are uncommon. Here are two examples:

Question: What could you call the blame leveled against all the people of a place?
Answer: population accusation

Question: What might you call it when all the people of a place are anticipating something?
Answer: population expectation

You might want to issue a "challenge of the week" to older students. Have them devise a hahinkety papinkety to try to stump their peers.

Category IV: Hink Hinks

Hink hinks are one-syllable homographs. Homographs are words that sound the same and are spelled the same but have different meanings.

Examples

Question: What might you call a particular color that is sad?
Answer: a blue blue

Question: What is it called when a roll of cloth runs away suddenly?
Answer: a bolt bolt

Hink hinks are plentiful because multiple-meaning words are so prevalent in the English language. Here are twenty hink hinks.

1. What is it called when a sauce for potato chips dives into a pool?
2. What is it called when a pile of snow moves around in a casual way?
3. What might you call a hyphen race?
4. What do you call it when jelly gets into a traffic snarl?
5. What might you call cheating done by thick, square candy?
6. What could you call a nervous verb form?
7. What is it called when people honor a crisp piece of bread?
8. What is a fenced-in area for ballpoints called?
9. What is a shrub, tree, and flower factory called?

10. What is it called when a label tells someone she or he is "it"?
11. What do you call a tie in a sketching contest?
12. What could you call a squashed British apartment?
13. What do you do when you tease a baby goat?
14. What might you call a sticky tree substance that behaves like a fool?
15. What might you call the lone whitefish?
16. What do you call a particular shellfish that is very tiny?
17. What could you call a wise person's favorite herb?
18. What could you call the underground part of a base word?
19. What is it called when a particular evergreen longs for something?
20. What is it called when a dried plum trims a tree?

Category V: Hinky Hinkies

Hinky hinkies are two-syllable homographs (words that have the same sound and spelling but different meanings).

Examples

Question: What is it called when boards of wood walk clumsily?
Answer: a lumber lumber

Question: What might you call it when a preserved cucumber is in a difficult situation?
Answer: a pickle pickle

As with hink hinks, many hinky hinkies can be created because of the large number of multiple-meaning words in our vocabularies. Here are twenty hinky hinkies to get you started.

1. What is it called when a particular bird gulps?
2. What might you call noise made by a tennis paddle?
3. What could you call it when an arrow case shakes?
4. What might you call trash improperly discarded by a group of puppies?
5. What could you call a particular yellow citrus fruit that is a dud?
6. What is it called when you leave a dark-red color on a lifeless island?
7. What is it called when a sewing tool teases someone?
8. What is it called when the metal part of a belt bends?
9. What might you call a large sled dog?
10. What might you call the bedspread for the lid of a kettle?
11. What do you call it when you tire out engine fumes?
12. What is it called when a particular fungus grows rapidly?
13. What is it called when you delight in a highly seasoned pickle sauce?
14. What might you call a firmly established place for horses?

15. What could you call a measuring device's leader?
16. What is a baseball player's container for liquids called?
17. What might you call a small copy of something that does not misbehave?
18. What might you call a flow of water that is up-to-date?
19. What is it called when you hold back a large basket?
20. What might you call an intestinal punctuation mark?

Category VI: Hinkety Hinketies

Hinkety hinketies are three-syllable homographs (same sound and spelling, different meanings).

Examples

Question: What might you call a round handbill?
Answer: a circular circular

Question: What could you call a music director who also is in charge of a train?
Answer: a conductor conductor

Hinkety hinketies are not as abundant as hink hinks and hinky hinkies. They require students to have a more sophisticated vocabulary. Here are ten hinkety hinketies for your most advanced students.

1. What could you call the final payment from a small village?
2. What might you call a hair salon process that is not temporary?
3. What might you call money available in a city denoted by a star on a map?
4. What could you call a commander who is not specific?
5. What might you call musical chords that do not disagree?
6. What could you call it when people are sad about a very difficult economic time?
7. What do you do when you provide a plan of fulfillment for a farm machine?
8. What might you call a written record of information about heat ducts?
9. What would you call the main school adminstrator in your district?
10. What might you call the group of people who are in charge of bonuses for sales?

Activity

Give younger students a list of one- and two-syllable homographs. As a group or in pairs, have students create questions for hink hinks and hinky hinkies. Have older students examine content-area materials to locate homographs and create hink hinks, hinky hinkies, and hinkety hinketies. Here is a hink hink from social studies: What would you call a piece of legislation about a bird beak? (a bill bill).

Category VII: Pink Pinks

Pink pinks are one-syllable homophones. Homophones have the same sound, but they have different spellings and meanings.

Examples

Question: What is a peeping sound that costs very little money?
Answer: a cheap cheep

Question: What might you call a reddish-purple vegetable that is exhausted?
Answer: a beat beet

Here are twenty pink pinks.

1. What might you call seven days in a row that are not strong?
2. How might you refer to tiny us?
3. What is it called when you brush away a sneaker?
4. What could you call an aircraft that is not fancy?
5. What is it called when you squeeze a piece of finger jewelry?
6. What is it called when a dog's feet stop for a moment?
7. What could you say when only a single person didn't lose?
8. What might you call a short look at a mountaintop?
9. What could you call it when glass in a window has an ache?
10. What might you call a particular animal that has a sore throat?
11. What might you call it when a branch bends at the waist?
12. What could you call a wild pig that is uninteresting?
13. What might you call a tall greeting?
14. What is it called when you are introduced to steaks and chops?
15. What might you call a rather colorless bucket?
16. What is a self-centered object for wind direction called?
17. What is it called when you look for a long time at a step?
18. What might you call a discount on a piece of ship canvas?
19. What does someone do who escapes from dog pests?
20. What might you call two of the same yellow fruit?

Category VIII: Pinky Pinkies

Pinky pinkies are two-syllable homophones (same sound but different spellings and meanings).

Examples

Question: What might you call a cold, spicy soup?
Answer: chilly chili

Question: What would you call a salesperson who works in a basement?
Answer: a cellar seller

Pinky pinkies are not as plentiful as pink pinks. Here are ten pinky pinkies.

1. What might you call a particular berry that is up-to-date?
2. What could you call a large rock that is more fearless?
3. What might you call an army commander's uncooked grains?
4. What might you call a very unusual marketplace?
5. What could you call an ice cream treat eaten on a particular weekend day?
6. What does a person do when he or she sells particular bicycle parts?
7. What might we call the strength of a particular shellfish?
8. What do you call grieving done before lunchtime?
9. What could you call a mule tunnel?
10. What happened when the person who wasn't brave cringed?

Category IX: Pinkety Pinketies

Pinkety pinketies are three-syllable homophones (same sound but different spellings and meanings).

Examples

Question: What could you call the continuing story of a breakfast food?
Answer: a cereal serial

Question: What might you call the main rule?
Answer: the principal principle

Question: What might you call paper that doesn't move?
Answer: stationary stationery

Activity ....

Homophones (pink pinks and pinky pinkies) are confusing to young learners. When working with lower elementary children, I often ask them to illustrate a homophone pair and then write the correct homophone under the corresponding picture. For example, "a high hi" might be illustrated as an elongated "h" and "i."

Older students might enjoy practicing their skills drawing cartoons with such pink pinks as "a boar bore" (e.g., a pig speaking and putting an audience to sleep). A collection of these cartoons could be used in a school newsletter or newspaper.

Giulio Maestro's *What's Mite Might?* (1986) and Marvin Terban's *Eight Ate* (1982) contain pink pinks and pinky pinkies. Share the books with your students and point out how pink pinks and pinky pinkies can introduce unfamiliar vocabulary. For example, *What's Mite Might?* includes the following question and answer: "Where's a frieze in a freeze? Under a cold cornice" (p. 47). "Frieze" and "cornice" probably will be "new" words to your students, but the pink pinks, pinky pinkies, and illustrations in Maestro and Terban's books provide context for the definitions.

Answers to Category I, Hink Pinks

1. a far star
2. a fine shine
3. a fast blast
4. frail mail
5. a fall ball
6. neat heat
7. hurt dirt
8. a shrill pill
9. a swift gift
10. a tame flame
11. a bright kite
12. a vase chase
13. a grouch couch
14. a late plate
15. a wee bee
16. a toad road
17. you sass grass
18. a quack stack
19. a lime rhyme
20. a hoot suit

Answers to Category II, Hinky Pinkies

1. the later gator
2. a llama drama
3. a toaster boaster
4. a ready Teddy
5. a salad ballad
6. a middle fiddle
7. a hopper stopper
8. a giant client
9. a fickle pickle
10. a gopher chauffeur
11. a crabby cabby
12. a colder folder
13. boring flooring
14. a ladle cradle
15. a maroon balloon
16. a merry berry
17. a quirky turkey
18. a silly lily
19. a stinker blinker
20. a witty city

Answers to Category III, Hinkety Pinketies

1. a percussion discussion
2. a credible edible
3. a banana bandanna
4. a vacation donation
5. curtailing inhaling
6. a contrary canary
7. a perfection reflection
8. a rotation location
9. a pollution solution
10. removal approval

Answers to Category IV, Hink Hinks

1. a dip dip
2. a drift drift
3. a dash dash
4. a jam jam
5. a fudge fudge
6. a tense tense
7. a toast toast
8. a pen pen
9. a plant plant
10. a tag tag
11. a draw draw
12. a flat flat
13. you kid a kid
14. a sap sap
15. a sole sole
16. a shrimp shrimp
17. a sage sage
18. a root root
19. a pine pine
20. a prune prune

Answers to Category V, Hinky Hinkies

1. a swallow swallow
2. a racket racket
3. a quiver quiver
4. litter litter
5. a lemon lemon
6. a maroon maroon
7. a needle needle
8. a buckle buckle
9. a husky husky
10. a cover cover
11. you exhaust exhaust
12. a mushroom mushroom
13. you relish relish
14. a stable stable
15. a ruler ruler
16. a pitcher pitcher
17. a model model
18. a current current
19. a hamper hamper
20. a colon colon

Answers to Category VI, Hinkety Hinketies

1. a settlement settlement
2. a permanent permanent
3. capital capital
4. a general general
5. a harmony harmony
6. a depression depression
7. you implement an implement
8. a register register
9. a principal principal
10. a commission commission

Answers to Category VII, Pink Pinks

1. a weak week
2. wee we
3. a shoe shoo
4. a plain plane
5. a ring wring
6. a paws pause
7. one won
8. a peak peek
9. a pane pain
10. a hoarse horse
11. a bough bow
12. a boar bore
13. a high hi
14. you meet meat
15. a pale pail
16. a vain vane
17. a stair stare
18. a sail sale
19. she/he flees fleas
20. a pear pair

Answers to Category VIII, Pinky Pinkies

1. a current currant
2. a bolder boulder
3. the colonel's kernels
4. a bizarre bazaar
5. a Sunday sundae
6. he/she peddles pedals
7. mussel muscle
8. morning mourning
9. a burro burrow
10. the coward cowered

....**Activity**

Divide the class into small teams (four to five students per team). Have the teams try to stump one another with original hink pinks using age-appropriate categories from the Fine Nine.

The Group Scoop:
Grouping Hink Pinks by Topics

Perhaps your students are studying a specific topic in depth (e.g., animals). Then you might want to work on hink pinks that evolve from your topic. The creation and sharing of hink pinks will increase your students' vocabularies and conceptual bases within the topic. Below are topics and hink pink family examples. The answer to each question is in parentheses after the question.

Animals and Insects: Hink Pinks

1. What could you call the giggle of a baby cow? (a calf laugh)
2. What could you call a spoiled rodent? (a rat brat)
3. What are stingy lambs called? (cheap sheep)
4. What might you call an excellent group of pigs? (fine swine)
5. What might you call a weak escargot? (a frail snail)
6. What is it called when a rabbit stares angrily at someone? (a hare glare)
7. What is it called when a bee's house jumps into a swimming pool? (a hive dive)
8. What would you call a pig run? (a hog jog)
9. What could you call good little rodents? (nice mice)
10. What could you call a dog kiss? (a pooch smooch)
11. What might you call an uncommon rabbit? (a rare hare)
12. What might you call a certain bashful insect? (a shy fly)
13. What is a stinker's suitcase called? (a skunk trunk)
14. What might you call a cozy insect? (a snug bug)
15. What is an extra cub called? (a spare bear)
16. What is a poem dedicated to a frog relative? (a toad ode)
17. What is a hot group of bees called? (a warm swarm)
18. What is a name for cattle food? (cow chow)
19. What could you call a feline conversation? (cat chat)
20. What might you call a muffler for a dog? (an arf scarf)
21. What is an adhesive used by gorillas? (ape tape)
22. What could you call an insect that is a bully? (a bug thug)
23. What would a flying mammal use for a cap? (a bat hat)
24. What could you call an exam for rats and cockroaches? (a pest test)
25. What might you call a hog dance? (a pig jig)

Animals and Insects: Hinky Pinkies

1. What could you call a very skinny young horse? (a bony pony)
2. What could you call a cross cat? (a crabby tabby)
3. What might you call a group who demonstrates against a particular chirping insect? (a cricket picket)
4. What is it called when a hare repeats the same behavior? (a rabbit habit)
5. What is a folktale about a certain animal with fur? (a sable fable)
6. What is a wringing-wet pooch called? (a soggy doggy)
7. What could a certain happy dog be called? (a jolly collie)
8. What might you call a conflict between steers? (a cattle battle)
9. What would you call a fake small horse? (a phony pony)
10. What could you call a horse made of onions? (a scallion stallion)

Animals and Insects: Hink Hinks

1. What might you call a porker that always takes more than its share? (a hog hog)
2. What is it called when a sea mammal tightly closes something? (a seal seal)
3. What might you call a fault-finding old horse? (a nag nag)
4. What is it called when you guide a young ox? (a steer steer)
5. What might you call a certain insect's baseball hit? (a fly fly)

Animals and Insects: Pink Pinks

1. What might you call the cry of a large sea mammal? (a whale wail)
2. What might a just-born antelope be called? (a new gnu)
3. What is the batter prepared by a female deer called? (doe dough)
4. What might you call the principal tuft of lion hair? (the main mane)
5. What might you call a thin candle used by a three-toed, long-snouted animal? (a tapir taper)

Activity ....

As a class or individually, have students write questions for the following animal/insect–related hink pinks, hinky pinkies, hink hinks, and pink pinks.

Hink Pinks

goat coat	mouse house
skunk bunk	toad road
wee bee	pup cup
cat bat	bug mug

Hinky Pinkies

city kitty	flabby tabby
jackal cackle	lizard wizard

Hink Hinks

    bug bug   mole mole

Pink Pinks

    flea flee   hare hair

More Topics for the Hink Pink Family

Here are more topics and examples to get you started on your collection of hink pinks. (What is a hinkety pinkety for thinking about a group of examples from the hink pink family? Answer: a collection conception)

Items Found in the Home

Hink Pinks

1. What could you call a chilly chair? (a cool stool)
2. What is it called when you squeeze a cup? (a mug hug)
3. What could you call an ordinary sink duct? (a plain drain)
4. What might you call a bed covering for a road? (a street sheet)
5. What could you call a timepiece made of stone? (a rock clock)

Hinky Pinkies

1. What might you use to weigh a drapery border? (a valance balance)
2. How might you describe a mischievous platter of snacks? (a playful trayful)
3. What do you call a person who steals only fine tin tableware? (a pewter looter)
4. What is the chubbier tray called? (the fatter platter)
5. What type of cookware is a stainless steel pot? (a metal kettle)

Hink Hinks

1. What is a hair grooming device made of branches? (a brush brush)
2. What is it called when a glass container is jolted? (a jar jar)
3. What is it called when an object with faucets goes underwater? (a sink sink)
4. What is it called when a window covering lightly colors a drawing? (a shade shade)
5. What could a prairie stove be called? (a range range)

Activity..

As a group or independently, have students write questions for the following household-related hink hinks.

fan fan   key key

file file   scale scale

light light

Your students might enjoy creating and collecting members of the hink pink family for the following categories:

1. Food

Examples

Question: (hink pink) What might you call a nasty type of legume?

Answer: a mean bean

Question: (hink hink) What is it called when a T-bone complains?

Answer: a beef beef

2. Music

Examples

Question: (hink pink) What could you call a well-used trombone?

Answer: a worn horn

Question: (hink pink) What could you call a dull, undistinctive combo?

Answer: a bland band

Other categories you might want to use are "School," "Sports and Games," "Actions," "Clothing and Accessories," "Machines and Tools," and "Geographic Names."

The Hint Mint:
Helpful Formats for Beginners

Younger students and students who are not proficient in English will appreciate a little help when they begin working with the hink pink family. The following formats have proved useful when introducing members of the categories:

Choose the Answer

A "hink pink" is a pair of one-syllable rhyming words. Read the word clue. Then choose the correct hink pink from the word box and write it on the lines.

Hink Pinks

Word Box

hot cot	tall wall	sick chick
glad dad	fair bear	camp lamp

Word Clues **Hink Pinks**

1. A high fence is a   _____ _____
2. A happy father is a   _____ _____
3. An ill baby hen is a   _____ _____
4. A tent light is a   _____ _____
5. A very warm bed is a   _____ _____
6. An honest cub is a   _____ _____

Find the Word

A "hink pink" is a pair of one-syllable rhyming words. Read each word clue. Choose one word from the word box to complete the hink pink. Then write the hink pink on the correct line.

Word Box

pool	slaw	rate	chum	chair	jump

Word Clues **Hink Pinks**

1. A chilly swimming place is a   cool _____
2. A dish price is a   plate _____
3. A sad friend is a   glum _____
4. To chew cabbage is to   gnaw _____
5. A landfill leap is a   dump _____
6. A grizzly seat is a   bear _____

Write the Answer

A "hink pink" is a pair of one-syllable rhyming words. Read each word clue. Choose two words from the word box to make a hink pink. Then write the hink pink on the correct lines.

Word Box

sad	crook	hot	small	song	plane
long	lane	mall	shook	pot	lad

Word Clues **Hink Pinks**

1. An unhappy boy is a   _____ _____
2. A nervous thief is a   _____ _____
3. A jet runway is a   _____ _____
4. A tiny shopping center is a   _____ _____
5. A very warm kettle is a   _____ _____
6. An endless tune is a   _____ _____

A Final Word

Teaching with hink pink riddles isn't always a quick trick. It can be a struggle to keep up with a class class that doesn't mind the brain pain that can result from creating and solving these little riddles. The next chapter examines the most common figure of speech and the most troublesome to children learning English as a second language: the idiom.

References

Augarde, T. *The Oxford Guide to Word Games.* Oxford, N.Y.: Oxford University Press, 1984.

Brandreth, G. *The Joy of Lex.* New York: William Morrow, 1980.

Burns, M., and M. Weston. *The Hink Pink Book.* Boston: Little, Brown, 1981.

Espy, W. R. *An Almanac of Words at Play.* New York: Clarkson N. Potter, 1975.

———. *Another Almanac of Words at Play.* New York: Clarkson N. Potter, 1980.

Geller, L. G. *Word Play and Language Learning for Children.* Urbana, Ill.: National Council of Teachers of English, 1985.

Golick, M. *Playing with Words.* Markham, Ontario: Pembroke Publishers, 1987.

Johnson, D. D., and B. v. H. Johnson. *Ginn Vocabulary Series.* Lexington, Mass.: Ginn and Company, 1986.

———. *In So Many Words Series.* Logan, Iowa: Perfection Learning, 1990.

———. *The Brain Train.* Elizabethtown, Pa.: Continental Press, 1994.

Lederer, R. *Get Thee to a Punnery.* Charleston, S.C.: Wyrick, 1988.

Pearson, P. D., and D. D. Johnson. *Teaching Reading Comprehension.* New York: Holt, Rinehart and Winston, 1978.

References:
Children's Books

Burns, M., and M. Weston. *The Hink Pink Book.* Boston: Little, Brown, 1981.

Maestro, G. *What's Mite Might?* New York: Clarion Books, 1986.

Terban, M. *Eight Ate.* New York: Clarion Books, 1982.

CHAPTER 3

Idioms

Walk on Eggs

Bertha and Elmer #1

Elmer: Hey, Bertha! Long time no see. What's up?

Bertha: Same old same old. I just got a gander at Henry—looks like he's at death's door.

Elmer: You can bet your bottom dollar his new girlfriend, Myrtle, is running him ragged. Rumor has it she always was a gold digger. Likes living high on the hog. Heard she ran her first husband right into the ground.

Bertha: Henry jumped out of the frying pan and into the fire. I thought he learned his lesson from his last fling. We'd better have a heart-to-heart with him—put the cards on the table.

Elmer: OK, but let's keep this under our hats. If Myrtle gets wind of us sticking our noses in, she'll hit the ceiling and probably fix Henry's wagon to boot.

Bertha and Elmer #2

Elmer: Good day, Bertha. I haven't seen you in a considerably extended period of time. What recently acquired information would you like to share?

Bertha: Indistinguishable information from the last time we spoke. I just saw Henry briefly. He looks as if he's close to expiring.

Elmer: You can be certain that his new significant other, Myrtle, is keeping him heavily engaged in activities. Foundationless beliefs suggest that she invariably has been avaricious in her relationships with men. She enjoys a sumptuous manner of living as well. I heard that she utterly exhausted her first husband because of her demands.

Bertha: Henry clearly has moved from an insufferable circumstance to an even more intolerable situation. I thought he had acquired knowledge and experience from his last period of self-indulgence. We must have a sincere, honest dialogue with him.

Elmer: Agreed. I suggest, however, that we keep this meeting confidential. If Myrtle learns of our concern, she'll become very angry and most likely will chastise Henry as well.

"Bertha and Elmer #1" is peppered with idioms. The playlet is easily comprehensible to adult, native, U.S. English speakers. It would be no picnic, though, for a child or nonnative speaker to comprehend the paragraphs. There is something about the use of idioms in the first playlet that makes us feel more comfortable with the speakers than with those in the second playlet. The language in the first playlet is colorful, lively, and familiar. Although we might think that Bertha and Elmer are somewhat meddlesome, we surmise that they are Henry's true-blue friends and have his best interests at heart. They don't want to see him taken for another ride.

"Bertha and Elmer #2" is devoid of idioms. The language is bloated and self-important. One gets the notion that this Bertha and Elmer are haughty bores. Henry might be unlucky in love, but anything would be better than to spend time with this pompous pair.

Activity

Divide your class into small groups. Tell each group to write a short story, a playlet, or a conversation that might take place in your school lunchroom or after school. Each group should create two versions: one with several idioms and the other with words to replace the idioms. Each group then can enact both versions of their work for the entire class. Ensuing discussions can compare interest, effectiveness, tone, impressions, and other elements. The *Scholastic Dictionary of Idioms* by Marvin Terban (1996) is a five-star, top-notch idiom resource for intermediate and middle school students. It contains more than 600 idioms, their meanings, and their origins.

Getting Down to Brass Tacks:
A Definition of "Idiom"

According to Crystal (1995), "Two central features identify an idiom. The meaning of the idiomatic expression cannot be deduced by examining the meanings of the constituent lexemes. And the expression is fixed, both grammatically ... and lexically" (p. 163). Simply put, an idiom is a saying whose meaning is different from the usual meanings of the individual words. If a person is a "stick-in-the-mud," that means he or she is a dull, fussy person, even though the usual meanings of "stick" and "mud" have nothing to do with the meaning of the idiom. Also, the words that make up the idiom cannot be changed. A "branch-in-the-mud," a "stick-on-the-mud," or a "stick-in-the-wet-soil" wouldn't cut it.

Activity

To demonstrate what happens to an idiom when even one word is replaced with a synonym, write the following five idioms on the chalkboard:

to break the ice (to make people more comfortable by a kind or friendly action)
to keep a stiff upper lip (to be brave)
to be in the driver's seat (to be in control of a situation)
to be full of hot air (to not talk sensibly)
to lead someone by the nose (to direct someone in a bossy manner)

As a full class, replace at least one word in each idiom with a synonym for that word (e.g., to break the frozen water, in the driver's chair). Point out that the phrases are no longer idioms because they become a collection of separate word meanings. You might want to tell the students that a major challenge of learning a foreign language is getting the words in idioms exactly correct. To "miss the boat" and to "miss the sailing vessel" are worlds apart.

Older than the Hills:
The Ages of Some Idioms

When were the following italicized idioms coined?

1. We're not *out of the woods* yet. Another storm is approaching from the west.
   a. circa 200 B.C.
   b. 1942
   c. 1967

2. La Tonda has been *down in the mouth* lately. Maybe we should try to cheer her up.
   a. 1649
   b. 1820
   c. 1935

3. Juto is upset with the boss. He really *gave her a piece of his mind.*
   a. 1667
   b. 1923
   c. 1976

In each item above, the answer is *a*. Ammer (1992) noted that "out of the woods" was used by the Roman playwright Plautus around 200 B.C., "down in the mouth" by Bishop Joseph Hall in 1649, and to "give someone a piece of one's mind" in 1667 by the playwright John Dryden.

The notion that idioms are rather recent additions to our language doesn't hold water. (Note: Writer John French used "hold water," according to Ammer, in 1626.) An historical linguist could recite examples of surprisingly old idioms "until the cows come home" (used in 1620 by Alexander Cooke; see Rogers 1985). Here are some examples. Please note that some idioms cannot be traced to the exact year. In those cases, an approximation is given.

to eat someone out of house and home	A.D. 40
dirt cheap	A.D. 60
in one ear and out the other	A.D. 80
at a snail's pace	1400
to be just skin and bones	1430
to beat around the bush	1520
to keep one's nose to the grindstone	1532
to be at loose ends	1546
too many irons in the fire	1549
to smell a rat	1550
to be left in the lurch	1576
to be in a pickle	1585
through thick and thin	1590

to change one's tune	1600
right under one's nose	1607
to walk on eggs	1621
to not hold a candle to	1640
to stretch one's legs	1653
to have bigger fish to fry	1660
to rack one's brains	1680
with flying colors	1692
to a T	1693

People who get cold feet about teaching idioms to children because they think that idioms are a flash in the pan should by now get the picture that most idioms have withstood the test of time. Their endurance is remarkable.

....**Activity**

Using a simple show of hands, survey your class to determine how many students think they know the meaning of each of the twenty-two idioms above. Tabulate the number who are familiar with or unfamiliar with each idiom. Engage students in a discussion about those idioms with which most are familiar. Then discuss those least familiar. Questions might include: Why are some idioms more famil- iar than others? (E.g., "With flying colors" refers to passing an exam in school; therefore, students might have heard the idiom before.) Are there any patterns in the familiarity of idioms? Where did you learn the idioms? When? How? Can you use each idiom in a sentence or short paragraph that helps identify the meaning?

More capable students might want to research the original meanings and uses of some of the idioms. Ammer's *Have a Nice Day—No Problem!* (1992) will be a valuable resource for students' idiom study. The book contains the origins of three thousand clichés, many of which are common idioms. A brief etymology is given for each entry.

Nothing to Sneeze At:
Writers Who
Introduced Commonly Used Idioms

Who was the first person to use the following idioms?

1. it's Greek to me
2. salad days
3. play fast and loose
4. love is blind
5. with bated breath
6. a foregone conclusion
7. green-eyed monster
8. at one fell swoop
9. the milk of human kindness
10. to go against the grain
11. strange bedfellows

If your guess is the Bard of Avon, William Shakespeare, you are right on the money. Idiom number 1, "it's Greek to me," is from *Julius Caesar*. Idioms 2 and 3, "salad days," and "play fast and loose," are from *Antony and Cleopatra*. "Love is blind" and "with bated breath" can be found in *Merchant of Venice*. *Othello* is the source of "a foregone conclusion" and "green-eyed monster." "At one fell swoop" and "the milk of human kindness" are from *Macbeth*, "to go against the grain" is from *Coriolanus*, and "strange bedfellows" can be found in *The Tempest*.

This might be a long shot, but I think that more high school students would buckle down and sink their teeth into Shakespeare if they knew he was the originator of such popular figures of speech. Not only does his use of idioms make his work seem less remote, but it certainly is also at least a part of why his work seems fresh even today.

Of course other well-known writers and orators have used but not necessarily originated idioms. Here are a few examples:

Cicero—to scrape the bottom of the barrel (to work with the least desirable of something or the leftovers)

John Milton—to add fuel to the fire (to make a bad situation worse)

Voltaire—the best of all possible worlds (a state in which everything is perfect)

Alexander Pope—to do the honors (to perform courtesies for quests, such as pouring them a drink)

Jonathan Swift—(don't) darken my door (again) (do not come to see me again)

Washington Irving—bright and early (very early in the morning)

Sir Walter Scott—to catch someone red-handed (to catch someone with evidence or doing something wrong); to give someone the cold shoulder (to be rather unfriendly toward someone); in the nick of time (just before the time was up); new lease on life (a more positive outlook)

Edgar Allan Poe—to go by the book (to follow the rules)

Henry Wadsworth Longfellow—to fold one's tents (to leave a place or give up)

Charles Dickens—apple-pie order (in place; well-organized); before you can say Jack Robinson (very quickly); behind the times (old-fashioned; not up-to-date); by the same token (in the same manner; also)

Mark Twain—to cut corners (to do something inexpensively); food for thought (something that requires reflection)

Bret Harte—cost a pretty penny (costly)

Arthur Conan Doyle—crystal clear (very clear or obvious)

Winston Churchill—business as usual (the normal routine)

Vanoni (1989) stated, "No other volume compares with the King James Version of the Bible in its influence upon speech. Its impact was especially great in the late eighteenth century, when religious leaders turned to Scripture for rules to govern every area of life" (p. 123). Some commonly used idioms that can be traced to the Bible include:

to raise Cain (to act in a wild manner; to misbehave)

a drop in the bucket (very little; a small amount)

apple of one's eye (a favorite person or thing)

after one's own heart (just the way one likes something)

to be beside oneself (to be worried or upset)

by the skin of one's teeth (just barely)

I hope that by now you are convinced beyond a shadow of a doubt of the historical significance of idioms. But I've just scratched the surface. Run-of-the-mill fictitious stories can't hold a candle to the intriguing real stories behind most idioms.

..........Activity

To activate the students' idiom schemata, share the meanings of several of the idioms above with your class. Divide the class into idiom teams. Each team then will brainstorm and make a list of idioms that come quickly to mind. For a week, teams should look and listen for idioms that can be added to the team list. Using the books previously mentioned and other idiom books such as Marvin Terban's *In a Pickle and Other Funny Idioms* (1983) and *Punching the Clock: Funny Action Idioms* (1990), teams should research the dates and original meanings of the idioms in their lists. Each team's "idiom dictionary" can become an ever-expanding source of idioms that students can use in their writing.

Reading Between the Lines:
The Stories Behind Some Idioms

I grew up learning how to divide words into syllables, how to diagram sentences, and how to put lengthy lists of sentences into proper sequence. Not once was I told a story about how a familiar idiom originated. I am not blaming my teachers for omitting these appealing tales. I spent a good many years teaching public school, and I know how curricular edicts often emanate from those who spend or have spent little time in classrooms with children. By not including the etymology of at least some figurative expressions, however, we are cheating children out of the historical richness of English. Knowing the etymology of common idioms seems to make the language more tangible and more captivating.

Many idioms originally had literal meanings. For example, "reading between the lines" was what people did when a message in invisible ink was written between visible lines of a message. The expression also referred to a message that was encoded not within every line but within every other line, or when readers thought that the intended message had something to do with the spaces rather than the words in a written communication. Etymologists trace the figurative meaning to the mid-1800s.

Here is a baker's dozen of idioms that originally had literal meanings.

baker's dozen—This idiom for "thirteen" originated in medieval England. During that period, unscrupulous bakers intentionally sold bread with more air holes than dough. The jig was up when a law was passed in 1266 that warned of strict punishment for airy loaves. To avoid having the book thrown at them, bakers gave their customers an extra loaf for every twelve purchased. This extra loaf would make up for any unintended lightweights.

to burn one's bridges—Ancient Roman military leaders would burn their boats upon landing on enemy soil so that their own armies could not beat a hasty retreat. Leaders used the same strategy when their invading armies crossed bridges.

to have something up one's sleeve—In the 1400s, there were no pockets on clothing. Full, puffy sleeves, therefore, became temporary storage areas for personal effects. Whether walking through the marketplace or meandering along the moat, most folks probably had something up their sleeves.

to strike while the iron is hot—Funk (1955) noted that this idiom was found in a work by Chaucer in 1386. The expression refers to the actions of blacksmiths, who had to quickly hit and shape metal before it cooled.

to go to rack and ruin—This idiom dates from the 1500s. "Wrack" was a form of the verb "wreck." According to Garrison (1992), if ships were wrecked (or wracked), their owners could be ruined by the losses.

to be called on the carpet—Before wall-to-wall became commonplace, only those areas occupied by the wealthy or the powerful were furnished with carpets. If an employee or servant was "called on the carpet," that person was summoned by a "superior" for a tongue-lashing or worse.

to give someone the cold shoulder—In the 1800s, a pesky visitor was often given an inexpensive shoulder portion of cold meat rather than a tantalizing warm meal in the hopes that the visitor would take a powder, or not linger.

run-of-the-mill—This idiom, meaning ordinary, originally meant the production from a mill before any quality control was put into effect. For example, run-of-the-mill flour might contain weeds, insects, or other unwanted items that an inspector would toss out.

to make the grade—Whether talking about a human on foot or a locomotive coughing out steam, special effort was (and is) required to climb the incline, or grade, of some steep hills.

to fork over—This American-sounding idiom actually can be traced to Britain. Tenants who could not pay the rent on the land they worked had to pay with their crops at harvest time. Landlords would demand that the farmers pick up pitchforks and fork over the grain or vegetables.

to know the ropes—One need only glance at a drawing of an old sailing vessel to realize that learning how its system of ropes operated was no piece of cake. It took an experienced sailor to know the ropes of his ship.

at the end of one's rope—A grazing animal, such as a horse, would be tied to a stake via a rope so that the animal could not wander. Often the animal would stretch the rope to its fullest length (i.e., to the end of the rope) to eat the grass within the rope's range.

to start from scratch—In any type of race, a runner, driver, or animal starts from a beginning point. Years ago, this starting point was scratched into the ground. To start from scratch, therefore, meant to start at the beginning.

■■■...**Activity**

Readers of all ages enjoy Fred Gwynne's *The King Who Rained* (1970) and *A Chocolate Moose for Dinner* (1976). The books are built around homophones (i.e., words with the same pronunciation but different spellings and meanings, such as "blue" and "blew") and homographs (i.e., words that have more than one meaning, such as a "fair" test or a county "fair"). The humor stems from the illustrations that portray the unintended meanings of the text. Read *The King Who Rained* or *A Chocolate Moose for Dinner* to your class. Then challenge students to write and illustrate a short idiom book with a mismatch between the intended meaning of the idiom (in the text) and the unintended meaning (portrayed in the illustrations). For example, if a student's text contains the sentence "Palo is *down in the dumps*" (meaning Palo is sad), the accompanying illustration might show a boy in a landfill. Having students share their illustrated "Gwynne-like" stories will reinforce the fact that idioms have distinct meanings that are different from the meanings of the words within the idioms.

■■■

More to It than Meets the Eye:
Inconsistencies in Explanations of Origins

Reference materials don't always agree on how idioms originated. For example, Ammer (1992) gives the following explanation of the meaning and the origin of *to eat one's hat*: "To declare one's readiness to consume one's headgear if a statement should prove false, an event should not occur, etc. The likelihood of actually doing so is presumably very remote, which is the very analogy being drawn (to a statement's being false, an event not occurring, etc.)" (p. 102).

Vanoni (1989) reported: "Napier's Boke of Cookery, an early British cookbook (1838), gives these directions: 'Hattes are made of eggs, veal, dates, saffron, salt, and so forth.' Exactly what these were is not too clear, but a strong stomach was probably needed to eat them. Even so, the early bragger who offered to eat a hatte had nothing as inedible as felt or straw in mind" (p. 23).

Funk (1955) gave this explanation: "Dickens could have coined the phrase, but it is more likely that it was merely his own adaptation of the older, 'I'll eat old Rowley's hat,' of the same general significance. Here 'old Rowley' referred to Charles II, a nickname given to him, it is said, from his favorite race horse, but cherished by his adherents from the long struggle against Oliver Cromwell, through punning connection with the familiar saying, 'a Rowley (Rowland) for an Oliver'" (p. 185).

I did not open such a can of worms each time I tracked down an origin. If I had, I would have thrown in the towel on etymology. Most sources do concur on how common idioms came about, and the sheer joy of knowing a little bit more about the expressions we use every day is worth the occasional disappointment when authors do not agree on origins.

One can only marvel at the scholarship and persistence of those who have helped preserve a part of our language's history by investigating the origins of idiomatic expressions. An example from Funk (1955) will shed some light on this scholarly commitment. Funk was trying to determine the origin of the phrase "to pull oneself up by one's bootstraps." He searched through dictionaries dated from 1611 to 1933 to determine a date and a definition for the word "bootstrap." No luck. He read books on bootmaking. Dead end. Finally, he "wrote to the Northampton Town (England) Footwear Manufacturers' Association, representing the center of English boot- and shoe-making since the early seventeenth century. My inquiry was ... turned over to Mr. John H. Thornton, ... a collector of historical items connected with the industry. ... Heavy riding boots, according to Mr. Thornton, were the first to be made with bootstraps and such boots did not come into use much before the end of the sixteenth century. The bootstrap, accordingly—or 'strap' as then called—had not been known long when Shakespeare mentioned it in *Twelfth Night,* written in 1601" (pp. xi–xii).

Activity..

Tell students how the idiom "baker's dozen" came about (see previous section). Then read *The Baker's Dozen: A Colonial American Tale* retold by Heather Forest (1988). The story is about a greedy baker who becomes well-off and then begins to scrimp on ingredients. An elderly woman scolds him, but he is unmoved. Business drops off. One of his cookies tells the baker that he is too greedy to become successful again. When the elderly woman comes back to the bakery, the baker gives her thirteen cookies for the twelve she ordered. Word spreads of the baker's generosity, and he prospers once more.

Discuss with the class the similarities between the actual origin of "baker's dozen" and the colonial tale. Then read the origins of several idioms from the previous section or from a source such as Ammer (1992). Some idioms might have more than one plausible origin. Have students write a tale that corresponds to the idioms of their choice (and in some cases, the origin of their choice).

Hopping on the Bandwagon:
Idioms That Originated in the United States

There are some idioms that are purely American. "To hop on the bandwagon," for example, was introduced in this country. In the 1800s, politicians and circus performers joined bands on wagons pulled by horses. Frequently, local politicians would hop on bandwagons to show support for particular candidates. The following idioms also are attributed to our clever, colorful forebears.

in the catbird seat (in an advantageous position)

from the word go (from the beginning)

to fly the coop (to leave)

to pay one's dues (to work hard and not take an easy route toward accomplishing something)

to bark up the wrong tree (to misdirect one's efforts or to ask the wrong person for something)

another day, another dollar (routine; this day is like any other)

to hightail it (out of somewhere) (to leave quickly)

to go along for the ride (to do something with another person but have no particular interest in the activity)

to fly off the handle (to become upset quickly)

to be all wet (to be mistaken)

that's for the birds (that's foolish or won't work)

at an all-time low (or high) (very low or high)

for the umpteenth time (as has been said or done many times before)

act your age (don't act so silly)

to do an about face (to change one's mind or actions)

a knock-down, drag-out fight (a serious confrontation)

to mend one's fences (to become friendly again with another person)

to be on the level (to be honest)

to be out in left field (to be far from accurate or normal)

to paint the town red (to celebrate wildly)

from the sublime to the ridiculous (from excellent to bad)

up for grabs (available to anyone or uncertain)

to keep up with the Joneses (to compete with one's neighbors)

to raise the roof (to become angry)

hook, line, and sinker (all; everything)

the real McCoy (something genuine)

hold your horses (please wait)

to pass the buck (to blame someone else)

to ride the gravy train (to gain much with little effort)

to play both ends against the middle (to pit people against each other for one's own benefit)

a tough act to follow (difficult to improve upon)

that hits the spot (that's just right)

head and shoulders above (someone or something) (much better than)

you can bet your boots (you can be certain)

This list is by no means exhaustive. Idioms that originated in the United States are a dime a dozen. As with other idioms, most have wonderful tales behind them.

Activity ....

Through group discussion, either in "idiom teams" or with the full class, have your students agree or speculate about the meanings of the American idioms above. Christine Ammer's *Have a Nice Day—No Problem!* (1992) is an indispensable resource for verification of meanings and origins of these idioms. Remind students that idioms are like words in that their meanings cannot be determined in isolation. Rich context is needed to give direction to the author's intended meaning. Assign each student two or three of the American idioms above. Students should use each idiom in a paragraph that helps readers figure out the intended meaning. Then ask groups of three students to tie their paragraphs together to form a coherent letter or article.

Activity ....

There are at least three explanations for the origin of the idiom "the real McCoy." Some experts believe the idiom refers to a late-nineteenth-century boxer whose nickname was Kid McCoy. Other etymologists think that the idiom originally referred to a brand of whiskey. A third explanation refers to the inventions of Elijah McCoy (1844–1929). Read *The Real McCoy: The Life of an African-American Inventor* by Wendy Towle (1993) to your class. Born to parents who escaped from slavery to Canada via the Underground Railroad, Elijah McCoy studied mechanical engineering in Scotland. After the Civil War, he moved to Michigan, where he worked for a railroad company. During that time, he invented a time-saving lubricating device for trains. There were imitators of McCoy's device, but discerning customers wanted only "the real McCoy." Elijah McCoy invented other useful items and eventually formed his own company.

Not from This Neck of the Woods:
Idioms in Other Cultures

Americans share many idioms with other cultures. Suzanne Brock, in *Idiom's Delight: Fascinating Phrases and Linguistic Eccentricities* (1988), pointed out that "Americans and Spaniards both cry crocodile tears. ... We both speak of a swan song and a stroke of luck. ... We both break the ice, ... swallow our pride, and have one foot in the grave" (p. 14). She also noted that several idioms in other languages have counterparts in American English. Here are some examples from Brock.

Spanish: *cogerlo con las manos en la masa* (to be caught with one's hands in the dough)
American English: to be caught red-handed

Spanish: *No quisiera estar en su pellejo* (I wouldn't want to be in your skin)
American English: I wouldn't want to be in your shoes

French: *Le champ est libre!* (The field is free!)
American English: The coast is clear!

French: *sur la paille* (on the straw)
American English: down and out, or on the skids

Italian: *inghiottire il rospo* (to swallow the toad)
American English: to eat crow

Italian: *rompere le uova nel paniere a qualcuno* (to break the eggs in someone's basket)
American English: to rain on someone's parade

Several German idioms have American English counterparts. Wiznitzer (1975) included the following idioms among his many examples.

German: *im Geld schwimmen* (swimming in money)
American English: rolling in money

German: *die Katze aus dem Sack lassen*
American English: to let the cat out of the bag

German: *Es liegt mir auf der Zunge*
American English: It's on the tip of my tongue

Collections of idioms from other cultures are as scarce as hen's teeth in many library reference sections and bookstores. Idioms seem to take a backseat in other languages as well. One cannot be considered proficient in a language, however, unless one understands its idiomatic expressions.

Any study of idioms across cultures reveals that deep down, we have many commonalities and are pretty much cut from the same cloth. It's a small world, and when it comes to feelings, experiences, and dreams, most of us speak the same language.

Activity

Perhaps you have students in your class who recently came to the United States from another country, or maybe your students know someone from another country who speaks a language other than English. Learning the idioms of a language is one of the most difficult things about learning that language. As a class, gather as many idioms from languages other than American English as you can find. For each idiom, decide if there is an American English–language counterpart.

The Whole Ball of Wax
(Shebang, Nine Yards, Kit and Caboodle):
Categories of Idioms

The sheer number of idioms cries out for some system of organization. In *NTC's American Idioms Dictionary* (Spears 1987), there are eighty-eight idiom entries just for the word "about" (e.g., to carry on about a person). I have culled common idioms from a variety of sources and have put them into categories that I think are the closest to most children's prior knowledge. I also have included the meanings of the idioms. The lists are by no means finite, and, as with any type of grouping, some members fit into more than one category.

Colors

to show one's true colors (to reveal what one is really like)

with flying colors (with complete success)

green with envy (jealous)

to give the green light to (to give permission)

to have a green thumb (to be a particularly successful (and often lucky) gardener)

to look green around the gills (to look ill)

to have a yellow streak (to be a coward)

to paint the town red (to celebrate)

to see red (to become very angry)

to be in the red (to owe money)

a red-letter day (an important day)

to catch someone red-handed (to catch someone doing something wrong)

to not have a red cent (to not have any money)

to roll out the red carpet (or to give someone the red-carpet treatment) (to treat someone especially well)

true-blue (to be loyal)

blue-ribbon (panel, cake, speech, and so on) (high quality)

once in a blue moon (very seldom)

to talk until one is blue in the face (to talk at length but have no effect on another person)

out of the (clear) blue (sky) (without warning)

to talk a blue streak (to talk a lot without stopping)

to wave a white flag (to want to settle some dispute or to want to surrender)

a white elephant (a useless or unwanted item)

to whitewash (to make a dishonest or inappropriate act seem less important)

in the black (not in debt)

purple passion (intense feeling)

to get a pink slip (to lose one's job)

to look through rose-colored glasses (to see things in an unrealistically optimistic way)

a golden opportunity (a rare opportunity of which one should take advantage)

born with a silver spoon in one's mouth (born into a privileged home)

a silver-tongued orator (a gifted speaker)

Numbers

one's days are numbered (one has only a short time left)

to have someone's number (to know the type of person someone is)

one's number is up (one has been unable to escape something certain such as death)

to zero in on (to concentrate on or to come closer to accomplishing)

A-number-one (the finest)

one-horse town (a small, boring town)

to have a one-track mind (to think of one thing to the exclusion of all else)

back to square one (back to the beginning)

from day one (from the beginning)

one-in-a-million (rare)

to put two and two together (to figure something out)

to put in one's two cents' worth (to give one's opinion)

no two ways about it (no alternatives)

to tell someone a thing or two (to tell someone off)

the three Rs (reading, writing, and arithmetic)

a three-ring circus (somewhat out of control)

on all fours (on one's hands and knees)

take five (take a pause or short break)

six of one, half dozen of the other (the same)

in seventh heaven (very happy; elated)

behind the eight ball (in trouble or in a bad situation)

nine-to-five job (a job that requires one to work typical business hours)

dressed to the nines (well-dressed, usually in expensive or showy clothes)

on cloud nine (ecstatic; overjoyed)

wouldn't touch it with a ten-foot pole (wouldn't consider getting involved with or commenting on it)

Food

sour grapes (disparagement of something one has been unable to get)

comparing apples and oranges (comparing two dissimilar things)

apple-pie order (well-organized)

to spill the beans (to tell a secret)

not worth a hill of beans (worth little)

to not know beans about (to not know anything about)

to dangle a carrot in front of someone (to try to get someone to do something by promising that person a reward) a hard nut to crack (someone who is difficult to get information from)

to walk on eggs (to be careful around someone or about something)

to have egg on one's face (to be embarrassed about something one did)

to bring home the bacon (to bring home a paycheck)

one's bread and butter (one's main source of income)

to butter up someone (to flatter someone)

icing on the cake (an unexpected or additional pleasant benefit)

pie-in-the-sky (unrealistic)

Activity...

Have teams of students locate idioms to place in the following categories.

Animals (e.g., to call off the dogs, to take the bull by the horns)

Birds, Fish, Insects (e.g., a wild goose chase, to have other fish to fry, to have a bee in one's bonnet)

The Body (e.g., over one's head, to keep a straight face, a sight for sore eyes)

Clothing (e.g., off-the-cuff, to be old hat)

A House, Its Parts, and Its Contents (e.g., on the house, to hit the roof, a wet blanket)

Money (e.g., to coin a phrase, to cost a pretty penny, that's money down the drain)

Plants (e.g., no bed of roses, to offer an olive branch, to turn over a new leaf)

Time (e.g., in the nick of time, to call it a day)

Students also can select their own categories and find idiom members for those categories. For example:

category: Show Business

members: the show must go on

get the show on the road

to steal the show

to get one's act together

When the students have several idioms in their categories, play charades. Have teams pantomime the idioms that they have compiled. The "audience" can try to guess each idiom being depicted and ultimately the category of the idioms.

A Final Word

My intent in this chapter (without making a federal case out of it) was to show how there is more to idioms than meets the eye. To write idioms off is to miss the boat on helping your students get a kick out of language without having to let learning take a backseat. When working with idioms, the sky's the limit. Speaking of "sky," what does "counting the rivets" mean? It is a pilots' slang for flying much too close to another plane. How about "Iowa"? According to Dunn (1997), the term is used by television and movie script writers to refer to a rather amateurish piece of work (e.g., "This play is really Iowa"). In the next chapter, we enter the world of established slang. Fasten your seat belts!

References

Ammer, C. *Have a Nice Day—No Problem!* New York: Plume Books, 1992.

Brock, S. *Idiom's Delight: Fascinating Phrases and Linguistic Eccentricities.* New York: Vintage Books, 1988.

Burke, D. *Street Talk-3: The Best of American Idioms.* Beverly Hills, Calif.: Optima Books, 1995.

Crystal, D. *The Cambridge Encyclopedia of the English Language.* Cambridge, Mass.: Cambridge University Press, 1995.

Dunn, J. *Idiom Savant: Slang as It Is Slung.* New York: Henry Holt, 1997.

Fry, E. B., J. E. Kress, and D. L. Fountoukidis. *The Reading Teacher's Book of Lists.* 3rd ed. Englewood Cliffs, N.J.: Prentice Hall, 1993.

Funk, C. E. *A Hog on Ice and Other Curious Expressions.* New York: Harper & Row, 1948.

———. *Heavens to Betsy! And Other Curious Sayings.* New York: Harper & Row, 1955.

Garrison, W. *Why You Say It: The Fascinating Stories Behind Over 600 Everyday Words and Phrases.* Nashville, Tenn.: Rutledge Hill Press, 1992.

Gulland, D. M., and D. G. Hinds-Howell. *The Penguin Dictionary of English Idioms.* New York: Viking Penguin, 1986.

Lyman, D. *The Animal Things We Say.* Middle Village, N.Y.: Jonathan David Publishers, 1983.

Rogers, J. *The Dictionary of Clichés.* New York: Wings Books, 1985.

Spears, R. A. *NTC's American Idioms Dictionary.* Lincolnwood, Ill.: National Textbook Company, 1987.

Urdang, L., W. W. Hunsinger, and N. LaRoche. *A Fine Kettle of Fish and Other Figurative Phrases.* Detroit, Mich.: Visible Ink Press, 1991.

Vanoni, M. *I've Got Goose Pimples: Our Great Expressions and How They Came to Be.* New York: Quill, 1989.

Wiznitzer, M. *Bildliche Redensarten.* Stuttgart, Germany: Ernst Klett Verlag GmbH, 1975.

References:
Children's Books

Beal, G. *The Kingfisher Book of Words.* New York: Kingfisher Books, 1991.

Forest, H. *The Baker's Dozen: A Colonial American Tale.* San Diego, Calif.: Gulliver Books, 1988.

Gwynne, F. *The King Who Rained.* New York: Simon and Schuster Books for Young Readers, 1970.

————. *A Chocolate Moose for Dinner.* New York: Simon and Schuster Books for Young Readers, 1976.

Terban, M. *In a Pickle and Other Funny Idioms.* New York: Clarion Books, 1983.

————. *Punching the Clock: Funny Action Idioms.* New York: Clarion Books, 1990.

————. *Scholastic Dictionary of Idioms.* New York: Scholastic, 1996.

Towle, W. *The Real McCoy: The Life of an African-American Inventor.* New York: Scholastic, 1993.

CHAPTER 4

Established Slang

Firebug

Health Nut

Greasy Spoon

As we were growing up, many of us were told to not use slang. We somehow knew, even with our limited experience, that if we didn't follow this directive, in the future we would be viewed by others as hopeless, unschooled dolts. The slang discussed in this chapter is not of the off-color, cheap-shot genre. That type of gross, sleazy, disgusto slang is better left to sickos, weirdos, and creeps—just the kind of scumbags we always were warned about. No, here we will take the high ground.

Not for Goof-offs, Lazybones, or Lightweights: The Study of Slang

Jonathan Evan Lighter, an English professor from the University of Tennessee, is compiling the ultimate reference on slang, the *Random House Historical Dictionary of American Slang*. The monumental work, when completed, will consist of three volumes. Malcolm Jones, Jr., in a *Newsweek* article (July 11, 1994), noted that Lighter's first volume (A–G) alone contains 20,000 definitions with 90,000 citations. Jones wrote, "Lighter's dictionary accords the nation's homemade language the respectful scrutiny it has so long deserved and so rarely enjoyed" (p. 49).

According to Lighter (1994), slang is "an informal, nonstandard, nontechnical vocabulary composed chiefly of novel-sounding synonyms for standard words and phrases" (p. xi). He pointed out: "Often, too, the use of slang suggests, as standard speech cannot, an intimate familiarity with a referential object or idea (compare, for example, the difference between *professional dancer* and *hoofer, wait tables* and *sling hash* ...). ... It pops the balloon of pretense" (p. xii).

Slang differs from jargon. Lighter defines jargon as "a vocabulary of technical terms" used by those who "share training or expertise" (p. xiii). For example, "alternative assessment techniques," "core curriculum," and "constructivist orientation" are a part of educators' jargon. These terms are not slang; they are not unique, less pretentious synonyms for more standard terms.

Eminent language scholars have not pooh-poohed the importance of slang in American English. S. I. Hayakawa (cited in Lighter 1994) said, "Slang is the poetry of everyday life" (p. xi). H. L. Mencken in *The American Language* (1977) noted, "What chiefly lies behind it is simply a kind of linguistic exuberance, an excess of word-making energy. ... The best slang is not only ingenious and amusing; it also embodies a kind of social criticism" (p. 702). Steven Pinker, in his widely acclaimed *The Language Instinct* (1994), stated, "As for slang, I'm all for it! Some people worry that slang will somehow 'corrupt' the language. We should be so lucky. ... When the more passé terms get cast off (from slang) and handed down to the mainstream, they often fill expressive gaps in the language beautifully" (p. 400). Professor Pinker is no piker. His brilliant book was selected by the editors of the *New York Times Book Review* as one of the "Best Books of the Year." As early as 1927, sociologists Sumner, Keller, and Davie, in *The Science of Society* (cited in Carruth and Ehrlich 1988), reported, "A people who are prosperous and happy, optimistic and progressive, will produce much slang; it is a case of play; they amuse themselves with the language" (p. 532).

Activity

Two books that will give your students a notion of slang in text are John Scieszka's *The True Story of the 3 Little Pigs! by A. Wolf* (1989), and Ruth Heller's *Color* (1995). Scieszka's book contains such slang as *jazzed up* and *the brains of the family,* and gives the reader a feel for the type of character the wolf is by its rather irreverent, "tough-guy" but humorous tone. Discuss "point of view" in a tale and how the reader might have a different impression of the wolf if he used formal English rather than slang.

Color contains such slang terms as *presto* and *change–o,* but this book is no twist on a fairy tale. It is an artistically designed and illustrated treasure that includes words such as "magentas," "cyan blues," and "achromatic." You might want to share this book with your class simply because of its sheer visual beauty. Heller also uses idioms such as "I'll eat my hat" and "by hook and by crook" in the text.

Activity

Write the word "big" on the chalkboard or on an overhead transparency. Tell students that there are many clever slang phrases in American English that use the word "big." Write down a few of the following examples and have students suggest others.

big bucks	Big Brother
big deal	big league
big name	big spender
yea big	talk big
big time	big of you

Have students write an advertisement for a *big-ticket item* that incorporates several of the "big" phrases. Ask students to do the same thing with "money" (e.g., *easy money*), "one" (e.g., *look out for number one*), and "story" (e.g., *sob story*).

Oldies but Goodies and Duds:
Time-Tested Slang and Quickly Forgotten Slang

Some slang has been around for a while; it is established. Here are some examples:

1. Alden is *cranky* today. I *haven't the foggiest* why.
2. The police have *the goods* on the suspect. That's one more *bad guy* headed for the *clink.*
3. Ms. Mabossa threw us a real *curveball* on the test. She asked when the slang term *chopper* first was used for "helicopter."
4. That *firebug* always was a *geek.*
5. My hotel room was a *cheapie.* It's no wonder I was a *basket case* after spending a night in that *fleabag.*

Here are the dates when the italicized slang above came into use.

Example 1.	*cranky*	1812
	haven't the foggiest	1917
Example 2.	*the goods*	1877
	bad guy	1944
	clink	1785
Example 3.	*curveball*	1944
	chopper	1951
Example 4.	*firebug*	1872
	geek	1876
Example 5.	*cheapie*	1942
	basket case	1952
	fleabag	1941

In referring to a book by Mario Pei, Dickson (1990) said Pei "points out that Shakespeare used the slang of his time, and by doing so gave us such words as *hubbub, fretful, fireworks,* and *dwindle*" (p. xiv). Dickson also noted that "English words as diverse as *snide, hold up, nice* (as in '*nice work*'), *bogus, strenuous, clumsy,* and *spurious* were regarded as slang not that long ago" (p. xiv).

Farb (1973) stated, "Occasionally some slang words—like *joke, fad, boom, crank,* and *slump*—become respectable items in the vocabulary. The Standard German word for 'head,' *Kopf,* was once slang" (p. 86).

Thumbing through Lighter's first volume of the *Random House Historical Dictionary of American Slang* (1994), I found the following former slang that has become part of Standard English: *bamboozle, alibi, (baby) boomer, boondocks, bore* (tiresome person), *chicken feed* (a small amount of money), *crowd* (many people), (to be in a) *crunch, cushy* (not difficult), (to) *doctor* (something up), *fake* (not real), *eatery, gooey,* and (to hear something via the) *grapevine*. There are oodles more.

Activity..

Many intermediate- and middle-grade students enjoy doing survey research. Slang provides a golden opportunity for your students to interview siblings, parents, grandparents, other relatives, and family friends about favorite slang terms that they used as children, teenagers, or adults. Interview questions might include some such as the following:

What slang do you remember using or hearing often?

How old were you then?

What year(s) was that?

What did the slang terms mean?

How did you use them?

On what occasions?

Other questions might deal with prevailing attitudes toward slang in speaking and writing.

In small groups or as a full class, the slang words, definitions, and dates can be compared, tabulated, and discussed. The result will be an historical profile of slang expressions known or used by people close to the lives of your students, bringing personal involvement to their study of language.

■ ■

Some slang is fleeting. Partin, in *The Social Studies Teacher's Book of Lists* (1992), lists slang from previous decades. A few examples from the 1920s through the 1960s that have fizzled out:

1920s

  darb (excellent)

  ham-and-egger (ordinary person)

  struggle buggy (car)

  wowser (prude)

1930s

  dinger (telephone)

  spinach (nonsense!)

  to unlax (relax)

  to woof (to chat)

1940s

  to ameche (to telephone)

  barouche (car, jalopy)

  grotty (new but useless)

  lettuce (money)

1950s

  boo (excellent)

  to iggle (to persuade)

  shim (one who dislikes rock-and-roll music)

  zorch (super)

1960s

  bat phone (police officer's phone)

  clanked (tired)

  gasser (the very best)

  shuck (a phony)

  tuff (excellent)

The following slang (from Dalzell's *Flappers 2 Rappers: American Youth Slang*, 1996) was hot in the 1970s and 1980s. These slang terms, too, turned out to be turkeys.

cozy (dull)

to grub (to eat in abundance)

junks (expensive basketball shoes)

load (a car)

melba (peculiar)

road dog (your best friend)

slaps (sandals)

to snake (to steal)

toast (in big trouble)

to woof (to boast)

Dalzell's collection of slang from the 1990s includes *blaze* (to leave), *bus one* (to leave), *circle of death* (a bad pizza), *epic* (great), *herb* (a social outcast), *home slice* (a good friend), *hoopty* (a car), and *weesh* (weak).

Activity..

Studying slang can lead to rich classroom discussion. Now would be a good time to discuss why some new words and slang expressions don't catch on. Students can speculate about why earlier terms such as *darb, woof, grotty, iggle, zorch, melba, slaps,* and *circle of death* didn't make it and faded from the language. Would they have used these words? Would they now? In contrast, why have such slang terms as *cranky, firebug, geek, haven't the foggiest, fleabag,* and *basket case* stood the test of time? What role might dictionaries have played? Did new slang need to be used by popular writers to become acceptable? Ask your students if they know of any slang that they once used but would be embarrassed to use now because no one speaks that way anymore. Add their terms to the Partin and Dalzell lists above. Individuals or pairs might enjoy writing short stories or poems using dead slang, supplementing them with appropriately creative illustrations. These could be shared with classes that haven't been studying slang.

Gone in a Jiffy or for Keeps?
Slang Longevity

Pearl's *The Jonathan David Dictionary of Popular Slang* contains "the most popular slang words and expressions in use today" (p. viii). Some examples:

1. bazoo (mouth)
2. cube (an old-fashioned person)
3. fliv (a car)
4. kadigan (something for which the correct name is unknown)
5. nerts (an interjection showing mild upset)

The copyright date of Pearl's book is 1980. Yet the book also includes the slang:

6. beanpole (a tall, skinny person)
7. a grand (a thousand; for example, two grand is $2,000)

8. graffiti (writing on public property)
9. greasy spoon (inexpensive, often untidy place to eat)
10. iffy (not certain)

Why are terms 1–5 seldom seen or heard but terms 6–10 are still common today? Dickson (1990) argued, "It is hard to sustain a 'new slang' without a group that continues to speak it" (p. xv). He gives the Valley Girl slang of the early 1980s as an example of ephemeral slang. There simply were not enough people in the country who used *gnarly* for "good" or *crill* for "not good," so Valley Girl slang faded from the scene, and its words and phrases did not make it into Standard English.

For particular slang terms to enjoy widespread usage and longevity, their creators must come in contact with many other people, and the terms must eventually reach the media. A slang term created by a loner living in a remote mountain cabin will not enjoy the exposure of a new slang term uttered by a well-known actor in a blockbuster film. It certainly must be true that slang enters our language more rapidly today because of our links to electronic media.

■■■**Activity**

Have your class try a small research project. As a group, create four or five nonsense slang words and give them meanings. They should look and sound like real words. For example, they might create the nonsense word *plurt* and give it the meaning "a very funny joke." Your students then should use their new slang words (e.g., "I heard a great *plurt* about a dumpster"). They can try them out around school, in the lunchroom, and elsewhere for a few days. The students should listen to hear if students from other classes begin to pick up these new "words" and use them in conversation or writing. Keep track of the words over the school year. Are any still alive in May?

■■■

Days Old, Legging, and Tooling Ringers:
Slang from Groups

Pinker (1994) stated, "Most slang lexicons are preciously guarded by their subcultures as membership badges. When given a glimpse into one of these lexicons, no true language-lover can fail to be dazzled by the brilliant wordplay and wit" (p. 400). Regardless of the type of group, it is likely that the members have their own lingo. Mencken (1977) reported, "Trappist monks, for whom silence is the rule, have introduced slang among themselves. In a collection of some 1,000 entries of sign language (much of it undoubtedly very ancient) used by Trappists, there are some which express attitudes and concepts which are more or less taboo and are not used in the presence of the Bishop" (p. 703). It probably is a safe bet to say that slang appears in every subculture within every culture.

The terms from the heading for this section have a sad origin. According to Dalzell (1996), they were slang terms used by "child tramps," that is, wandering homeless children during the Great Depression. *Days old* referred to stale baked goods, *legging* meant walking, and *tooling ringers* referred to ringing doorbells.

Lighter (1994) attributes much of our slang to the military. Even though some words and phrases might have originated earlier, slang from wars became better known simply because so many Americans were engaged, one way or another, in the wars. *Foxhole* and *chow* (food) became popular during World War I, *brass* (officers of high rank) and *goof up* during World War II, *chopper* during the Korean War, and *care package* (treats sent from home) from the Vietnam War (Dickson 1990).

The music world has added some oomph to our vocabulary. *Jam session* (an often unscheduled gathering of musicians who usually improvise on musical selections), *tin ear* (one not musically inclined), and *skins* (drums) come from the 1930s swing era; *gofer* (one who fetches things for another), *sleeper* (a surprise musical hit), and *bouncer* (one who keeps order at an event) were popularized during the 1960s.

Westward expansion and films and books based on the Old West gave rise to a wealth of cowboy and cowgirl slang. *Dogie* (a calf, sometimes a stray), *rustler* (a cattle thief), and *tenderfoot* (an inexperienced individual) were popularized by real and Hollywood-made *cowpunchers* (cowboys and cowgirls). Mariani (1994) noted that cowpokes also had numerous slang terms related to cooking. The *chuck wagon* or *mess wagon* or *growler* (wagon carrying food and cooking gear) was run by the *cookie, bean master, dough roller,* or *stomach robber* (cook). *Grub* (food) included *hot rocks* (biscuits), *immigrant butter* (grease, water, flour), *skunk eggs* (onions), *swamp seed* (rice), and *poor doe* (tough venison).

Activity..

Younger students enjoy listening to tall tales. You may want to read *Pecos Bill* by Steven Kellogg (1986) or any other tall tale to the class. Ask students to listen in particular for Western-style slang such as *flea–bitten outlaws* and *horsefeathers*. Later, discuss the possible and probable meanings of the slang expressions.

A "must read" for this section is *Saving Sweetness* by Diane Stanley (1996). It is a hilarious tale about how an orphan finagles her way into a sheriff's heart and home. The tale abounds in Wild West slang.

Activity..

If you have an oven available, try the following recipe for Cowboy Toast with your students. The recipe is from John F. Mariani's *Dictionary of American Food and Drink* (1994).

"Break 6 cold biscuits in half, place in bread pan, and brown in hot oven. Sprinkle with sugar, and replace in oven until sugar is browned. Cover with $1^1/_2$ c. milk, sprinkle with a dash of allspice, pour melted 1 T. butter over the dish, replace in oven, and let simmer for 10 min."

Although the nutritional level of the toast is nothing to write home about, according to Mariani, the dish was found in a 1937 cookbook and touted by the cookbook authors as being "enjoyed in ranch homes and cow camps in the west for many years" (p. 98).

If no oven is available, a Cowpuncher's Sandwich can substitute. The following recipe is from Craig Claiborne (cited in Mariani 1994, p. 99).

"Slice red onions about one-quarter-inch thick. Put them in a bowl with a generous sprinkling of crumbled oregano. Add equal amounts of ice water and vinegar to cover and let stand overnight. Drain the onions, sprinkle with salt and pepper, and use as a filling for two slices of buttered bread."

Ethnic groups contributed to the rich patchwork of American slang. *Nitty-gritty* (the basics; the gist), *badmouth* (to speak about someone in an unkind way), and *chump change* (a small amount of money) are African American in origin. *Macho* (aggressively masculine) and *barrio* (neighborhood) are Mexican American. *Chatterbox* (a very talkative person) and *fluke* (unexpected good luck) are British, and *schmooze* (to chat) and *schlep* (to carry; to lug) are from the Yiddish language. *Klutz* (a clumsy person) and *spiel* (talk that is intended to persuade) are from German. Lighter (1994) noted the American colonists even picked up a few slang terms (e.g., *netop*, Algonquian for "friend") from Native Americans.

Activity

As mentioned earlier, slang is not unique to American English. Many British people enjoy a good feed of *bangers and mash* (wieners and mashed potatoes) with onion gravy. Australians refer to teachers as *chalkies,* to tomatoes as *marties,* and to something easy to accomplish as *all cush.* You probably have students from other cultures who speak languages other than American English in your school. Invite some of these speakers to share slang expressions from their native languages. In what ways are the types and categories of slang expressions in other languages and cultures the same as in American English? In what ways are they different?

Criminals have contributed to American slang. *The big house, slammer, joint, big cage, clink, cooler, pen, hoosegow, pokey, tank, boarding school, academy, jug,* and *icebox* (all slang for jail or prison) is where many criminals *do time* (remain behind bars). A *rat* is one who gives police information about a criminal or crime, and a *mark* is a victim. An inexperienced prisoner is a *fish* or a *pigeon.* A *big cough* is a bomb, and *Mr. Ed* (after the TV series about a talking horse) is unidentifiable meat served to prisoners.

Jerry Dunn has written the quintessential book on the slang of subcultures in America. *Idiom Savant: Slang as It Is Slung* (1997) is a doozy. It is not surprising that gamblers, Harley-Davidson riders, wrestlers, and pool hustlers have their own slang—

but stone skippers, bird-watchers, and creators and solvers of crossword puzzles? Here are some examples from Dunn:

Stone Skippers
> skronker (a thrown stone that doesn't touch anything)
> to plonk out (to have a stone sink with no skips) (p. 214)

Bird-watchers
> gashawk (a plane)
> TV dinner (roadkill (TV stands for turkey vulture)) (pp. 225, 227)

Crossword Puzzle Creators and Solvers
> dirty double-crosser (intersection of two difficult words)
> six down (term for well-known puzzle constructors who have died) (p. 238)

If *six down* seems somewhat insensitive, Dunn's collection from highly respected professions are downright surprising. Here are some from just two professions:

Medical Workers
> eating in (being fed intravenously) (p. 7)
> gone camping (patient in an oxygen tent) (p. 8)
> organ recital (hypochondriac's medical history) (p. 10)
> sidewalk soufflé (patient who has fallen from a building) (p. 12)

Pilots
> chop and drop (a fast descent) (p. 24)
> sniffing for asphalt (seeking a runway in inclement weather) (p. 29)
> cumulo-granite (clouds that hide mountains; flying into cumulo-granites spells death) (p. 25)
> when the rubber band breaks (aircraft engine failure) (p. 31)

Activity..

To build class lists of occupational slang, a good place to begin is with the local newspaper, phone book, advertising circulars, or other listings of occupations. Students can first list the various occupations that exist locally and then choose the ones of greatest interest. As an authentic letter-writing activity, each student could write to one person from a selected occupation asking if the recipient would be willing to share with the class any occupation-related slang and definitions familiar to people in their line of work. The resultant class compilation will reveal the variety of slang expressions in use locally and will serve as an additional "slang word bank" resource. It is highly likely that plumbers, lawyers, car salespeople, nurses, restaurant servers, firefighters, hair stylists, and others will contribute interesting job-specific slang.

Younger students will find Alexandra Day's *Frank and Ernest* (1988), *Frank and Ernest Play Ball* (1990), and *Frank and Ernest on the Road* (1994) loaded with occupational slang. In the first title, Frank (a bear) and Ernest (an elephant) operate a woman's diner while she is gone. Frank and Ernest learn and use diner slang such as *mats* (pancakes), *one from the Alps* (a Swiss cheese sandwich), and *put out the lights and cry* (liver and onions). The second title contains such baseball–related slang as *the meal ticket* (the best pitcher on a team) and *lumber* (a baseball bat). The third title contains trucker slang (e.g., a milk truck is a *thermos bottle*, a *muck truck* is a cement-mixing truck). Students might speculate on slang that Frank and Ernest would use in a variety of occupations.

Although not related to a specific job, occupational realms have dished up some dandy slang that we use without thinking of it as slang.

The Business World

bear market, bull market (a *bear market* goes down; a *bull market* goes up)

to go belly up (to close a business, usually because of financial difficulties)

the books (the financial records of a business)

to get canned (to lose one's job)

cash cow (a product that consistently makes money)

kickback (money received for promoting or selling a product)

paper pusher (person whose main tasks involve a lot of paperwork)

plastic (credit cards)

to plug a product (to publicize a product)

to pound the pavement (to look for a job)

word-of-mouth advertising (happy customers who tell others about a service or product)

The Sports World

batting a thousand (doing well)

benchwarmer (someone who wants to participate in an activity but isn't asked to)

cheap seats (seating for those who bought inexpensive tickets to an event)

good sport (one who is positive and upbeat even under bad circumstances)

neck-and-neck (close)

to pinch hit (to take someone's place, usually temporarily)

to tackle a problem (to begin trying to solve a problem)

to call a timeout (to cease doing something for a period of time)

zip (zero)

Activity..

Have students name their favorite sports. Divide the class members into groups according to the sport each member enjoys the most, either through participating or just watching. Then have them list slang words or phrases common to each sport. For example:

Basketball	**Football**
boards (backboards)	flanker (end position)
skyhook (hook shot)	gridiron (playing field)

In addition, they can interview coaches, managers, players, parents of players, cheerleaders, and fans to add to their repertoires of sports slang.

Activity..

In small groups, have students examine print media, explore computer databases, or listen to radio or television broadcasts for slang terms that would fit under the following headings. Which "world" has the most slang known to the students?

The World of Computers (e.g., *hacker* [someone who can break into a computer system], *crash* [when a computer program stops functioning], *hard copy* [a paper copy])

The World of School (e.g., *apple polisher* [one who flatters the teacher], *snap course* [an easy class], *teacher's pet* [a teacher's favorite student])

The World of Weather (e.g., *twister* [a tornado], *mercury* [the temperature], *thunderboomers* [thunderstorms])

The World of Traffic (e.g., *bumper-to-bumper traffic* [heavy, slow-moving traffic], *rush hour* [heavy traffic before and after common working hours], *bottleneck* [a slowdown in traffic movement, usually caused by a lane closing or narrowing of a lane]).

What Are the Damages for This Rabbit Food?
Slang Related to Food and Eating

The writer James Fenimore Cooper (1789–1851) said, "The Americans are the grossest feeders of any civilized nation known" (Lasky 1977). He didn't mean "disgusting," because this shade of meaning for "gross" did not exist until it was created by students in 1959. I suspect that Cooper meant that, assuming our financial picture was rosy, we weren't picky about what and how much we packed away.

As with other categories of slang, those related to food have some old, rarely used members. Examples include *Chicago* for pineapple (1920s), *chicken fixins* for fancy food (1830s), *common doings* for plain food (1830s), *cut straw and molasses* meaning poor-quality food (1857), *flat car* for pork chops (1936), and *army chicken*, which was World War II slang for beans and wieners (Mariani 1994). Two food-related slang terms not in use today deserve special mention: *slumgullion* and *liberty cabbage*. Mariani (1994) said, "In *Roughing It* (1872) Mark Twain wrote of being offered a drink of slumgullion by a station keeper in Nebraska who said it was like tea. But, Twain remarked, 'there was too much dish rag, and sand, and old bacon-rind in it to deceive the intelligent traveller'" (p. 288). As a patriotic measure, *liberty cabbage* was coined as a replacement for the German *sauerkraut* during World War I.

Not all modern food-related slang is familiar to the masses. The airline industry has some catchy slang that is rarely heard among us grounders. A *galley queen* or *galley king* is a slothful flight attendant who lingers in the plane's kitchen rather than helping the other attendants. *Leather or feather* refers respectively to a beef or chicken meal, and *pilot pellets* are peanuts. If you don't like to eat while flying, prior to boarding you might grab something from a *food simulator* (vending machine in an airport) or an airport restaurant that serves a *hundred-dollar hamburger* (so called because food at airport eateries tends to be costly). The term *airline food* actually has become slang for tasteless, unimaginative eats. Chalmers (1994) reminds us that "taste buds are dulled by high altitude and the cabin pressure" (p. 15), so maybe fliers can be a tad more forgiving.

Whether divey or fancy-schmancy, perhaps no other location serves up as much food-related slang as does a restaurant. Diners at a plush establishment would not use a *boardinghouse reach* (i.e., snatching food quickly and without asking for it to be passed). Regulars and *high muckety-mucks* (i.e., "important" people) at these *table-cloth restaurants* would not be seated in *Siberia* (i.e., in undesirable locations such as the *back of the house* [i.e., the kitchen]).

In less cushy surroundings, one might hear the following slang:

"Where's the opened box of *birdseed* (cereal)?"
"Your *bowwow* (hot dog) is ready."
"Better refill the *lumber* (toothpick) holder, the *twins* (salt and pepper shakers), and the *sand* (sugar) bowls."
"A glass of *city juice* (water). *Hold* (don't add) the *hail* (ice)."

The following slang could be heard in either the posh restaurant or the less ritzy one:

to get stiffed (to not get a tip or an appropriate tip)
fluff and fold (customers who require special attention)
campers (diners who sit at their table for a long time)
sweet spot (the place to which a menu designer tries to draw the customers' eyes first)

The following words and phrases are common food-related slang that your students will encounter.

bite (a small meal)
to brown bag it (to bring one's own lunch to work or to school)

burger joint (a casual restaurant where hamburgers are sold)

carbo load (to eat carbohydrate-rich food before strenuous exercise)

cement doughnut (a bagel)

chief cook and bottle washer (one who cooks and cleans)

chocoholic (a person who likes to eat a lot of chocolate)

to chug-a-lug (to drink something quickly)

doggie bag (leftovers from a restaurant meal that are taken home)

downhome cooking (simple but tasty food)

early-bird special (reduced price on a meal for those who eat early in the evening)

empty calories (usually high-calorie food that has a small amount of nutrients)

fast food (food that can be purchased quickly and is mostly prepared ahead of the customer's arrival)

health nut (a person who eats carefully to avoid illnesses and weight gain)

junk food (food that has little nutritional value)

moo juice (milk)

mom-and-pop (run by a wife-and-husband team)

to have the munchies (to be hungry, usually for snack foods such as potato chips)

mystery meat (meat from an unidentifiable animal source)

rubber-chicken dinner (dinner served at a large gathering, especially a political fund-raiser)

veggies (vegetables)

yo-yo dieting (a cycle of losing weight and then regaining it)

Activity...

Fiction writers, contemporary poets, and writers of song lyrics frequently make use of appropriate slang. This might be a good time for your students to engage in some creative writing—either a short story, poem, or song lyrics. The topic: something to do with food, eating, dining, picnicking, restaurants, recipes. The challenge: to use several of the slang expressions found in the above lists, from the earlier class compilation of occupational slang, or from your students' own prior knowledge. This activity lends itself to the five steps of the writing process: prewriting, drafting, revising, editing, and publishing. Your class might find peer editing to be helpful. Finally, students can publish their works and share them within the classroom and elsewhere, either visually or vocally.

Activity...

As a pre-class-session warm-up, display a different bag of nonperishable packaged food (e.g., dry soup, pretzels) every day for a week or two. Have students quickly think of slang terms for each package. For example, two slang terms for potato chips might be "spud flakes" and "tater baiters."

Out-and-Out Razzle-dazzle:
Repeating Slang and Rhyming Slang

Burke (1992) pointed out that we often use rhyming slang (e.g., *jet set*) without noticing the rhyming elements. The same probably is true for repeating slang (e.g., *over and over*). Here are some common repeating slang and rhyming slang phrases and their meanings.

Repeating Slang

buddy-buddy (overly friendly)

goody-goody (a person who is so nearly perfect that he or she is rather boring)

ha-ha (an interjection indicating laughter, often sarcastic)

hush-hush (secret)

lulu (extraordinary, often in a negative sense)

neck-and-neck (so close as to be a tie)

no-no (something one shouldn't do)

out-and-out (complete)

over and over (many times)

to pooh-pooh (to disregard something or someone)

rah-rah (to cheer; overly enthusiastic)

so-and-so (a name substitute; or a phrase used in place of a nasty word)

so-so (average)

through and through (completely; without a doubt)

up-and-up (legitimate, honest)

yum-yum (to express that something tastes good)

Rhyming Slang

boo-hoo (an expression suggesting crying, usually used in a sarcastic way)

to dilly-dally (to waste time by being slow or not paying attention to the task at hand)

fender bender (a car accident that isn't serious)

fuddy-duddy (a person who is persnickety or too old-fashioned)

handy-dandy (convenient and helpful)

to hobnob (to socialize)

hoity-toity (snobbish, upper-class)

hotshot (someone who is adept)

hubbub (noise or confusion)

humdrum (boredom)

hustle and bustle (a lot of activity)

to kowtow (to humble oneself)

lean and mean (to be fast and efficient)

local yokel (someone from the town one is referring to)

lovey-dovey (showing a lot of affection, sometimes in a sappy way)

nitwit (a foolish person)

okey-dokey (OK)

palsy-walsy (overly close or friendly)

peewee (a very small thing)

ragtag (not organized; not well-dressed)

roly-poly (chubby but cuddly)

wear and tear (heavy usage resulting in something's not being in perfect condition)

wheeler-dealer (someone who makes many deals)

Activity . . . .

You can get instructional and assessment mileage out of the following activity. For each repeating and rhyming slang expression (e.g., *goody–goody, lulu, so–so*), ask volunteers for a definition or a sentence or two containing the expression. Many of the slang terms on these pages probably will be known to all your students, but others (e.g., *hoity–toity, kowtow, ragtag*) may be known to few of them. Ask students to speculate about why so many of these slang terms share common sounds. What makes them fun? Have each student create a clever poster that illustrates the meaning and usage of one less-familiar expression. Invite other classes to visit the poster display.

Some slang doesn't quite rhyme and the word is not repeated, but often only a letter (or two) is changed within the word. Here are some examples:

chitchat (conversation that isn't serious talk)

flip-flop (a complete turnaround; or to reverse)

ho hum (dull; or an interjection meaning that something is boring)

jibber-jabber (unimportant chatter)

mishmash (a group of dissimilar things; a hodgepodge)

riffraff (undesirable, often dishonest people)

rinky-dink (poor-quality, second-rate)

shipshape (in order, tidy)

tip-top (good condition)

wishy-washy (indecisive)

to zigzag (to follow a course full of short sharp turns; or having such turns)

Activity . . . .

Marvin Terban's *Superdupers! Really Funny Real Words* (1989) is filled with repeating slang, rhyming slang, and near-rhyming slang (e.g., *whippersnapper*). The book also gives the origins of many of the words. Terban asks the reader (p. 7):

"Do you know what this sentence means?

"The *roly–poly bigwig pooh–poohed* his *humdrum* life and wanted to go to a *razzle–dazzle wingding.*"

"It means: The chubby important person hated his boring life and wanted to go to an exciting party."

Using words from Terban's book and from the "Out-and-out Razzle-dazzle" section above, have students create sentences laden with repeating slang, rhyming slang, and almost-rhyming slang. Then have them exchange their sentences with another student. Each student should "interpret" the other's slang sentences and write them in Standard English.

A Final Word

This chapter has pointed out that there is no need to freak out over using established slang. The next time you talk about nuking your dinner, watching the tube, owning a gas guzzler, or knowing a bean counter, you can give credit to the indomitable American creativity that coins such terms, and, in so doing, keeps our language fresh and alive. The next chapter examines multiple-meaning words. Sounds blah? Then visualize the action in this headline in two different ways:

Attorney Presents Case in Circus Suit

References

Burke, D. *Street Talk-1: How to Speak and Understand American Slang.* Los Angeles: Optima Books, 1992.

———. *Street Talk-2: Slang Used by Teens, Rappers, Surfers, & Popular American Television Shows.* Los Angeles: Optima Books, 1992.

———. *Biz Talk-1: American Business Slang & Jargon.* Los Angeles: Optima Books, 1993.

———. *Street Talk-3: The Best of American Idioms.* Beverly Hills, Calif.: Optima Books, 1995.

Carruth, G., and E. Ehrlich. *American Quotations.* New York: Wings Books, 1988.

Chalmers, I. *The Great Food Almanac: A Feast of Facts from A to Z.* San Francisco: CollinsPublishers, 1994.

Chapman, R. L. *Thesaurus of American Slang.* New York: HarperPerennial, 1989.

Dalzell, T. *Flappers 2 Rappers: American Youth Slang.* Springfield, Mass.: Merriam-Webster, 1996.

Dickson, P. *Slang! Topic-by-Topic Dictionary of Contemporary American Lingoes.* New York: Pocket Books, 1990.

Dunn, J. *Idiom Savant: Slang as It Is Slung.* New York: Henry Holt, 1997.

Farb, P. *Word Play: What Happens When People Talk.* New York: Alfred A. Knopf, 1973.

Jones, M., Jr., "Red, White and Very Blue." *Newsweek*, 11 July 1994, p. 48–49.

Lasky, M. S. *The Complete Junk Food Book.* New York: McGraw-Hill, 1977.

Lighter, J. E. *Random House Historical Dictionary of American Slang: Volume 1, A–G.* New York: Random House, 1994.

Mariani, J. F. *The Dictionary of American Food and Drink.* New York: Hearst Books, 1994.

Mencken, H. L. *The American Language.* New York: Alfred A. Knopf, 1977.

Partin, R. L. *The Social Studies Teacher's Book of Lists.* Englewood Cliffs, N.J.: Prentice Hall, 1992.

Pearl, A. *The Jonathan David Dictionary of Popular Slang.* Middle Village, N.Y.: Jonathan David Publishers, 1980.

Pinker, S. *The Language Instinct.* New York: HarperPerennial, 1994.

Spears, R. A. *NTC's Dictionary of American Slang and Colloquial Expressions.* Lincolnwood, Ill.: National Textbook Company, 1989.

References:
Children's Books

Day, A. *Frank and Ernest.* New York: Scholastic, 1988.

———. *Frank and Ernest Play Ball.* New York: Scholastic, 1990.

———. *Frank and Ernest on the Road.* New York: Scholastic, 1994.

Heller, R. *Color.* New York: Putnam & Grosset, 1995.

Kellogg, S. *Pecos Bill.* New York: Mulberry, 1986.

Scieszka, J. *The True Story of the 3 Little Pigs! by A. Wolf.* New York: Viking, 1989.

Stanley, D. *Saving Sweetness.* New York: G. P. Putnam's Sons, 1996.

Terban, M. *Superdupers! Really Funny Real Words.* New York: Clarion Books, 1989.

CHAPTER 5

Multiple-Meaning Words

Loot Found by Trash Can

It's down.

The simple sentence above can mean many things.

1. The computer isn't working.
2. It's on a lower level of the building.
3. The sun has set.
4. It's south on the map.
5. I swallowed it.
6. I tied it securely.
7. The stock market has lost points.

8. I recorded it in writing.
9. The shade has been pulled.
10. It's feathers.

If the *It's* is dropped, *down* also can mean:

11. to the ground (The house burned *down*.)
12. out of one's hands (Please put the toy *down*.)
13. finding (She's *tracking down* a thief.)
14. completely (Tom scrubbed *down* the house.)
15. from generation to generation (The necklace was handed *down* from her great-great-grandmother.)
16. to make thinner (Company's coming. Better *water down* the soup.)
17. to bet on (Karin *put* her money *down* on the black.)
18. a down payment (The customer put $50 *down*.)
19. to press (Today's edition of the *Cedar Tribune* has gone *down*.)
20. be seated ("*Down* in front," he shouted.)
21. a play in football (They made a first *down*.)
22. not in top form (Bilius is feeling *down* today.)
23. behind in scoring (Their team is six points *down*.)
24. finished, over ("One exam *down* two to go," said Genna.)

When idioms and slang are included, we can add:

25. *down* and out (without money)
26. *down* in the mouth, *down* in the dumps (sad)
27. *down* on one's luck (having a temporary streak of bad luck)
28. *down* the drain, *down* the tubes, *down* the chute (gone for good, usually in a wasteful way)
29. *down* for the count (not conscious or not active)
30. *down* to the wire (up to the last minute)
31. *down* under (Australia)
32. to get *down* (to get comfortable with something or someone; to relax)
33. brought the house *down* (was very pleasing to an audience)
34. to buckle *down* (to get serious and do something constructive)
35. to back *down* (to not do something one said one would do)
36. to break *down* (to lose control and cry or to have a car stop running)
37. to clamp *down* on someone (to become less easygoing with someone)
38. *down* to earth (practical)
39. to fall *down* on the job (to not do something in a satisfactory way)
40. to get *down* to work, to get *down* to business (to begin working hard)
41. to go *down* in history (to be remembered by future generations)

42. to let one's hair *down* (to become less formal)
43. to wind *down*, to die *down* (to slow)
44. to tone something *down* (to make something less intense or strong)
45. to talk *down* to someone (to speak to someone as if he or she is inferior)
46. to step *down* (to resign)
47. to simmer *down* (to become less angry)
48. to run someone or something *down* (to speak badly about someone or something)
49. to talk someone *down* (to get someone to lower a price)
50. to flag someone *down* (to stop someone for assistance)
51. to go *down* fighting (to try hard until the end)
52. a hand-me-*down* (something not new, usually previously used by a family member)
53. to lay *down* the law (to be firm about something, such as behavior or rules)
54. to never live something *down* (to be unable to overcome others' memories of one's misbehavior)
55. to come *down* in the world (to move to a less prestigious position)
56. to come *down* hard on someone (to be very strict or critical toward someone)
57. to be *down* on (to be unhappy with)
58. *Down* with ... (Do not support ...)
59. hands *down* (completely; without a doubt)
60. Please pipe *down*! (Be less noisy or don't interrupt.)
61. to pull *down* an amount of money (to earn an amount of money)
62. to hunker *down* (to get secure or to earnestly begin a task)
63. to wolf *down*, to scarf *down*, to chow *down* (to eat quickly or hungrily)
64. to shake someone *down* (to intimidate someone in hopes of getting information or goods)
65. Something's going *down* (Something out of the ordinary or extraordinary is happening.)
66. to turn thumbs *down* (to reject or disapprove of something)
67. to turn a place upside *down* (to thoroughly search a place)
68. to be shot *down* (to be belittled or rejected)
69. to throw *down* the gauntlet (to challenge someone to do something)
70. to be tied *down* (to be very busy or to be unable to change one's lifestyle)
71. to vote *down* (to defeat)
72. to shut a place *down* (to close a place)
73. to scale *down* (to make smaller or less ambitious)
74. to mark *down* (to reduce the price)
75. to put one's foot *down* (to be unyielding)
76. to play something *down* (to minimize something)
77. to pin someone *down* (to exert pressure on someone for desired information)
78. to look *down* one's nose at (to show a superior attitude toward)

79. to breathe *down* someone's neck (to watch someone closely)
80. to be bogged *down* (to have too many tasks)
81. to boil *down* to (to reduce to the essential)
82. to dress *down* (to dress in an informal way or to scold)
83. to crack *down* on someone (to be harder on someone than in the past)
84. to cut someone *down* to size (to make someone less arrogant and more humble)
85. to get something *down* (to understand something or to become adept at something)
86. to jump *down* someone's throat (to scold or yell at someone)
87. to hold *down* a job (to have a job, usually one that isn't temporary)
88. to let someone *down* (to disappoint someone)
89. to lay *down* one's life (to give one's life)
90. to lead someone *down* the garden path (to fool someone)

There are more meanings of *down*. Before the reader's interest wears *down*, it should be noted that adding compound words with *down* (e.g., *down*beat, *down*grade, *down*cast, *down*fall, *down*town, *down*trodden, and so on) would lengthen the list even further.

The Lowdown on Multiple Meanings

I have pointed out to my students that often the longer the word, the fewer the definitions of the word. I'm certain there are exceptions, but consider the following words: *hippopotamus, philanthropist,* and *valedictorian.* A *hippopotamus* is a large mammal native to Africa. A *philanthropist* helps others, usually by donating money to a cause, and a *valedictorian* has the highest grades in a graduating class and gives a speech at commencement. Even the longest words in the English language have only one meaning.

Ash (1996) listed the longest word in the English language. It has 1,909 letters and is "the scientific name for tryptophan synthetase A protein, an enzyme made up of 267 amino acids" (p. 108). The second-longest word is 1,185 letters long and is "the word for Tobacco Mosaic Virus, Dahlemense Strain" (p. 108). Hepaticocholangiocholecystenterostomies (a mere 39 letters) is "the word for surgical operations to create channels of communication between gall bladders and hepatic ducts or intestines" (p. 108). The next time your students complain about spelling long words, you might want to put the 39-letter word on the chalkboard.

Now for the words with the most meanings. In the *Oxford English Dictionary,* the word *set* has 464 meanings, *run* has 396 meanings, *take* has 343 meanings, and *stand* has 334 meanings (Ash, 1995). *Down* isn't even listed among the ten words with the most meanings. Words such as *run* and *take* are common in beginning reading books, but one can understand the confusion that arises when a first-grader encounters a different meaning of *run* from the one he or she learned.

Pinker (1994) stated, "Though most common words have many meanings, few meanings have more than one word. ... No one really knows why languages are so stingy with words and profligate with meanings" (pp. 156, 157). The topic of multiple-meaning words can become rather sticky when one enters a linguist's realm. Linguists refer to multiple meanings as polysemy (pah-LISS-uh-mee) and multiple-meaning words as polysemous (pah-LISS-uh-muss) words.

McArthur (1996), in *The Concise Oxford Companion to the English Language*, defined polysemy as "a term in linguistics for words or other items of language with two or more senses, such as *walk* in *The child started to walk* and *They live at 23 Cheyne Walk*" (p. 715). Linguists refer to meanings of a word that are "close" or "distant." McArthur stated, "*Walk* (action), *walk* (street) are relatively close, but *crane* (bird), *crane* (machine) are much farther apart" (p. 715). Carter (1987) said, "*Line* can be associated with drawing, fishing or railways, and share physical properties of material covering space between two points where the different senses are close; but *race* (run in a race; ethnic group) has meanings which are so distant as to be only arbitrarily related through the formal identity of the word" (p. 11).

Aitchison (1994), a psycholinguist from the University of Oxford, although not referring specifically to closeness or distance, clearly understood the concepts. She wrote:

The word *old* is an old problem. Consider: Pauline was astonished to see—

—an old woman (an aged woman)
—an old friend (a long-standing friend)
—her old boyfriend (former boyfriend)
—old Fred (Fred whom she knew well).

The old woman is aged, but the others may be young. The old friend is still a friend, but the old boyfriend might now be an enemy. ... In the case of *old Fred*, English speakers have to know that *old* attached to proper names is a mark of friendly affection (p. 62).

Linguists also speak about the "muzziness" of some words. This means that some words have somewhat vague meanings, but the meanings aren't distinct enough to classify the word as polysemous, or multiple meaning.

Johnson and Moe (1983) examined nine thousand words "common to lists of children's oral vocabulary, story books and school textbooks for children, and various sources of general printed English" (p. 11). The investigators found that 72 percent of the nine thousand words were polysemous or had more than one "unmuzzy" meaning. How can educators handle multiple meanings without teaching every meaning of every word? Johnson and Pearson (1984) suggested the most commonsensical approach that I have found. They said, "Teachers need to help children develop a mind-set for diversity when it comes to word meaning" (p. 29). The remainder of this chapter provides activities that you can use with your students to establish a mind-set for word-meaning diversity when they are reading, listening, speaking, or writing.

Activity ....

To develop a "mind-set" for polysemy, there are four books you might want to share with your students. *Buz* by Richard Egielski (1995) is a story for younger learners. It tells the tale of an insect, Buz, who is eaten with a boy's breakfast cereal. The boy is treated by a physician and given pills to help the boy get rid of the "bug" (i.e., Buz). Buz eventually escapes from the boy's body, but something is wrong with Buz. A "bug" (i.e., insect) physician gives Buz pills for the "germ" that is inside Buz.

Learners new to wordplay will enjoy Michael Rosen's *Walking the Bridge of Your Nose: Wordplay, Poems, Rhymes* (1995). "Foolish Questions," an American folk rhyme adapted by William Cole, uses multiple-meaning words such as *nails, pupils,* and *crook* in questions that seem silly if one uses inappropriate meanings for the multiple-meaning words in the questions. Readers are asked, for example, where one can "buy a cap" for one's knee and a key for a "lock" of hair.

Jumbo, by Rhonda Blumberg (1992) is a nonfiction book about Jumbo, an enormous elephant who was brought from England to America in 1881 by P. T. Barnum. Although *jumbo* does not fit the definition of an eponym because Jumbo wasn't a person, his name has become a synonym for *huge.* After reading the book, ask students to look at large boxes of laundry detergent, paper towels, and other products to see what synonyms for *jumbo* (e.g., *king-size, giant-size, family-size*) are in vogue with package designers.

Linda Bourke's *Eye Count: A Book of Counting Puzzles* (1995) is a counting book for more sophisticated learners. Going through the numerals 1 to 12 requires familiarity with homophones (e.g., *chord, cord*) and multiple-meaning words. For the numeral 8, for example, the word *scale* is pictured with eight different meanings. The reader must identify a *musical scale, a scale model,* to *scale a mountain,* and so on. The book is unique and the artwork is engaging.

Activity ....

Play the *narf* game (Johnson and Pearson, 1984) with your students. First have the participants make up a nonsense word (e.g., *narf, blig, flump, murlb, crulp*). Then use the word in several sentences. The nonsense word will take the place of an actual multiple-meaning word. Here are some examples to get you started.

1. Please *narf* the newspaper article.
2. These papers need a *narf.*
3. "Don't *narf* your opponent," said the football coach.
4. She was traveling at a good *narf.*
5. Big Buck Food Store is a *narf* joint.
   (*Narf* is *clip.*)

1. We got a new *blig.*
2. Her artistic *blig* is remarkable.
3. Those animals graze on the *blig.*
4. The Wasatch *blig* is spectacular.

5. The temperature will *blig* from 70 degrees Fahrenheit to 90 degrees Fahrenheit.
   (*Blig is range.*)

1. Did she *flump* the phone lines?
2. She just put a new *flump* on that shoe.
3. If you *flump* that pencil, it will annoy him.
4. This pipe needs a new *flump*.
5. I've heard that type of *flump* is painful.
   (*Flump is tap.*)

1. The racers got into the *murlb*.
2. A *murlb* was found on the old battlefield.
3. Please fill that *murlb* with whippped cream.
4. That man is just a *murlb* of his former self.
5. Maybe we can bring LaMoine out of his *murlb*.
   (*Murlb is shell.*)

1. That old *crulp* music is from Mr. Tune's attic.
2. The construction worker ruined a large *crulp* of wood.
3. *Crulp* lightning lit up the sky.
4. Can I get that *crulp* in 100 percent cotton?
5. A *crulp* of rain made driving dangerous.
   (*Crulp is sheet.*)

Throughout the game, you might want to point out that a multiple-meaning word can be different parts of speech. For example, *season* can be a noun (e.g., It's been a dry *season*) or a verb (e.g., Let's *season* the stew with paprika). Some students might want to create their own sets of sentences to challenge others.

Activity

Tell your students that riddles often are dependent on the multiple meanings of words. Give the following example:

Why did the ice cream always carry a geometry book?

Answer: It liked cones.

Read the following riddles to your students. Have them supply the missing multiple-meaning words, which are in parentheses.

1. Why was the building popular?

   It had a lot of (stories).

2. Why did the scissors put people to sleep?

   It was (dull).

3. Why did no one pay attention to the cliff?

    It was a (bluff).

4. Why was a fish on a branch with birds?

    It was a (perch).

5. Why did Shantelle use a map to open a door?

    It had a (key).

6. Why did the players always slip on home plate?

    It has an oil (base).

7. Why did the army officers hang around Fred's Discount Market?

    It was a (general) store.

8. What did the gelatin say to the old cheese?

    "Can't you get rid of that (mold)?"

9. Why did the teacher keep the blueberries after school?

    They had been (wild) all day.

10. What did the boastful pan say to the best-seller?

    "I have a more attractive (cover) than you."

11. Why were the lobsters extra nice to Maurice?

    He was a (crab).

12. What did the horse say to the drill?

    "Want to borrow a (bit)?"

13. What did two and four say to one and three?

    "You're (odd)."

14. What did the dog say to the sixteen ounces?

    "I'll trade this (pound) for yours."

15. What do traffic and angry wolves have in common?

    They both can (snarl).

16. Why was the music teacher asked to run six hospitals?

    She had a lot of experience with (staffs).

17. Why are commercials so experienced in rowing boats?

    They're on a lot of (channels).

18. Why does the banker want to go to Japan?

    She has the (yen).

19. What did the potato chip say to the diver?

    "That (dip) was refreshing."

20. What did the punctuation mark tell the cook?

    "Just add a (dash)."

21. Why were the maple-syrup bucket and the bike running away?

    They were tired of carrying some (sap).

22. What did the shellfish say to the rounded, half-circle border?

    "I like your (scallops)."

23. Why was there so much talk at the meeting of plywood?

    It was a (panel) discussion.

24. What did the barbecue chef ask the tennis fans?

    "Where's the (match)?"

25. What did the billiard player say to the actor?

    "Let's discuss this (cue)."

■■■

■■.....Activity

Divide your students into teams of four. Tell them you are going to have a Multiple-Meaning Mind-Mangler Match. You or a volunteer will read two words or phrases. Each team will think of a multiple-meaning word that fits each of the words or phrases.

Example Words		Multiple-Meaning Word
sailors	gloves	hands

Explanation: Sailors are sometimes referred to as "hands," and gloves are worn on one's hands.

The first team to raise its hand with the correct multiple-meaning word and with both meanings used in one explanatory sentence (such as the "hands" example above) gets a point. Here are many mind-manglers and the correct multiple-meaning words. Your teams might want to devise their own to try to stump the other teams. Multiple-Meaning Mind-Mangler Matches can introduce players to new meanings for familiar words.

Words or Phrases		Multiple-Meaning Words
1. wheel	speaker	spoke
2. whole wheat	to do nothing	loaf
3. unusual	fiction	novel
4. to observe	reminder	note
5. corn	manufacturing	plant
6. not trained	forest	green
7. unclear	peach	fuzzy
8. evening	film	star
9. shore	to drift	coast
10. direct	hot dog	frank
11. to slant	skinny	lean
12. lion	to follow	tail
13. gulp	hook, line, and sinker	swallow
14. harmless	money and jewels	safe
15. a deed	to perform	act
16. group	cave dwellers	club
17. gateway	foot	arch
18. limbs	weapons	arms
19. toe	pencil	stub

Words or Phrases		Multiple-Meaning Words
20. price	game	tag
21. clock	deer	tick
22. to eat	contents	table
23. liquids	grain	straw
24. to cheer	underground	root
25. wild dogs	journey	pack
26. cook	airport	apron
27. most important	officer	major
28. to stop	city	block
29. sun	brown	tan
30. ship	newsperson	anchor
31. curve	to fold up	bend
32. travel	to slip	trip
33. bed	nonsense	bunk
34. dim	dizzy	faint
35. marsh	to overwhelm	swamp
36. window	to look at carefully	screen
37. fog	to confuse	cloud
38. rides	not good or bad	fair
39. icy	feet	cold
40. to filter	muscle	strain
41. grade	punctuation	mark
42. car	water	pool
43. thick	not bright	dense
44. land	area of study or work	field
45. not tidy	to fool with	mess
46. to cry	fat	blubber
47. to get bigger	excellent	swell
48. lamp	tulip	bulb
49. crop	vehicle front and back	bumper
50. ordinary	cold	common
51. young students	rating	grade
52. wedding	to clean	groom
53. sour	car	lemon
54. chip	time	nick
55. calm	hospital	patient
56. sugary	wealthy	rich
57. only	shoe	sole
58. dance	water	tap
59. to bend over	feeling about the future	hunch
60. cork	parade	float

Multiple-Meaning Words

	Words or Phrases		Multiple-Meaning Words
61.	fence	notice	post
62.	candy	coins	mint
63.	rough plan	chilly air	draft
64.	to watch carefully	tags	tabs
65.	store	electrical plug	outlet
66.	thin	punishment	fine
67.	great	thousand	grand
68.	ground seeds	lunch	meal
69.	opening	baby bird	hatch
70.	eye	pan	lid
71.	slow animal	lazy	sloth
72.	equal	bow	tie
73.	to push	magazines, newspapers	press
74.	clothes	failures	duds
75.	buds	a liking for	taste
76.	to hold back	along a street	curb
77.	noise	solid	sound
78.	gown	thought	train
79.	flat bill	to dodge	duck
80.	cloth	small area	patch
81.	to pull	boat	tug
82.	to walk	stairs	steps
83.	story	bank	teller
84.	yet	quiet	still
85.	bread	to congratulate	toast
86.	full of pickles	difficult	thorny
87.	to wash	small plants	scrub
88.	hasty	spots	rash
89.	finest ones	to not eat much	pick
90.	to overeat	things	stuff
91.	quick bite	bud	nip
92.	to leave alone	string	strand
93.	matches	to reserve	book
94.	food	insect	grub
95.	to bark	body of water	bay
96.	pie	sharp	tart
97.	water	nose	bridge
98.	evidence	to read	proof
99.	valley	not solid	hollow
100.	candidates	speeding	ticket

Activity . . . .

Multiple-meaning words are found in all areas of study and in all areas of work. Here are some from the entertainment realm:

fan (one who admires an entertainer and follows her or his career closely)

star (a well-known, popular, and usually highly paid actor or actress)

soap (a soap opera)

to pan (to give a performance a bad review)

bomb (a flop)

the house (the audience, usually in person)

a hit (a success)

number (musical selection usually chosen by the performer)

to plug (to promote a product or production)

ham (a person who enjoys acting so much that he or she sometimes overacts)

sleeper (a show that wasn't expected to do as well as it did)

lines (what an actress or actor says in a production)

spot (an advertisement between portions of a program)

Individually or in small teams, have students select a topic such as "Plants" and list as many multiple-meaning words connected with the topic as they can. Group members might want to refer to books on the topics for help. Here are a few examples of topics and multiple-meaning words that can be associated with the topics.

Topic	Multiple-Meaning Words
Animals	shell, claw, antennae, prints, hide, scales, fawn, lark
Human Body	leg, hand, colon, appendix, foot, head, back, vessel
Physical Geography	coast, harbor, bay, swamp, gap, range, gorge
Computers	boot, crash, chip, file, bit, menu, load, mouse
Travel	coach, deck, rail, course, fly, rates, ticket, gate
Cooking	measure, stir, loaf, menu, drain, degrees, roll, coat

Corn Market Worried About Small Ears:
Ambiguous Headlines

Headlines often are ambiguous because there are so many multiple-meaning words in our language. The ambiguity can result in unintended hilarious meanings. For example, the writer of the headline above probably meant that those who deal with the trading of corn in an economic market are concerned because underdeveloped ears of corn will bring in less money than larger, more mature cobs. The writer most likely did not mean that a store made of corn is losing sleep over tiny organs of hearing.

Multiple-Meaning Words

In a few editions of my local newspaper, I found the following ambiguous headlines:

Food section: "Chicken to the Rescue" and "What a Ham"

Entertainment section: "Hot Dogs on Film, with Relish" and "Second Banana (person's surname) Lands Plum Role"

Business section: "Chamber Keeps Lid on Finalists for Top Job"

Advertising section with coupons: "No Penalty for Clipping"

In a widely circulated state newspaper, I found "Stressful Time for Elevators" and "Farmers, Elevators Urged to Settle" in the business section. For readers who are not agronomists, the "elevator" in the headlines is a structure built for grain storage. It does not refer to the lift that plays zippy tunes as one travels from floor to floor.

......Activity

Give your students the following ambiguous headlines. Ask volunteers to explain the meaning the writer intended and at least one ridiculous meaning that the writer probably did not intend. (Note: The unintended meanings of ambiguous headlines are fun to illustrate.)

Golf Club to Host Banquet

Police Acting on Tip from Neighbor

Ace Serves Ball with Flair

Loot Found by Trash Can

Calf Still Nags Player

Do You Toast Your Bread?

Game to Be Moved Back to Forest

Fisher Runs for School Board

Bill Sails Through Congress

School Brass Stick to Budget

Branch Manager to Leave Bank

Ordering a Sub to Go

Suspect Held in Jewelry Case

Celebrity Catches Wrong Plane

Squash Requires Racket

Slides Reveal Colon Bug

Local Woman Upsets Match

Crooks' Short Sentences Rankle Board

Tie Frustrates Coach

Batter Draws Crowd

School Group Visits Mint

Gobbler Arrives at White House

Steep Prices Annoy Shoppers

Hill: "I Was Framed!"

Dense Population Causes Traffic Problems

Activity..

Give your students some or all of the following multiple-meaning words. They have more than one meaning as nouns, so they are simpler to work with than a noun/verb multiple-meaning word (e.g., *sink*) or an adjective/verb (e.g., *lean*) is. Have group members use the words in ambiguous headlines. Ask an impartial judge to rank the top three headlines according to cleverness and humor.

pen	palm	school
trunk	scale	ring
brush	gear	glasses
litter	horns	wave
needle	bat	bed
pitcher	pool	block
log	deck	rest
jam	band	coat
legends	bureau	title
ticket	snap	gift

Activity..

As a change of pace for a birthday party or any other celebration, play Headline Deadline. Divide the students into teams of three or four. Give each team magazines, newspapers, or access to the Internet. The teams have a specified amount of time (preferably at least 30 minutes) to find as many ambiguous headlines (or subheads) as they can. Advertisement "one-liners" (e.g., "Could Your House Use Another Coat?") also are acceptable. The team with the most headlines at the conclusion of the time allotted is the Reigning Multiple-Meaning Marvels and should be given a hand.

A Final Word

All's well that ends well.

When the well is dry, we know the worth of water.

These sayings illustrate two of the meanings of *well.* We know only too well that it's all well and good to know one definition of a word, but we might as well admit it: one well-grounded in the English language understands the concept of polysemy as well.

Well, what do you know? The two sayings above are proverbs, the subject of the next chapter.

References

Aitchison, J. *Words in the Mind.* 2nd ed. Oxford, England: Blackwell Publishers, 1994.

Ash, A. *The Top 10 of Everything: 1996.* London: Dorling Kindersley, 1995.

———. *The Top 10 of Everything: 1997.* London: Dorling Kindersley, 1996.

Carter, R. *Vocabulary: Applied Linguistic Perspectives.* London: Routledge, 1987.

Johnson, D. D., and A. J. Moe. *The Ginn Word Book for Teachers.* Lexington, Mass.: Ginn and Company, 1983.

Johnson, D. D., and P. D. Pearson. *Teaching Reading Vocabulary.* 2nd ed. Fort Worth, Tex.: Holt, Rinehart and Winston, 1984.

McArthur, T. *The Concise Oxford Companion to the English Language.* Oxford: Oxford University Press, 1996.

Pinker, S. *The Language Instinct.* New York: HarperPerennial, 1994.

References:
Children's Books

Blumberg, R. *Jumbo.* New York: Bradbury Press, 1992.

Bourke, L. *Eye Count: A Book of Counting Puzzles.* San Francisco: Chronicle Books, 1995.

Egielski, R. *Buz.* New York: A Laura Geringer Book, 1995.

Rosen, M. *Walking the Bridge of Your Nose: Wordplay, Poems, Rhymes.* New York: Kingfisher, 1995.

CHAPTER 6

Proverbs

Let Sleeping Dogs Lie.

Well Begun Is Half Done:
What Is a Proverb?

A proverb is a saying that gives advice or offers an observation about life. "Better late than never" is a proverb. It means that it is better to do something late than to not do it at all. Proverbs:

1. are not wordy or syntactically complicated
2. often rhyme or are alliterations
3. are sometimes stated metaphorically
4. often are very old and anonymous
5. deal with tangible, unpretentious topics
6. are a part of every culture
7. are timeless and are universal in their application

Let's examine each enumerated point above.

1. Proverbs are not wordy or syntactically complicated. The French mathematician, scientist, artist, and philosopher Blaise Pascal (1623–1662), referring to a correspondence, said, "I have

made this letter longer than usual because I lack the time to make it shorter" (Evans 1968). Anyone who has composed any message via the written word knows how difficult it is to be succinct. Certainly anyone who has sat through a speech or lecture that is saturated with tiresome, muddled, makes-you-want-to-scream gobbledygook appreciates clear, concise verbal messages. One of the reasons proverbs have survived as a language device is because they are brief, direct, and simply worded.

(Note: In the remainder of the chapter, proverbs are defined in parentheses if their meanings are not literal or if they are difficult to express in another way. If a proverb has more than one meaning, each meaning is given.)

2. Proverbs often rhyme or are alliterations. Nursery rhymes have been remembered through generations because of their pleasingness to the tongue and ear. Often we have no notion of where the rhymes originated, nor are we curious. They simply are fun to repeat and hear—even if their origin is less than cheery. For example, "Ring Around a Rosy" a charming little ditty, refers to a form of plague that was prevalent in the 1660s. The "ring" was a rash, the "posies" were supposed to protect one from the disease, "fall down" meant to drop dead (Panati 1987). On a more upbeat note, the originators of proverbs, too, always have been attuned to the value of catchy couplets and other ear-piquing devices. Here are some examples of proverbs that rhyme:

> Health is better than wealth.
> Haste makes waste. (If you hurry, unexpected problems might occur.)
> Many strokes fell great oaks. (Persistence can overcome large obstacles.)
> No pain, no gain. (Success doesn't come easily.)
> Rain before seven, fine before eleven. (Don't let problems get you down; things will get better later.)
> A friend in need is a friend indeed. (Good friends stick with you even in difficult times.)
> No joy without annoy. (Most happiness is accompanied by some aggravations; or one person's happiness causes other people's envy.)
> Penny and penny laid up will be many. (If you save just a little regularly, you'll eventually have a large sum of money.)
> Great spenders are bad lenders. (Spendthrifts make unwise loans.)
> Two in distress makes sorrow less. (Problems don't seem as serious when shared by someone else.)

Several proverbs use alliteration to engage the listener or reader:

> Live and learn. (We learn from our experiences, or experience helps you to not make the same mistake twice.)

Travel teaches toleration. (Going outside your local environment helps you appreciate diversity.)

Peace makes plenty. (War costs a lot in lives and money.)

They know most who know they know little. (Intelligent people are humble.)

Never trouble trouble till trouble troubles you. (Stay away from potential problems unless you can't avoid them.)

Good finds good. (Nice things come to good people, or good people find the good in others.)

Skill is stronger than strength. (Talent will get you further than muscle power.)

Like likes like. (Similar people appreciate and get satisfaction from each other.)

Live and let live. (We should mind our own business and enjoy life.)

Patience is plaster for pain. (Time will make things better.)

Much coin, much care. (Wealth can bring worry.)

Willful waste brings woeful want. (If we're wasteful, we will end up with nothing.)

3. Proverbs sometimes are stated metaphorically. For example, "A small leak will sink a ship" is a metaphorical proverb. Its literal meaning is evident, but metaphorically, or through implied comparison, it means that a small, seemingly insignificant problem, if not corrected, eventually can have disastrous consequences. Metaphorically stated proverbs probably are popular because they fit a variety of situations. Here are some metaphorical proverbs:

Without thorns, no roses. (Without struggle, no triumph.)

A good pilot is best tried in a storm. (We learn from experience.)

A library is a group of silent friends. (Books are fine companions.)

A handsome shoe often pinches the foot. (Good looks can be a hindrance.)

Greedy people have long arms. (Selfish people take more than their fair share.)

Flies come to the feast uninvited. (Pests show up where they're not wanted.)

Much rain wears the marble. (Annoyances can lead to major difficulties.)

Don't judge a tree by its bark. (Looks aren't everything.)

4. Proverbs often are very old and anonymous. Mansoor (1994) stated, "All authors and speakers—including this compiler—who use and quote proverbs are in fact plagiarizing the ancient sources" (p. vi). Certain proverbs are remarkably old, and their originators' names are long lost. Although the words might not have been precisely those used today, the ideas are the same. The following proverbs are from ancient Greece:

Actions speak louder than words. (What you do and not what you say is most important.)

A bird in the hand is worth two in the bush. (It is better to have a little than to wish for a lot.)

Leave well enough alone. (We shouldn't look for trouble, or we shouldn't stick our noses in other people's business.)

Eat to live; do not live to eat. (Don't be a glutton.)

In unity there is strength.

Don't count your chickens before they are hatched. (Don't count on something that might not happen.)

Other very old proverbs include:

400s B.C.

Every dog will have its day. (Every person is important in some way, or every person will eventually have a say in a situation.)

40s B.C.

Familiarity breeds contempt. (The better you know someone, the more apparent the person's faults are.)

1100s

All roads lead to Rome. (Regardless of what decisions you make, the result will be the same.)

You can lead a horse to water, but you can't make it drink. (You can introduce something to a person, but you can't make that person do that thing or like it.)

1200s

Don't cut off your nose to spite your face. (Don't cause unnecessary problems for yourself just to make a point.)

Out of sight, out of mind. (We forget about people and situations when we are away from them.)

First come, first served. (It pays to be early.)

An ounce of prevention is worth a pound of cure. (It's easier to prevent a problem than to resolve it.)

1300s

Time heals all wounds. (In time, hurtful things seem less painful.)

All good things must come to an end. (Nothing lasts forever.)

Easy come, easy go. (If things come easily, we don't assign them much importance.)

1400s

Still waters run deep. (Quietness hides underlying emotion.)

April showers bring May flowers. (Bad times are followed by good times.)

1500s

Bad news travels fast. (People like to gossip.)

Feed a cold, starve a fever. (Eat to get rid of an illness.)

There's no accounting for taste. (Each person has her or his own preferences.)

Tomorrow is another day. (We regularly get second chances to change things.) (Note that this one is not a Scarlett O'Hara original.)

Beauty is in the eye of the beholder. (People value different things.)

You can't make a silk purse out of a sow's ear. (You can't turn something ugly or of little worth into something beautiful or valuable.)

Don't make a mountain out of a molehill. (Don't make problems seem worse than they are.)

Don't let the grass grow under your feet. (Stay active.)

1600s

Business before pleasure. (Work before you play.)

Where there's a will, there's a way. (If you want something enough, you'll figure out a way to get it.)

Let bygones be bygones. (Forgive past injustices.)

Don't cry over spilled milk. (Don't worry about things you can't change.)

As with some idioms and some established slang, the creators of proverbs are not always traceable. Even figures in ancient history who used proverbs in their writing are not cited as the originators. In referring to the proverb "Misery loves company," Ammer (1992) stated, "This observation dates from ancient Greek and Roman times or even earlier; Sophocles (*Oedipus at Colonus,* c. 408 B.C.) and Seneca (c. A.D. 54) both wrote words to that effect" (p. 233). The proverb means that unhappy people like to find others who feel the same way.

Activity.....................................

Share *A Word to the Wise and Other Proverbs* by Johanna Hurwitz (1994) with your students. Several proverbs are illustrated in the book, but the endpapers (i.e., the inside of the front and back covers) are especially entertaining. Both endpapers feature the same illustration, which depicts several well-known proverbs (e.g., "A watched pot never boils," "Don't look a gift horse in the mouth," "A new broom sweeps clean"). Hurwitz explains that she saw a large painting at Belvoir Castle in England that contained many "proverbial scenes," and this provided the inspiration for her book. The painting Hurwitz refers to probably is the work titled, *Dutch Proverbs,* completed by David Teniers in 1647. There are 45 Dutch proverbs illustrated in Teniers's work. Flavell and Flavell (1993) reported that a print completed by a French artist in 1570 contained 71 proverbial expressions.

Divide your students into teams. Give each team several proverbs from this chapter, or have them locate proverbs on their own. Tell each team to incorporate the proverbs into a large drawing. Then have the teams try to identify the proverbs in each other's drawings.

5. Proverbs deal with tangible, unpretentious topics. Sayings that refer to esoteric subjects or use highfalutin language would not make it as proverbs. Here are two examples:

Proverbs

Deipnosophy, not abligurition, makes the aristologist.

Myrmecophobics should avoid Myrmecophagidae members.

How refreshingly simple and close to home "An apple a day keeps the doctor away" sounds. It clearly means that eating apples is good for one's health. You probably are wondering what my two deficient "proverbs" above mean. The first one means "Clever conversation—not spending a lot—makes one a scientist and artist of dining." The second means "One who fears ants should avoid anteaters."

....**Activity**

First Things First: An Illustrated Collection of Sayings Useful and Familiar for Children, by Betty Fraser (1990), can be used with younger learners who are unfamiliar with the utility of proverbs. Fraser states and illustrates a circumstance (e.g., "What to say when you spill it, drop it, or break it"). She then cites proverbs that fit the scenario (e.g., "Accidents will happen," "Forgive and forget," "Nobody's perfect").

Give your group several proverbs from this chapter or from a source listed in the reference section at the end of this chapter. Ask group members to describe one or more situations that would fit each proverb.

For a more challenging activity, have a group member describe a situation and ask others to recite an appropriate proverb for that situation. Here are some examples:

Situation	Proverb
You want to change your mind about something, but it might cause difficulties.	Don't change horses in midstream.
You haven't heard anything recently from a relative who is not one of your favorite people.	No news is good news. Let sleeping dogs lie.
A very important, wealthy person was caught doing something illegal.	The bigger they are, the harder they fall.
You can't seem to solve a problem that you've been working on alone for days.	Two heads are better than one.
Your noisy neighbor often complains about your dog barking.	People who live in glass houses shouldn't throw stones.

The "Proverbs" section of *The Kingfisher Book of Words* (Beal 1991) can help your group with this activity. The section lists and explains many common proverbs.

6. Proverbs are a part of every culture. Perhaps every culture has proverbs because it is characteristic of cultures to pass wisdom on from one generation to the next. Older, more experienced people often believe that they can save younger members of a group from some of life's hard knocks. Proverbs are a clever way to attempt to do so. Here is a sprinkling of proverbs from around the globe.

Better to ask twice than to lose your way once. (It's best to be sure of something.) (Danish proverb)

The person who says it cannot be done should not interrupt the person doing it. (A doubter should not pester a doer.) (Chinese proverb)

No choice is also a choice. (If you do nothing, you are taking a stand.) (Jewish proverb)

One who cannot dance will say the drum is bad. (Some people blame others for their own inadequacies.) (Ashanti proverb)

Be happy with what you have and you will have plenty to be happy about. (Irish proverb)

Rain does not fall on one roof alone. (Everyone has problems.) (Cameroonian proverb)

They who are being carried don't realize how far the town is. (You have to work to appreciate something.) (Nigerian proverb)

Old habits are iron shirts. (It's hard to break old habits.) (Yugoslavian proverb)

Good bargains empty our pockets. (A thing isn't a bargain if you don't need it.) (German proverb)

A day is lost if one has not laughed. (Laughter is an important part of living.) (French proverb)

Listening requires more intelligence than speaking. (People should know when to say nothing.) (Turkish proverb)

Eggs have no business dancing with stones. (Try to avoid dangerous people.) (Haitian proverb)

If we knew beforehand where we were going to fall, we could lay down a rug. (We can't predict the future.) (Russian proverb)

Do not call to a dog with a whip in your hand. (Use kindness—not force—to persuade others.) (Zulu proverb)

Since my house must be burned, I may as well warm myself at it. (Make the best of a bad situation.) (Italian proverb)

Many proverbs from one culture have counterparts in other cultures. In his discussion of proverbs, McArthur (1996) pointed out, "A common idea may be given different local references: English *carrying coals to Newcastle* (is) equivalent to Greek *sending owls to Athens*" (p. 736). Both expressions warn against pointless, unnecessary activities: Newcastle upon Tyne, a city in England, has been known for its rich coal supply, and apparently at one time many owls resided in Athens, Greece. The Spanish "If you give someone a hand, that person takes a foot" is "If you give someone an inch, they'll take a mile" in English. The proverbs mean that we shouldn't give in to bullies. The French warn, "Don't bother a sleeping cat"; we say, "Let sleeping dogs lie." Both tell us to not look for trouble. Italians note that "Dogs don't eat dogs"; Americans say, "There's honor even among thieves." Although we might not agree with the proverbs, they mean that unsavory people look out for one another. The English "When the cat's away, the mice will play" is "Cat outside the house, repose for the mouse" in Germany; "When the cat is not in the house, the mice dance" in Italy and Spain; and "When the cat runs on the roofs, the mice dance on the floors" in France (Flavell and Flavell, 1993). All of these proverbs mean that people do things they wouldn't ordinarily do when they know they won't get caught doing them.

Activity

Read *A Chinese Zoo: Fables and Proverbs* (Demi 1987) to your class. The exquisitely illustrated book contains thirteen Chinese fables—some as old as the seventh century B.C. Each fable concludes with a "moral" that is a proverb. Examples include: "Small creatures must live by their wits" and "Beware of judging by appearance."

Verna Aardema has retold two African folktales that have proverbs as the morals of the stories. *Jackal's Flying Lesson: A Khoikhoi Tale* (1995) is about a nasty jackal, a naive dove, and a clever crane. The proverb of the story is "Whoever sows evil will see it come forth in his own garden." Aardema's *This for That: A Tonga Tale* (1997) tells of a conniving rabbit who gets his comeuppance. The proverb at the end of the story is "A lie may travel far, but the truth will overtake it."

Have your students write fables. Tell students to end their pieces with a proverb that exemplifies the moral of the tale.

7. Proverbs are timeless and are universal in their appeal and application. Brock (1988) stated, "When it comes to the matters of heart and soul ... we the people of the world think alike. Not only that, we always have. 'A liar should have a good memory' says a Roman sage to his dinner guests. Nearly two thousand years later we nod in agreement" (p. 10). "You can't have your cake and eat it too" can be traced to before the 1540s, when it appeared in print, yet modern parents might still use the proverb when they are telling children that they can't have something both ways. Ancient Romans said, "Don't put the cart before the horse" (i.e., don't do things out of sequence), and even though few of us use carts or horses for conveyance, we still use the same admonishment.

Too Many Cooks Spoil the Broth or Many Hands Make Light Work?
Contradictory Proverbs

McArthur (1996) said, "Two proverbs may seem contradictory when in fact they contain truths applicable to different situations" (p. 736). "Too many cooks spoil the broth" fits when several eager "experts" only waste time and complicate a situation. "Many hands make light work" makes sense when more helpers will ensure that a task will be completed easily and quickly. "Two's company, three's a crowd" is an apropos proverb when one wants to spend time with just one special person. "The more the merrier" fits when one is planning a large, festive celebration.

Activity ···

Share pairs of the following proverbs with your group. Ask when each of the proverbs in the pair might be relevant.

Ignorance is the peace of life. (People don't worry about what they don't know.)
Ignorance is the night of the mind. (Not knowing things dulls the mind.)

A great tree attracts the wind. (Prominent people attract the most criticism.)
Big fish eat little fish. (Prominent people overpower less prominent people.)

A heavy purse makes a light heart. (With enough money, people don't have to worry.)
Money isn't everything. (People can't buy happiness.)

Good advice never comes too late. (It's never too late to consider wise suggestions.)
When a thing is done, advice comes too late. (When something is completed, suggestions will not help.)

Beauty is only skin deep. (There's more to a person than his or her appearance.)
Beauty opens locked doors. (People with good looks have advantages in life.)

A tree often transplanted bears little fruit. (You must be settled to be productive.)
A new broom sweeps clean. (Change is good for us.)

One enemy is too many, one hundred friends too few. (It's good to have many friends.)
Friends are the thieves of time. (It takes time to maintain friendships.)

In the land of hope, there is no winter. (People who have hope see the world more positively.)
They who live by hope will die of hunger. (Hope can't take the place of work.)

Proverbs

Late is often lucky. (Don't always try to be first.)
The early bird catches the worm. (First is best.)

Revenge is sweet. (It feels good to get even.)
Revenge never repairs an injury. (Getting even won't make us feel better.)

The squeaky wheel gets the grease. (If you have a problem, tell others.)
Silence catches a mouse. (Be quiet and patient and rewards will come.)

Absence makes the heart grow fonder. (We care about certain people more when we are
     not with them.)
Out of sight, out of mind. (We forget about certain people when we are away from them.)

You're never too old to learn. (Being able to learn has nothing to do with getting older.)
You can't teach an old dog new tricks. (Older people become set in their ways.)

Slow and steady wins the race. (Take your time and do something correctly.)
Slow help is no help. (Help that is not quick can be a hindrance.)

Faults are thick where love is thin. (People who love each other overlook each other's flaws.)
A fault once excused is twice committed. (If we overlook an unpleasant action, it will be repeated.)

A day is lost if one has not laughed. (Laughter is important to survival.)
Laugh and show your ignorance. (People who laugh a lot look like fools.)

Nothing ventured, nothing gained. (We must take risks to get rewards.)
Better safe than sorry. (Taking risks can lead to trouble.)

Last but not least. (Being last is OK.)
It is the last person the dogs attack. (If you don't stay with the group, you could have difficulties.)

Strike while the iron is hot. (Take action—do not delay.)
Haste makes waste. (Think things through before taking action.)

Look before you leap. (Think of possible outcomes before doing something.)
Those who hesitate are lost. (If you ponder a situation too long, you might miss an opportunity.)

Children are poor people's riches. (Children brighten poor people's lives.)
Small birds must have meat; children and chicken must always be pickin'. (It costs a lot of
     money to raise children.)

It Is a Striking Coincidence
That the Word "American" Ends in "Can":
American Proverbs

When we think of proverbs originated by Americans, we think of Benjamin Franklin and his *Poor Richard's Almanack*. Mansoor (1994) pointed out, however, that Franklin recognized the proverbs were "'the wisdom of many ages and nations'" (p. vi). Mansoor noted that "Franklin gives many of them in the form in which they are now best known, embellished with new wit, rhyme, and sparkle" (p. vi). For example, "Early to bed and early to rise makes a man healthy, wealthy, and wise" can be traced to 1496. "Little strokes fell great oaks" was first seen in print around 1370. Both dates are well before Franklin's time (1706–1790). But let's give credit where credit is due (an American proverb originated in 1777 by Samuel Adams). We are an inventive people who don't like to wallow in wordiness, and we are a nation composed of all cultures. Creating proverbs should fit us to a T—and it does. Here are some proverbs "made in America" and the earliest dates they were found in written communication.

To each his or her own. (Each person has his or her own tastes.) (1713)

Money doesn't grow on trees. (Money is hard to come by and shouldn't be wasted.) (1750)

Small ships should stay near the shore; larger ships may venture more. (Less experienced people should not take big risks.) (1751)

Where sense is wanting, everything is wanting. (Without common sense, problems are certain to occur.) (1754)

A bad penny always comes back (or turns up). (It's difficult to get rid of a pest.) (1766)

United we stand, divided we fall. (A group that supports its members and stands together is stronger than any individual.) (1768)

Don't shout until you are out of the woods. (Don't let down your guard until you are out of danger.) (1770)

If the shoe fits, put it on (or wear it). (If a description fits a person, that person should accept it.) (1773)

Oil and water (or vinegar) don't mix. (People with similar ideas get along best.) (1783)

Don't give up the ship. (Don't be a quitter.) (1814)

Look out for the minutes and the hours will look out for themselves. (Pay attention to details and you won't have to worry about difficult or overwhelming situations.) (1827)

An apple never falls far from the tree. (Children are like their parents.) (1839)

If at first you don't succeed, try, try again. (1840)

Cream always comes (or rises) to the top. (The best in anything becomes evident.) (1841)

It is easy to repeat, but hard to originate. (Creativity is rare; copying is not.) (1842)

Talk is cheap. (It's easier to say something than to do something.) (1843)

Necessity does everything well. (When we must do something, we are able to accomplish it.) (1844)

We never feel the shoe unless it pinches our own foot. (We don't understand other people's suffering unless we experience suffering ourselves.) (1846)

Don't cross the bridge till you come to it. (Don't worry about something until it happens.) (1850)

There is no luck in laziness. (There is no advantage to being lazy.) (1859)

It is better to remain silent and be thought of as a fool than to speak and prove the same. (1862)

Nothing succeeds like success. (Success tends to repeat itself.) (1867)

The show must go on. (Even in trying circumstances, people should finish what they start.) (1867)

Better to be a big frog (or fish) in a little pool (or pond) than a little frog (or fish) in a big pool (or pond). (It's better to have prominence among a few than to be unnoted among many.) (1871)

Build a better mousetrap and the world will beat a path to your door. (If you are inventive, you will be successful.) (1871)

Cheap things are not good; good things are not cheap. (1875)

Much profit, much risk. (You must take chances to make money.) (1875)

Fish or cut bait. (Do something or admit you cannot or will not.) (1876)

If you want something done right, do it yourself. (1880)

Let the chips fall where they may. (Don't worry about the consequences of an action.) (1880)

Smile and the world smiles with you, weep and you weep alone. (No one likes to be around an unhappy or self-pitying person.) (1883)

All words are pegs to hang ideas on. (We use words to express thoughts.) (1887)

Everybody talks about the weather, but nobody does anything about it. (It's easier to complain about something than to remedy it.) (1890)

It's always fair weather when good friends get together. (People are happy when they are with their friends.) (1894)

There's always room at the top. (Everyone has a chance to be successful.) (1900)

Curiosity killed the cat. (Being nosy can get you into trouble.) (1909)

A good offense is the best defense. (Some people protect themselves by attacking others.) (1928)

You can't unscramble eggs. (Some problems can't be fixed.) (1928)

You can't judge a book by its cover. (You can't judge quality by appearance.) (1929)

Don't take any wooden nickels. (Watch out for swindlers and phonies.) (1930)

Money can't buy happiness. (1930)

Don't stick your neck out. (Don't take risks for someone else.) (1939)

Better to be neat and tidy than tight and needy. (1940)

One who slings mud loses ground. (Gossips and slanderers never are admired.) (1940)

The best things in life are free. (1940)

A picture is worth ten thousand (a thousand) words. (Visuals sometimes tell you more than words do, or real life is better than vicarious experiences.) (1921)

If you can't beat 'em, join 'em. (Be a good loser, or know when to quit.) (1941)

You are what you eat. (We can learn something about people through their eating habits.) (1941)

Haste is slow. (Being in a hurry can cause delays.) (1948)

Say what you mean and mean what you say. (1948)

Since we cannot get what we like, let us like what we can get. (Be satisfied with what you have.) (1948)

The reward is in the doing. (Work is fulfilling, or helping others is satisfying.) (1948)

If anything can go wrong, it will. (1949)

The truth hurts. (Sometimes it is painful to hear the truth about oneself.) (1956)

Another day, another dollar. (This day will be like many others.) (1957)

Variety Is the Spice of Life:
Proverbs from States

Occasionally one runs across a work massive in scope and noble in scholarship. Mieder, Kingsbury, and Harder's *A Dictionary of American Proverbs* (1992) is one of those works. The *Dictionary* is dedicated to Margaret M. Bryant, who chaired the American Dialect Society's Committee on Proverbial Sayings from 1945 to 1985. For forty years, Bryant and her colleagues collected, through field research, potential proverbs. After ten additional years, the team narrowed 150,000 citations down to 75,000 actual proverbs. There are 15,000 of these proverbs in the *Dictionary*. Not all of the 15,000 proverbs originated in America, but all are used by Americans. Here are some examples from states in each geographic region that the paremiologists (proverb scholars) and paremiographers (collectors of proverbs) recorded.

Pacific States

California: Behind the clouds the sun is shining. (Troubles are temporary.) (p. 573)

Oregon: A business is like a car: it will not run by itself except downhill. (One must work to make a business succeed.) (p. 75)

Washington: Worry is like a rocking chair. Both give you something to do, but neither gets you anywhere. (p. 679)

Rocky Mountain States

Colorado: If you don't say anything, you won't be called upon to repeat it. (Sometimes it is wiser to say nothing.) (p. 525)

Utah: Keep your temper; nobody else wants it. (No one likes a hothead.) (p. 586)

North-central States

Illinois: When the outlook isn't good, try the uplook. (A positive attitude will get you through rough times.) (p. 443)

Iowa: You can't be a howling success simply by howling. (Success requires effort—not bragging.) (p. 571)

Wisconsin: The only difference between stumbling blocks and stepping stones is the way you use them. (Be optimistic and seize opportunities.) (p. 570)

South-central States

Mississippi: Abusive language is the abuse of language. (Harsh words are a poor use of language.) (p. 359)

Texas: Friends you can count on you can count on your fingers. (Most people have few reliable friends.) (p. 236)

Louisiana: To know everything is to know nothing. (Braggarts and blowhards usually are ignorant.) (p. 185)

Southeastern States

South Carolina: Don't waste ten dollars looking for a dime. (Don't spend more effort on something than what it is worth.) (p. 163)

North Carolina: The same sun that will melt butter will harden clay. (Sweet or soft-appearing people can be mean or tough.) (p. 573)

Northeastern States

New York: Better late than before anyone has invited you. (Don't go where you're not wanted.) (p. 360)

New Jersey: Hidden life, happy life. (People need privacy.) (p. 373)

. . . . **Activity**

Have your students compile proverbs used in their state. These can be put into a book for your school library or can be used in student-illustrated books for parents. You might want to ask community members who have lived in your area for a long time to serve as consultants.

A Place for Everything and Everything in Its Place:
Categories of Proverbs

Activity..

Perhaps you would like to integrate proverbs into a topic being discussed in your classroom. Here are some categories of proverbs and several members of the categories. As with any categorization, some members belong to more than one group. Have your students add more proverbs to each category.

Home

Home is where the heart is. (Home is where we are happiest; or wherever one is content, that is home.)

There's no place like home. (We like home better than any other place.)

Charity begins at home. (Be kind to those close to you first.)

East or west, home's the best. (Home is the best place to be.)

Plants

The grass is always greener on the other side of the fence. (People often think that things are better someplace else.)

Make hay while the sun shines. (Don't delay doing something.)

No rose without a thorn. (Nothing is perfect.)

Great oaks from little acorns grow. (Small actions can lead to mighty accomplishments.)

Flowers leave fragrance in the hand that bestows them. (Giving to others will bring rewards.)

Little strokes fell great oaks. (Persistence can overcome large obstacles.)

If you have two loaves of bread, sell one and buy a lily. (If you have the necessities of life, spend your money on beautiful things.)

Virtues

Honesty is the best policy.

Bad workers always blame their tools. (Incompetent people never blame themselves for problems.)

Don't start anything you can't finish.

Never tell tales out of school. (Keep a friend's secret.)

Practice what you preach. (Do what you say should be done.)

There are no gains without pains. (Success requires work and sacrifice.)

Virtue is its own reward. (Being good makes us feel good.)

Better to light one candle than to complain about the darkness. (Don't just complain about a bad situation; do something.)

One lie leads to another.

It's not whether you win or lose but how you play the game. (Being fair and honest is more important than being a champion.)

Never put off until tomorrow what you can do today.

Liars are not believed even when they tell the truth.

Weather

Lightning never strikes the same place twice. (Unusual occurrences don't happen more than once.)

It never rains but it pours. (A little trouble often is followed by more trouble.)

Every cloud has a silver lining. (Good things can result from unpleasantness.)

After a storm comes a calm. (Trouble doesn't last forever.)

Don't throw caution to the wind. (Don't take unnecessary risks.)

Save for a rainy day. (Save your money for future misfortune.)

Appearance

Appearances are deceptive. (We can't judge people by the way they look.)

A handsome shoe often pinches the foot. (Good looks can be a hindrance.)

Clothes don't make the person. (We can't judge people by the way they are dressed.)

Beauty is only skin deep. (There is much more to a person than physical appearance.)

Beauty is in the eye of the beholder. (What some find beautiful, others find ugly.)

Beauty is another's good. (Good people are perceived as beautiful.)

Handsome is as handsome does. (One cannot be considered good-looking without doing good.)

Animals

Don't count your chickens before they're hatched. (Don't count on anything before it has happened.)

Don't cast pearls before swine. (Don't give to those who are unappreciative.)

A bird in the hand is worth two in the bush. (It's better to have a little than to wish for a lot.)

A cat has nine lives. (Some people lead lucky lives, or cats are survivors.)

The leopard can't change its spots. (People don't change their personalities.)

Every dog has its day. (Every person is important in some way, or every person eventually will have a say in a situation.)

Let sleeping dogs lie. (Don't look for trouble.)

If it looks like a duck, walks like a duck, and quacks like a duck, it's a duck. (People can't pretend to be what they are not.)

Don't let the fox guard the henhouse. (Don't trust untrustworthy people.)

If you lie down with dogs, you will get up with fleas. (You tend to take on the characteristics of the people with whom you associate.)

Don't kill the goose that laid the golden egg. (Don't destroy something good or useful.)

Don't look a gift horse in the mouth. (Don't question a good person's motives.)

Food

Half a loaf is better than none. (Be happy regardless of how little you have.)

People do not live by bread alone. (There is more to life than the necessities.)

One rotten apple spoils the bushel. (A bad person can make a group of people appear undesirable.)

You can catch more flies with honey than with vinegar. (Kindness will get you more than meanness.)

Give people fish and you feed them for a day; teach them how to catch fish and you feed them for a lifetime. (It's better to learn to do something than to have someone do it for you.)

That's the way the cookie crumbles. (That's the way life is.)

Don't put all your eggs in one basket. (Don't invest all of your effort or money into one person or situation.)

There's no such thing as a free lunch. (Everything costs something—in either money, time, or emotion.)

Take the bitter with the sweet. (Take the bad with the good.)

Fire

Don't jump from the frying pan into the fire. (Learn from your mistakes or your troubles might get worse.)

Don't play with fire. (Avoid dangerous people or situations.)

Fight fire with fire. (Protect yourself.)

Where there's smoke, there's fire. (There is some truth behind a rumor.)

Money

Lend your money and lose a friend.

Money is the root of all evil. (Money brings out the worst in people.)

Fools and their money are soon parted. (Wise people save.)

Money talks. (Money gives one power or influence.)

A good reputation is more valuable than money.

Activity

McArthur (1996) stated, "Proverbs in present-day usage may often be regarded as clichés, but their persistence indicates their sociolinguistic importance. Commonly, when they occur in informal conversation, only the opening phrase is used: *Well, a stitch in time, you know; Don't count your chickens* (before they hatch)" (p. 736).

Give your group the beginning of a proverb (e.g., "Still waters ..."). Have a volunteer complete the proverb (i.e., "Still waters run deep"). If your group is well versed in proverbs, only the first word can be given. For example:

Don't ...

add insult to injury. (Don't make things more difficult for those having hard times.)

make a mountain out of a molehill. (Don't make a problem seem worse than it is.)

bite off more than you can chew. (Don't attempt more than you can accomplish.)

shut the barn door after the horses have run away. (Don't wait to do something till after it is too late.)

build castles in the air. (Don't be a daydreamer.)

make the same mistake twice.

air your dirty linen in public. (Don't discuss personal matters with those who are not your relatives or close friends.)

hit someone when they're down. (Don't be unkind to a person who is having difficulties.)

let the grass grow under your feet. (Stay active.)

buy a pig in a poke. (Don't buy something unless you have seen it.)

wish for something too hard; you might just get what you wished for. (If you get what you want, you might not be satisfied with it.)

cut off your nose to spite your face. (Don't cause unnecessary problems for yourself just to make a point.)

lead with your chin. (Don't show your weaknesses.)

burn your bridges behind you. (Don't move on without keeping some connections to the past.)

do as I do, but do as I say. (Listen to my advice, but don't use my actions as examples of the way you should behave.)

wear your heart on your sleeve. (Don't show your emotions.)

throw the baby out with the bathwater. (Don't dismiss important things that might be found in everyday surroundings.)

hide your light under a bushel. (Don't cover up your talents.)

Activity

Roget's Student Thesaurus (1994) is intended for ages 10 to 14. In addition to providing the part of speech, definition, example sentence, synonyms, antonyms, and cross-references for each entry, the *Thesaurus* contains twelve recurring features designed to appeal to early adolescents. Among the features are "Have You Heard?" (which presents full meanings of proverbs and sayings), "Idioms," "Words at Play" (verses and rhymes), and "Word Story" (the origins of words). Although more than five hundred pages long, the book is clearly organized and inviting, and contains a wealth of information about words. Have your group check this work or other available thesauri for treatment of proverbs and other figurative expressions.

Time Will Tell:
Potential Proverbs

Some relatively new sayings and quotations fit at least three of the characteristics of proverbs listed at the beginning of this chapter. They are not wordy or syntactically complicated; they deal with tangible, unpretentious topics; and they are timeless and universal in their application. In addition, some are anonymous. "Time changes everything" (American proverb), so perhaps the following words of wisdom will pass from quotation or expression status to that of proverbs.

1. "What goes around comes around." Although this saying is not listed in *A Dictionary of American Proverbs*, it is American in origin and has been in use since the

1970s. It means that one's unthinking behavior in the present may cause problems in the future.

2. "Be nice to people on your way up because you'll meet them on your way down." According to the *Random House Dictionary of Popular Proverbs and Sayings* (Titelman 1996), Wilson Mizner (1876–1933), a writer in Hollywood and on Broadway, first used this saying. It means that one should be considerate to all—especially to those in "subordinate positions," because someday those people might be one's supervisors or colleagues.

3. "The price of your hat isn't the measure of your brain." Mansoor (1994) listed this saying as an African American proverb, but it cannot be found in *A Dictionary of American Proverbs* or in any of the references cited at the end of this chapter. It means that wealth has no bearing on intelligence.

4. The American comedian Eddie Cantor (1892–1964) said, "It takes twenty years to become an overnight success" (Mansoor 1994). This quotation tells us that there is no such thing as a quick route to accomplishment.

5. U.S. tennis player Arthur Ashe (1943–1993) said, "From what we get, we can make a living; what we give, however, makes a life" (Mansoor 1994). Ashe wisely pointed out that it is more fulfilling to share our time and money than it is to simply work and get a paycheck.

6. Humanitarian Eleanor Roosevelt (1884–1962) said, "No one can make you feel inferior without your consent." This quotation means that if we think well of ourselves, no one can make us feel any other way.

7. Will Rogers (1879–1935), an American humorist, said two things that I think should be proverbs: "Everyone is ignorant, only on different subjects" and "I would rather be the one who bought the Brooklyn Bridge than the one who sold it." The first quotation tells us that no one knows everything, and the second says that it is better to be the dupe than the one who dupes.

8. Norman Vincent Peale said, "The trouble with most of us is that we would rather be ruined by praise than saved by criticism." Sometimes constructive criticism hurts our pride, but it is the impetus for a lot of learning, and as Vernon Law said, "When you're through learning, you're through."

9. There are two quotations on laughter that are self-explanatory and would make fine proverbs. Paul B. Lowney said, "Laughter has no foreign accent." The quotation "They who laugh—last" has been attributed to both Wilfred Peterson and Mary Pettibone Poole.

10. A British publisher, Henry G. Bohn, said, "One of these days is none of these days." His quotation can be found under "Procrastination" in many volumes.

11. "When the going gets tough, the tough get going." Although this saying is not in *A Dictionary of American Proverbs* (1992), it is given proverb status in the *Random House Dictionary of Popular Proverbs and Sayings*, which attributes the saying to President John F. Kennedy's father, Joseph P. Kennedy (1888–1969). The

expression means that when difficulties arise, it is the strong who dig in to overcome obstacles.

12. American baseball player Yogi Berra said, "It's not over till it's over." Like the previous entry, it is considered a proverb by the *Random House Dictionary of Popular Proverbs and Sayings* but is not found in *A Dictionary of American Proverbs*. It means that no matter how late in the "game," one must not quit until the event is actually finished.

The last four quotations have no recorded authors; they are anonymous:

13. People will believe anything if you whisper it. (People tend to believe gossip.)
14. Experience is a hard teacher; she (he) gives the test first, the lesson afterward. (We learn from our mistakes.)
15. A closed mouth gathers no feet. (Staying quiet will keep one out of trouble.)
16. Procrastination is hardening of the oughteries. (Some people intend to do things but never get them finished.)

Activity

People whom your students know—for example, parents, teachers, relatives, neighbors, or friends—often make wise statements that might deserve to become proverbs. For a week, tell your class to record any wise sayings voiced by someone they know. At the end of the week, compile a class list of these sayings. After discussing their meanings and the contexts in which they were used, you might want to have the class cast ballots to select the sayings most deserving of proverb status.

A Final Word

It is fitting to conclude this chapter on proverbs with some proverbs about proverbs.

A proverb is the wit of one and the wisdom of many.
A proverb is to speech what salt is to food.
A proverb is the child of experience.
The genius, wit, and spirit of a nation are discovered in its proverbs.
(Sir Francis Bacon, 1561–1626)
A proverb is a short sentence based on long experience.
(Miguel de Cervantes, 1547–1616)
A proverb distills the wisdom of the ages, and only a fool is scornful of the commonplace. (William Somerset Maugham, 1874–1965).

Someone once said, "Wit consists of knowing the resemblance of things that differ, and the difference of things that are alike." A West African proverb says that no two things are exactly alike. Nor are any two things totally different. In the next chapter, we will explore the notions of alike and very different.

References

Agel, J., and W. D. Glanze. *Pearls of Wisdom: A Harvest of Quotations from All Ages.* New York: Harper & Row, 1987.

Ammer, C. *Have a Nice Day—No Problem! A Dictionary of Clichés.* New York: Plume, 1992.

Baz, P. D. *A Dictionary of Proverbs.* New York: Philosophical Library, 1963.

Brock, S. *Idiom's Delight: Fascinating Phrases and Linguistic Eccentricities.* New York: Vintage Books, 1988.

Brussell, E. E., ed. *Webster's New World Dictionary of Quotable Definitions.* 2nd ed. Englewood Cliffs, N.J.: Prentice Hall, 1988.

Byrne, R. *1,911 Best Things Anybody Ever Said.* New York: Fawcett Columbine, 1988.

Crystal, D. *The Cambridge Encyclopedia of the English Language.* Cambridge, England: Cambridge University Press, 1995.

Elster, C. H. *There's a Word for It!* New York: Scribner, 1996.

Evans, B. *Dictionary of Quotations.* New York: Delacorte Press, 1968.

Fergusson, R. *The Penguin Dictionary of Proverbs.* New York: Penguin Books, 1983.

Flavell, L., and R. Flavell. *Dictionary of Proverbs and Their Origins.* New York: Barnes & Noble, 1993.

Gleason, N. *Proverbs from Around the World.* New York: Carol Publishing, 1992.

Hendrickson, R. *Animal Crackers.* New York: Penguin Books, 1983.

Leslau, C., and W. Leslau, comps. *African Proverbs.* White Plains, N.Y.: Peter Pauper Press, 1985.

Mansoor, M. *Wisdom from the Ancients: Proverbs, Maxims and Quotations.* Madison, Wisc.: Mayland Publishing, 1994.

McArthur, T. *The Concise Oxford Companion to the English Language.* Oxford: Oxford University Press, 1996.

Mieder, W., S. A. Kingsbury, and K. B. Harder, eds. *A Dictionary of American Proverbs.* New York: Oxford University Press, 1992.

Panati, C. *Panati's Extraordinary Origins of Everyday Things.* New York: Harper & Row, 1987.

Rogers, J. *The Dictionary of Clichés.* New York: Wings Books, 1985.

Sperling, S. K. *Tenderfeet and Ladyfingers: A Visceral Approach to Words and Their Origins.* New York: Penguin Books, 1981.

Titelman, G. Y. *Random House Dictionary of Popular Proverbs and Sayings.* New York: Random House, 1996.

References:
Children's Books

Aardema, V. *Jackal's Flying Lesson: A Khoikhoi Tale.* New York: An Apple Soup Book, 1995.

————. *This for That: A Tonga Tale.* New York: Dial Books for Young Readers, 1997.

Beal, G. *The Kingfisher Book of Words.* New York: Kingfisher Books, 1991.

Demi. *A. Chinese Zoo: Fables and Proverbs.* New York: Harcourt Brace Jovanovich, 1987.

Fraser, B. *First Things First: An Illustrated Collection of Sayings Useful and Familiar for Children.* New York: Harper & Row, 1990.

Hurwitz, J. *A Word to the Wise and Other Proverbs.* New York: Morrow Junior Books, 1994.

Scott Foresman and Company. *Roget's Student Thesaurus* (rev. ed.). New York: HarperCollins Publishers, 1994.

CHAPTER 7

Alike and Different

Search

Snoop

How are the words *boanthropy* and *groak* alike?

Both words are obsolete (Wallechinsky and Wallace, 1993).

How are *boanthropy* and *groak* different?

They had different meanings. *Boanthropy* described a mental condition in which one thought that he or she was an ox. With oxen less in use as a mode of transportation nowadays, this word slipped from our lexicon. *Groak* meant to quietly observe others eating and to wish that the diners would invite you to their table. It is a puzzlement why this useful word fell out of favor.

How are the words *sap* and *crunch* alike?

In a poll of speech teachers, the words were listed among "the ten worst-sounding words in the English language" (Berent and Evans 1997, pp. 33, 137). Also, both words can be nouns and verbs. Someone might *crunch* potato chips and *sap* our energy. A community might be in a budget *crunch* because the *sap* in the sugar maples was less than expected for the season.

How are the words *sap* and *crunch* different?

Sap is a military term for a covered trench. There are *sap* beetles (insects) and *sap*suckers (birds). If a *y* is added, there is *crunchy* peanut butter—no *sappy* peanut butter. We hear *sappy* tales—not *crunchy* ones.

How are the words *kite* and *yo-yo* alike?

They belong to the category *Toys*. Also, they both have a string and were invented in China by at least 1000 B.C.

How are the words *kite* and *yo-yo* different?

Chinese military personnel used a *kite* to signal each other from a distance. This was done with the kite's colors, designs, and movements. Although originally a toy, large *yo-yos* were used by hunters to ensnare animals by the legs from a safe distance (Panati 1987). *Yo-yo* also is a slang term for a foolish or annoying person.

How are the words *bully* and *browbeater* alike?

They are synonyms for *intimidator*.

How are the words *bully* and *browbeater* different?

Bully did not always have a negative connotation. It originally meant a kind, upstanding person (Room 1986). *Bully* was an antonym for its current meaning. Since the 1500s, the word's definition has gradually changed to the opposite of what it meant when it entered the English language. Today, an antonym for *bully* is *samaritan*.

In this chapter, the notions of alike and different are explored within four categories: synonymous words (e.g., *bully, browbeater*), superordinate-subordinate words (e.g., *Toys, kite*), antonyms (e.g., *bully, samaritan*), and words that are alike in one way but very different in other ways (e.g., *sap, crunch*). To form the categories, I relied on information from the linguists Carter (1987) and Aitchison (1994), from the educators Pearson and Johnson (1978), and from my own work with words.

Results from word-association experiments provided three of the categories: synonyms, superordinate-subordinate words, and antonyms. Here is a short word-association task: What word do you think of first when you hear or see the word *cloudy*? If you thought of the word *overcast*, you thought of a synonym. If *weather* came to mind, you were in the superordinate-subordinate category. If *cloudy* elicited *sunny*, your choice was an antonym.

Word-association tasks are not the be-all and end-all of alike and different categorization. Aitchison pointed out that context holds the key to how we form word associations. If, for example, *cloudy* had appeared with *vague, indefinite,* and *ambiguous,* you probably would not have thought of *overcast, weather,* or *sunny*. It is unlikely, however, that the stimulus *cloudy* would have elicited *broom* or *the* or *attach*. So, for our purposes, we'll forge ahead with the categories of synonyms, superordinate-subordinate words, and antonyms. They form what Pearson and Johnson refer to as simple associations of concept-level comprehension. The category of *alike but very different* is my own. Words that are alike in some way but very different in other ways include *bee* and *mosquito*. Both are insects and both can be a nuisance, but a bee serves useful purposes to humans, whereas a mosquito can carry diseases.

One and the Same?
Synonyms

Words are synonyms if they mean nearly the same thing. If two words meant exactly the same thing, one probably would be phased out; our language isn't bloated with redundancies. Urdang (Rodale 1978) stated, "Those who work with language know that there is no such thing as a true 'synonym.' Even though the meanings of two words may be the same—or nearly so—there are three characteristics of words that almost never coincide: frequency, distribution, and connotation" (Introduction).

Tie and *tether* are examples of differences in frequency among synonyms; the word *tie* is seen and heard more often than the word *tether*. *Flexible* and *fictile, passive* and *biddable* are other examples. Distribution refers to how widely circulated the synonyms are. A word such as *resumé* enjoys far-reaching use. *Vita* is a synonym for *resumé,* but primarily those in the academic realm use it. Connotation, according to Johnson and Pearson (1984), "refers to the 'excess baggage' or emotional tone a word carries with it" (p. 23). This differs from denotation, which is the literal meaning of a word. Here are some examples of denotation and connotation:

> Denotative meanings: Mayar bought a new *plant* yesterday. The *plant* closes at 5:00 P.M. Please *plant* those tulips today.

The denotative meanings of *plant* as used above are, respectively, a member of the vegetable kingdom, an industrial operation, and to bury. Of course, there are other denotative meanings of *plant*; it is a multiple-meaning word.

> Connotative meanings: Sanoi is a *funny* person. Sanoi is a *hilarious* person. Sanoi is a *witty* person. Sanoi is a *silly* person. Sanoi is a *zany* person.

Each adjective for *funny* has a different connotation—a different shade of meaning. *Hilarious* connotes side-splitting humor. *Witty* connotes a quicker and more intellectual sense of humor. If one is a *silly* person, one might seem goofy or immature. A *zany* person could be capable of absurd, prankish behavior.

Activity ......

Tell your group that synonyms are words that are similar but not exactly the same. For example, *search* and *snoop* are synonyms for *look*. *Search* means to look for something that is lost, but *snoop* means to look at others' property or lifestyle in a nosy way. *Search* has a more positive meaning than *snoop*. Put the italicized words in each sentence below on the chalkboard or on the overhead. Then have students answer the questions. Discuss the differences in meaning between the two synonyms in each sentence. Then ask students to contribute other synonyms for each underlined word pair.

1. Would you rather have an *unwasteful* friend or a *cheap* friend? (*Unwasteful* because it means thoughtful about spending money; *cheap* means stingy. Other synonyms: saving, economical, frugal, scrimping, tight-fisted, penny-pinching, miserly, moneygrubbing)

2. Is it better to be thought of as *strong-willed* or *mulish*? (*Strong-willed* because it means that a person is firm in her or his beliefs; *mulish* means stubborn. Other synonyms: unbending, unchangeable, inflexible, rigid, pigheaded, headstrong)

3. Who is more tired: someone who is *drowsy* or someone who is *exhausted*? (Someone who is *exhausted*. *Drowsy* means sleepy; *exhausted* means to be completely worn out. Other synonyms: weary, fatigued, half-asleep, dog-tired, burned out, tuckered out, wiped out)

4. Would you rather eat in a place that is *filthy* or in one that is *messy*? (One that is *messy*. *Filthy* means so dirty as to be sickening. *Messy* means untidy. Other synonyms: sloppy, grungy, unkempt, disorganized, disheveled, unclean, grimy, piggish)

5. Would you rather be thought of as *uninformed* or *ignorant*? (*Uninformed* because it means unaware of information. *Ignorant* means empty-headed and sometimes rude. Other synonyms: uneducated, unschooled, unlettered, untutored, unenlightened, unknowing)

6. Which is more important: a discovery that is *significant* or one that is *earthshaking*? (One that is *earthshaking* because it means of enormous importance. *Significant* means notable. Other synonyms: memorable, momentous, foremost, paramount, distinguished, noteworthy, prominent)

7. How might a designer describe the bright colors of his or her clothing: *gaudy* or *bold*? (*Bold* because it implies freshness and daring. *Gaudy* implies poor taste. Other synonyms: showy, flashy, eye-catching, garish, vivid, loud)

8. Would you rather spend a night in a mountain *shack* or a mountain *cabin*? (A mountain *cabin* because *cabin* means a small vacation home. *Shack* usually means a roughly constructed dwelling, although in some parts of America, *shack* is used facetiously to describe a comfortable second home. Other synonyms: cottage, shanty, bungalow, hut)

9. Would a *quarrel* or a *fight* be more dangerous? (A *fight* because it implies physical combat. *Quarrel* means that the disagreement was conducted through words alone. Other synonyms: debate, argument, conflict, brawl, row, squabble, altercation)

10. Would you rather be thought of as *unexcitable* or *easygoing*? (*Easygoing* because it means relaxed and happy-go-lucky. *Unexcitable* implies that one is unfeeling. Other synonyms: calm, unworried, laid-back, carefree, unruffled, accepting)

11. Would you rather have a friend who is *blunt* or one who is *direct*? (One who is *direct* because it connotes honesty. *Blunt* connotes frankness without thought of others' feelings. Other synonyms: straightforward, clear, forthright, candid, no-nonsense, unmistakable)

12. Would you rather have a *pesky* insect problem or a *worrisome* insect problem? (A *pesky* insect problem because it would be merely annoying. One might lose sleep over a *worrisome* insect problem. Other synonyms: bothersome, troublesome, nagging, disturbing, disquieting, irksome)

13. Who would have more friends: a person who is *chatty* or one who is *sociable*? (A person who is *sociable* would have more friends because that person would be thought of as pleasant and

outgoing. A *chatty* person is thought of as too talkative and maybe even gossipy. Other synonyms: agreeable, neighborly, cordial, warm, chummy, conversational)

14. Would you rather be called *sensitive* or *edgy*? (*Sensitive* because it connotes a person who is easily moved by emotional situations. An *edgy* person is one who is nervous and somewhat grouchy. Other synonyms: high-strung, touchy, temperamental, excitable, thin-skinned, irritable)

15. Which seems less threatening: a *mob* or a *crowd*? (A *crowd* seems less threatening. *Mob* implies that the members are violent or lawless. *Crowd* implies just a large group of people. Other synonyms: horde, mass, gathering, bunch, herd)

16. Would you rather be called *fussy* or *exacting*? (*Exacting* because it means that a person is concerned about details. *Fussy* means that a person is too concerned about these things. Other synonyms: particular, picky, discriminating, selective, demanding, painstaking)

17. Would you rather have someone *encourage* you to do something or *prod* you to do it? (*Encourage* because it means to cheer one on. *Prod* means to hound one to do something. Other synonyms: prompt, spur, motivate, urge, influence, egg on)

18. Who would you rather have as a co-worker: someone who is *sluggish* or someone who is *lazy*? (Someone who is *sluggish* because it implies that the condition might be temporary. *Lazy* implies hopeless sloth. Other synonyms: idle, dillydallying, unambitious, foot-dragging, inactive, listless)

19. Would you rather have a friend who is a *borrower* or a *freeloader*? (A *borrower* because that person might return what he or she borrowed. A *freeloader* depends on another for material things and is unlikely to repay the lender. Other synonyms: cadger, leech, sponger, parasite, moocher)

20. Which is worse: a *tragic* event or an *unfortunate* one? (A *tragic* event is worse because it usually involves shock and sorrow. An *unfortunate* event is upsetting but not uncommon or disastrous. Other synonyms: disturbing, crushing, luckless, miserable, pitiful, pathetic, distressing, troublesome, unlucky)

Ask group members to be on the lookout for word connotations by listening to people talk. Many individuals show their feelings and biases through subtle uses of words. After a week, compile a list of connotations your group has heard and discuss the situations in which the connotations were used.

....**Activity**

Some words in a group of synonyms are more extreme in their effect or power; they are more intense. For example, food that is *putrid* seems more rotten than food that is *rancid*.

Divide your class into teams. Hand out a list with the following 20 sets of synonyms. Have each team number the synonyms in each group according to their extremeness. The numeral 1 is the most extreme.

1.	chip	(3)	11.	dislike	(2)
	break	(2)		slight	(3)
	destroy	(1)		despise	(1)
2.	barbarous	(1)	12.	torment	(1)
	crude	(2)		tease	(3)
	uncultured	(3)		irritate	(2)
3.	overprotect	(2)	13.	comfortable	(3)
	corrupt	(1)		plush	(2)
	dote on	(3)		luxurious	(1)
4.	swallow	(3)	14.	immaculate	(1)
	guzzle	(1)		clean	(3)
	swig	(2)		scoured	(2)
5.	sickening	(2)	15.	swift	(2)
	distasteful	(3)		breakneck	(1)
	revolting	(1)		fast	(3)
6.	bashful	(3)	16.	angry	(3)
	anxious	(2)		furious	(2)
	fearful	(1)		crazed	(1)
7.	despondent	(1)	17.	ask	(3)
	miserable	(2)		demand	(1)
	unhappy	(3)		urge	(2)
8.	intelligent	(2)	18.	vicious	(1)
	brilliant	(1)		rowdy	(2)
	smart	(3)		mischievous	(3)
9.	munch	(3)	19.	splurge	(2)
	consume	(2)		spend	(3)
	devour	(1)		squander	(1)
10.	condemn	(1)	20.	overlook	(3)
	frown upon	(3)		disregard	(2)
	criticize	(2)		neglect	(1)

Have the teams compare their rankings of each set of words. To do this, you may want to tally and average the rankings. Lively discussion will ensue over word sets that received diverse rankings. Discuss the situations or contexts in which the most and least extreme words in each set occur. Such discussions help learners realize the vitality and richness of English.

Activity..

You might have noticed in the Activity above that the most familiar and most frequently used words have little intensity. They have broad-based utility, but they are bland in comparison to their synonyms. Tired words are a problem when students engage in writing. As Mark Twain said, "The difference between the right word and the almost right word is really a large matter. It's the difference between lightning and the lightning bug."

The following words in parentheses are synonyms for the italicized, common word. Select some of the synonyms for which you think discussion would be appropriate. Which words have your students heard before? Which words have they used in their speaking and writing? Which words do they not like to use? Why not? Are they aware of the slight or large differences among the synonyms? How would they use some of the less familiar words to "spruce up" their writing? Ask group members if they know of additional synonyms to add to each list.

Only a *bad* person would do that. (dishonest, crooked, untrustworthy, disloyal, treacherous, dangerous, wicked, evil, sinister, malicious, spiteful, fiendish, villainous, cruel, inhuman, brutal, detestable, contemptible)

That's a *little* animal. (puny, runty, stunted, lean, wee, peewee)

"Tomorrow," Parina *said*. (announced, responded, remarked, stated, declared, mentioned, whispered, replied, claimed, testified, reported, promised)

The travelers were *sick*. (bedridden, ill, out-of-sorts, injured, under the weather, queasy, unhealthy, diseased, ailing, debilitated)

Josine was *surprised*. (astonished, stunned, shocked, speechless, flabbergasted, astounded, startled, amazed, overwhelmed, thrown for a loop, blown away, bowled over, caught off guard)

It was an *excellent* meal. (classic, first-rate, top-notch, incomparable, magnificent, sensational, unsurpassed, superb)

The best-seller is *interesting*. (spellbinding, enchanting, intriguing, gripping, riveting, engaging, absorbing, engrossing, thought-provoking, captivating)

Our leader is a *good* person. (honorable, noble, upstanding, respectable, commendable, admirable, deserving, reliable, trustworthy, solid, honest, likable, kind, considerate, humane, virtuous, moral, well-behaved, decent)

That's a *big* animal. (great, enormous, gigantic, towering, monstrous, mammoth)

Parina *looked* at the bird. (gazed, stared, gawked, peeked, glared, glanced, squinted, peered, glimpsed, observed [delete "at"], examined [delete "at"], noticed [delete "at"])

Josine is *nice*. (kind, charitable, pleasant, delightful, amusing, gracious, understanding, generous, compassionate, congenial, cheerful, sympathetic, charming)

The travelers were *afraid*. (alarmed, panic-stricken, uneasy, tense, cowardly, edgy, jittery, frightened, fearful, terrified)

The new play is *exciting*. (inspiring, moving, compelling, electrifying, thrilling, spine-tingling, stirring, exhilarating)

They will *hate* it. (dislike, detest, despise, abhor, loathe, have an aversion to, shrink from, deprecate, disapprove of, blench from)

Have teams compile their own lists for *walk, run, hungry, noise,* and any other overused words. Probably the best source of "fresh" words is a thesaurus. Two of my favorites are *Roget's Children's Thesaurus* (1994), intended for ages 8 to 12 and *Roget's Student Thesaurus* (1994), intended for ages 10 to 14. These volumes provide parts of speech, definitions and context sentences, idioms, and antonyms. Additional information sprinkled throughout includes word histories, writing tips, famous quotations, and verses and rhymes. A thesaurus is an invaluable resource for speakers and writers of any age.

Johnson and Johnson (1989) stated, "A person who can read effortlessly, but who cannot evaluate the accuracy or importance of what is read, is not a thinking reader. Critical comprehension means making judgments about what one reads. These judgments have to do with the accuracy, acceptability, point of view, worth, suitability, intent, or quality of what is read" (p. viii).

The authors included "detecting and evaluating bias" as one of six elements that should be addressed in teaching critical comprehension. (The other five are distinguishing between fantasy and reality, distinguishing between fact and opinion, analyzing propaganda, detecting fallacies of reasoning, and determining source credibility.)

Synonyms chosen by writers and speakers reflect their biases. For example, one writer might comment that salespeople at a new store are *enterprising*. A second writer might describe them as *pushy*. *Enterprising* and *pushy* are synonyms for aggressive. The first writer probably admires the salespeople's energy and ambition or has a financial or familial interest in the new store. The second writer regards the salespeople's efforts as over-bold and brassy. Just one word could influence whether people will shop at the new store.

Activity

Have your group look in newspapers, in magazines, or on the Internet for critics' reviews of movies, TV shows, books, or restaurants. Tell them to locate words that show the writers' biases. Ask the group to supply synonyms for these words and then note the change in tone of the reviews as you or a group member reads the original review and the review with the "new" synonyms.

Activity

Read the following two restaurant reviews (adapted from Johnson and Johnson 1989, p. 76) to your group.

Writer 1

Mother Murphy's Moo Burger restaurant is difficult to miss because of the building's bright colors. Once inside, the customer is greeted by the aroma of the hamburgers. A favorite on the menu is the Marvelous Moo burger. It is served well-cooked on a warm, moist bun. The Marvelous Moo's sauce is mild, and the pickles are tart. No visit would be complete without a slice of Mother Murphy's peach pie. Its chewy crust is the talk of the town.

Writer 2

You can't miss Mother Murphy's Moo Burger restaurant because of its gaudy colors. The stench of Mother Murphy's burgers hits you when you walk in the door. Mother Murphy's best-selling hamburger, the Marvelous Moo, is served on a warmed-over, soggy bun. A tasteless sauce and bitter pickles cover this heat-tortured burger. For dessert, stay away from Mother Murphy's peach pie unless you like a really tough crust.

	Writer 1	Writer 2
restaurant's outer appearance	vivid colors	gaudy colors
word for smell inside	aroma	stench
how meat is cooked	well-cooked	heat-tortured
bun	warm, moist	warmed-over, soggy
pickles	tart	bitter
pie crust	chewy	tough

What would the tone of the paragraphs be if Writer 3 were a vegetarian and Writer 4 served on a board that promoted beef?

Have your group write two paragraphs about the same topic. One paragraph will treat the topic favorably, the other unfavorably. Tell students to use corresponding synonyms in the paragraphs. They might want to construct a comparison grid such as the one above. Topics your group might consider for this activity include a particular pet store, vacation spot, a new theme park, a sports team, and school exams.

Categorically Speaking:
Superordinate-Subordinate Words

What are Kentucky wonders, English runners, and pintos? In a word-association exercise, a typical response might be "types of horses." Actually, the three terms refer to types of beans. The category label, "Beans" in this example, is a superordinate word, or hyperonym. Words within the category (i.e., Kentucky wonders, English runners, pintos) are referred to as subordinate words, or hyponyms (Carter, 1987; Aitchison, 1994).

Initially the superordinate-subordinate category of alike and different may seem to be worth beans. As with any knowledge, however, there is more to this matter than meets the eye. Carter (1987) stated, "Even a very ordinary and widely used word can have a complex relationship with its 'referents' and with the other words in which it exists in a structured semantic network" (p. 21). The "semantic network" that Carter refers to is a wondrous linguistic concept.

I'll use the lowly *bean* as an example. Here are some superordinate and subordinate words and phrases associated with the word *bean.*

superordinate:	Baseball
subordinate:	beanball (a baseball aimed at a batter's head)
superordinate:	Clothing
subordinate:	beanie (a small, tight-fitting cap)
superordinate:	Slang for Body Shape
subordinate:	beanpole (a tall, skinny person)
superordinate:	Insects
subordinate:	bean weevil, bean-pod borer, bean leaf roller, bean leaf beetle, bean fly, bean aphid, bean cutworm
superordinate:	Plant Diseases
subordinate:	bean blight, bean anthracnose, bean mosaic
superordinate:	Slang for "Accountant"
subordinate:	bean counter
superordinate:	Idioms
subordinate:	to spill the beans (to tell a secret), full of beans (full of nonsense), to not know beans about (to not know anything about), not worth a hill of beans (not worth much)
superordinate:	Slang for "Head"
subordinate:	bean
superordinate:	Verbs Meaning "To Hit on the Head"
subordinate:	bean
superordinate:	British Slang for "Person"
subordinate:	bean
superordinate:	American Frontierspeople
subordinate:	Judge Roy Bean
superordinate:	Fairy Tales
subordinate:	*Jack and the Beanstalk*
superordinate:	Slang for Inexpensive Restaurant
subordinate:	beanery
superordinate:	Field Beans
subordinate:	navy, kidney, black
superordinate:	Garden Beans
subordinate:	string, lima, wax
superordinate:	Nicknames for Boston
subordinate:	Beantown
superordinate:	Bean Dishes
subordinate:	American three-bean salad, Mexican *frijoles refritos*, Austrian bean and herring salad
superordinate:	Organizations
subordinate:	National Dry Bean Council, American Dry Bean Board
superordinate:	Game Pieces

subordinate:	beanbag
superordinate:	Furniture
subordinate:	beanbag chair
superordinate:	Parts of a Bean
subordinate:	leaf, pod, stem, blossom
superordinate:	Seafood
subordinate:	bean clam (a small clam found in California)
superordinate:	Potentially Harmful Toys
subordinate:	bean shooter
superordinate:	Celebrations
subordinate:	bean feast (an annual meal for employees paid for by the employer)

Forming superordinates (categories) and subordinates (members of the categories) helps us organize information that otherwise would be disjointed and overwhelming. Superordinates-subordinates also help us make links among familiar and unfamiliar words that at first seem to have little in common. These links, supported by the proper context, help us to remember the "new" words. The links emanate from our prior knowledge and expand it.

Activity..

Divide your group into small teams. Have the teams find as many superordinate and subordinate words or phrases as they can for *green, potato, block, hold,* or *big*. When the teams are finished, they can share their findings with the whole group. Each compiled list is an additional source for writing tasks. Here are some examples for *green*.

superordinate:	**Figurative Language Containing "Green"**
subordinate:	green stuff (money), green light (approval to do something), green thumb (good at growing things), greenbacks (dollar bills), greenwash (money laundering), greenhorn (beginner), green-eyed monster (jealousy)
superordinate:	**Vegetables and Herbs**
subordinate:	spinach, broccoli, celery, asparagus, cabbage, sage, thyme, parsley, arugula, lemon balm, marjoram, chives
superordinate:	**Shades of Green**
subordinate:	lime, kelly, forest, olive, moss, avocado, emerald, pea
superordinate:	**Immigration Terms**
subordinate:	green card
superordinate:	**Salad Dressings**
subordinate:	green goddess
superordinate:	**Cities**

subordinate:	Green City, Missouri; Green Bay, Alabama; Green Bay, Virginia; Green Bay, Wisconsin; Green Camp, Ohio; Green Bottom, West Virginia; Green Bank, New Jersey; Green Bank, Washington; Green Bank, West Virginia
superordinate:	Animals and Birds
subordinate:	green iguana, green turtle, green woodpecker
superordinate:	Vermont
subordinate:	Green Mountain State, Green Mountain Boys
superordinate:	Synonyms for "Green"
subordinate:	verdant, grass-covered, inexperienced, unsophisticated, campus, common, golf course, turf
superordinate:	Famous Characters
subordinate:	Kermit, Jolly Green Giant, Sprout
superordinate:	Environmental Concerns
subordinate:	greenhouse effect
superordinate:	Nicknames for Political Parties
subordinate:	the Greens
superordinate:	Proverbs
subordinate:	Green apples are better than none; distant fields look greener.
superordinate:	American Surnames
subordinate:	Green, Greenbaum, Greenlaw, Greenspan, Greenberg, Greenwald, Greenwood
superordinate:	Pottery
subordinate:	greenware (unfired pottery)
superordinate:	Problems with Tomatoes
subordinate:	green shoulder (uneven coloration)
superordinate:	Theater and TV Talk
subordinate:	greenroom (the room where stars or guests wait before going on stage)

Activity

Have your students look through the Yellow Pages of available telephone directories for superordinates and their subordinates. Here is a partial listing for "Physicians." Other possible superordinates include "Automobiles," "Contractors," "Office," and "Restaurants."

superordinate:	Physicians
subordinate:	anesthesiologists, cardiologists, dermatologists, hematologists, neurologists, radiologists, rheumatologists

As always, discuss the meanings of any "new" words.

Activity...

Tell your group that you will name three members (subordinates) of a category (superordinate). Then they should name the superordinate. You might have them try to guess the category after you give them the first word, and again after the second and third word in each category. For some subordinates, students may guess the superordinate after hearing only the first word (e.g., "interjection" in number 1 below), but they may need to hear all three words for some subordinates such as number 3. Unfamiliar words such as *oomiak* often motivate learners to consult a dictionary.

1. interjection, verb, adjective (Parts of Speech)
2. light-year, fortnight, decade (Time Periods)
3. catamaran, oomiak, tug (Boats)
4. mustard, amber, canary (Shades of Yellow)
5. sole, bass, anchovy (Fish)
6. publisher, author, editor (Book-Related Jobs)
7. gila monster, crocodile, alligator (Reptiles)
8. Appalachians, Andes, Alps (Mountain Ranges or Proper Names That Begin with "A")
9. tall tale, fable, myth (Fiction)
10. dogwood, apple, cherry (Trees)
11. lounge, range, key (Multiple-Meaning Words)
12. tambourine, cymbal, chime (Percussion Instruments)
13. greasy spoon, diner, deli (Eateries)
14. wastebasket, thermos, vase (Containers)
15. funny, hungry, honest (Adjectives)
16. pheasant, turkey, chicken (Poultry or Birds)
17. river, gulf, bay (Bodies of Water)
18. sleet, hail, snow (Precipitation)
19. plateau, mountain, mesa (Landforms)
20. luncheon, supper, brunch (Meals)
21. minuscule, immense, miniature (Sizes)
22. slide, catch, bunt (Things Baseball Players Do)
23. Pollock, Renoir, van Gogh (Famous Artists)
24. Cassiopeia, Gemini, Orion (Constellations)
25. worth a bundle, on Easy Street, rolling in dough (Slang for "Rich")

Now divide your class into teams of four. Tell each team to write down three subordinates (members of a category), and then ask another team to name the superordinate (category).

Alike and Different

Read the following groups of words to your students. In each group, one word does not belong. Ask volunteers to tell which word doesn't belong, explain why it doesn't belong, and suggest another word that would belong.

1. Velcro, staples, tape, pencil, thread (*Pencil* because it doesn't hold things together. *Button* or any other fastener would belong.)

2. cone, grass, branch, leaf, bark (*Grass* because it is not part of a tree. *Needle* or any other part of a tree would belong.)

3. swan, pelican, hawk, loon, duck (*Hawk* because it is not a water bird. *Crane* or any other water bird would belong.)

4. beret, kilt, okra, cardigan, vest (*Okra* because it is a vegetable, not an article of clothing. *Shirt* or any other article of clothing would belong.)

5. magenta, mauve, maroon, mill, coral (*Mill* because it is not a color. Any other color would belong.)

6. nutmeg, cumin, turnip, pepper, paprika (*Turnip* because it is not a spice. *Cloves* or any other spice would belong.)

7. petunia, carp, gladiolus, zinnia, dahlia (*Carp* because it is a fish, and the others are flowers. Any other flower would belong.)

8. monsoon, husk, cirrus, typhoon, barometer (*Husk* because it is not a weather term. *Meteorologist* or any other weather term would belong.)

9. pineapple, peach, banana, pear, persimmon (*Banana* because although it is a fruit, it doesn't begin with the letter "p." *Plum* and *pomegranate* would belong.)

10. garbage, junk, can, trash, refuse (*Can* because it isn't a word for discarded matter. *Rubbish* would belong.)

Now have your students write their own groups of words using the format above. Encourage them to use words from content areas they have studied.

Share David Macaulay's *Cathedral: The Story of Its Construction* (1973) with your group. The entire book lends itself to the study of superordinate-subordinates. The cathedral, of course, is the superordinate. Subordinates found in the work include craftspeople, tools, areas of the floor plan (e.g., apse, nave), mortar composition, sequence of building, gargoyles, bells, doors, and so on. Placing and discussing subordinates in the book under the superordinate helps to organize the wealth of information found in this remarkable work.

As Different as Night and Day:
Antonyms

I have found an exception to the British proverb "All things are difficult before they are easy." The study of antonyms is the exception. Delving beyond the familiar definition of antonyms as opposites is akin to opening Pandora's box and a can of worms simultaneously.

Pearson and Johnson (1978, pp. 55–56) stated that there are five types of "opposition": contradiction, contrary pairs, reverse terms, counterparts, and contrasted terms. Carter (1987, pp. 19–20) listed and defined four "demarcations within antonymic sense relations": complementarity, converseness, incompatibility, and antonymy. Cook (1997) cited D. Cruse's work (1986) with opposites. Cruse divided opposites into two categories: complementaries and antonyms. Interactives and satisfactives are subcategories of complementaries. Antipodals, counterparts, reversives, and converses are subcategories of antonyms. Can you believe this? When Cook (1997) remarked that "one of the most complex areas of meaning is opposites" (p. 93), she wasn't kidding.

Johnson (in press) mercifully boiled down the types of antonyms into three major, easy-to-understand categories: contradictory antonyms, counterparts, and contrary antonyms. Contradictory antonyms are those that exclude one another, such as *complete-incomplete, alive-dead, perfect-imperfect.* If we are half-dead from working on a project that is incomplete, we are still alive and the project is still not finished. Counterparts are antonyms that show a reciprocal relationship, such as *employer-employee.* If you are an employee, chances are you have an employer. Contrary terms, according to Johnson, differ in degrees. Antonyms such as *earsplitting-inaudible* belong to this category. *Earsplitting* can be found on one end of the "Sound" continuum and *inaudible* on the other end. In between are degrees, such as the following:

earsplitting   blaring   loud   toned down   soft   inaudible

The point of all this is not to teach categories of antonyms. Antonym activities, however, should be included in the curriculum. As Johnson and Pearson (1984) stated, "Activities based on antonyms offer students practice in the type of thinking that will be valuable when they must sort through contrasting concepts and statements from reading assignments in all areas of study" (p. 26).

Activity...

Tell students that antonyms are words with nearly opposite or opposite meanings. Have students create rhymes using pairs of antonyms. This is a challenging activity, and you might want to use the following examples, asking students to supply the word in parentheses. If your students create their own rhymes, a rhyming dictionary such as *The New Comprehensive American Rhyming Dictionary* (Young 1991) would be helpful.

1. *Fierce is to gentle as physical is to (mental).*
2. *Support is to balk as peek is to (gawk).*
3. *Capture is to release as decline is to (increase).*
4. *Interesting is to boring as ceiling is to (flooring).*
5. *Start is to complete as advance is to (retreat).*
6. *Heavy is to light as weakness is to (might).*
7. *Spicier is to blander as praise is to (slander).*
8. *Relaxed is to delirious as happy is to (furious).*
9. *Smooth is to creaky as straightforward is to (sneaky).*
10. *Lesser is to greater as hill is to (crater).*
11. *Dud is to sparkler as "good dog" is to (barker).*
12. *Silent is to chatty as tidy is to (ratty).*
13. *Dismiss is to recruit as gullible is to (astute).*
14. *Calm is to quiver as chunk is to (sliver).*
15. *Ignore is to nurture as surefooted is to (lurcher).*
16. *Warmth is to chilliness as wisdom is to (silliness).*
17. *Uncomfortable is to snug as humble is to (smug).*
18. *Happy-go-lucky is to grouch as upright is to (slouch).*
19. *Good is to naughty as modest is to (haughty).*
20. *Add is to delete as refill is to (deplete).*

The rhymes above are analogies. Analogies show the relationships among words. The relationships above are words that rhyme and words that are antonyms. There are several types of analogies: synonyms, part-whole, superordinate-subordinate, and so on. You might want to introduce the well-known analogy symbols to your group. Write the following sentences on the board:

> Adult is to child as tame is to wild.
> Adult : child :: tame : wild.

Tell students that the symbol : takes the place of the words "is to". The symbol :: takes the place of the word "as".

■ ■

■ . . . .**Activity**

Finding degrees among antonyms is a vocabulary-building activity. Through discussion, it can help students understand the nuances among words. Here is where a synonym finder and a thesaurus come in handy.

Have your group develop a continuum for each of the following antonym pairs: *cry-laugh, hot-cold, fast-slow, hate-love, happy-sad, dark-light, heavy-light.* Two example continua are below.

Dry-Wet	Inexpensive-Expensive
least wet	**least expensive**
parched	dirt-cheap
dry	reduced
unmoistened	inexpensive
damp	high
wet	expensive
soggy	exorbitant
sopping	**most expensive**
most wet	

From Soup to Nuts:
Alike but Very Different

How are potato chips, penicillin, bricks, and the town name Jellico (Tennessee) alike? They were "invented" unintentionally or accidentally. Potato chips were created in response to a disgruntled diner who wanted thinner, crispier spuds from a chef. Alexander Fleming inadvertently discovered penicillin when he left a mold-collecting microscope slide near an open window. Archaeologists think that ancient Egyptians noticed hardened mud chunks near the Nile and thought they'd make strong building material. Jellico, Tennessee, was supposed to be Jericho, Tennessee. It was written "Jerrico" by a poor speller and typed "Jellico" by an even poorer typist.

Activity

Read *Mistakes That Worked: 40 Familiar Inventions and How They Came to Be* by Charlotte Foltz Jones (1991) to your group. It will set the tone for this section on words that are alike but very different. All of the inventions or discoveries in the book (e.g., cheese; aspirin; paper towels; the name for Nome, Alaska; trouser cuffs) are alike in at least one way: they were originally mistakes. The book is an International Reading Association and Children's Book Council Children's Choice award winner.

"Alike but very different" activities enhance interest in vocabulary, encourage students to look for relationships among words, and often require research. The remainder of this section consists of activities of varying degrees of difficulty. Answers are provided for your convenience, but your group may find even more connections among the words. Throughout the activities, the spelling and length of the words used should not be included in how the words are different.

Alike and Different

Read the two words to your group. Discuss how the words are alike and how they are different.

1.   astronomer   stargazer

Alike: Both look at the evening sky.

Different: An *astronomer* is a scientist; a *stargazer* might be an amateur astronomer, an astrologer, or a daydreamer.

2.   editing   revising

Alike: Both involve correcting or improving work.

Different: *Editing* often is done by an editor; *revising* is done by the writer. Film is usually edited, not revised.

3.   goggles   eyeglasses

Alike: Both protect the eyes.

Different: *Goggles* have side shields and usually are worn in a lab or under water. *Eyeglasses* improve vision.

4.   tornado   hurricane

Alike: Both storms can cause disasters.

Different: A *tornado* is funnel-shaped and usually has higher winds and a more narrow path than a *hurricane*. There is a shorter warning when a tornado is approaching. Hurricanes have names.

5.   orchard   field

Alike: Food can be grown in both.

Different: Fruit and nut trees are found in *orchards*; there are few of these found in fields. A field can be an open space for an athletic event. If a field is cultivated, grain or vegetables usually are grown in it.

6.   clown   comedian

Alike: Both often make people laugh.

Different: A *clown* is usually found in a circus or a parade, wears outlandish clothes and makeup, and pays more attention to children than to adults. A *comedian* usually just tells jokes and appears on TV or in comedy clubs.

7.   expedition   trip

Alike: Both are types of journeys.

Different: A *trip* is shorter. An *expedition* usually involves exploration.

8.   kennel   pen

Alike: Both are places where animals are kept.

Different: A *kennel* usually is for dogs and cats and provides temporary boarding. A *pen* usually is for animals raised for food and is found out-of-doors.

9.   buffet   banquet

Alike: Both are meals.

Different: A *buffet* usually has no waitpeople, and most of the other diners are strangers to each other. A *banquet* usually is more formal and often is for a special occasion.

10.   fable   tall tale

Alike: Both are fictitious stories.

Different: *Fables* usually include animal characters and have a moral. *Tall tales* involve exag geration and often have a singular human protagonist.

11.   rustler   thief

Alike: Both steal.

Different: A *rustler* steals cattle. A *thief* steals anything (e.g., jewelry, cars).

12.   bed   hammock

Alike: Both are places to stretch out, rest, or sleep.

Different: A *hammock* usually is found strung between two trees, and it swings. A *bed* has a mattress and is sold in furniture stores.

13.   name   signature

Alike: Both refer to the words by which someone is known.

Different: A *signature* usually is written in cursive and often is found on letters or formal documents.

14.   jam   honey

Alike: Both are put on bread and are sweet and sticky.

Different: *Honey* usually is yellow and is made by bees. *Jam* usually is made from fruit, whereas honey is made from nectar.

15.   museum   gallery

Alike: Both can display art.

Different: A *museum* can display objects from all the arts and sciences. A *gallery* exhibits and usually sells only works of art.

16.   ballet   square dance

Alike: Both are types of dancing.

Different: There usually is a theme or story in a *ballet*. *Square dancing* often requires four couples, and a "caller" tells the dancers which moves to make.

17.   ladder   escalator

Alike: Both have steps and take one to a different level.

Different: An *escalator* moves and is able to carry many people.

18.   cook   chef

Alike: Both prepare food.

Different: A *chef* often wears a white hat and is the head cook in a somewhat fancy restaurant.

19.   cafeteria   cafe

Alike: Both are places that serve food.

Different: In a *cafeteria,* customers form a line and serve themselves or are served at a counter. *Cafes* usually are smaller than cafeterias, waitpeople serve the customers, and the menu often is more limited.

20.   cockroach   cricket

Alike: Both are insects with long antennae, and both can be pests.

Different: *Crickets* make appealing chirping sounds and are not often seen in big cities. *Cockroaches* make no sound and are found everywhere.

21.   referee   umpire

Alike: Both are officials who have authority at sports events.

Different: An *umpire* is associated with baseball.

22.   opponent   foe

Alike: Both are rivals.

Different: An *opponent* isn't necessarily an enemy; a *foe* is.

23.   banjo   guitar

Alike: Both are instruments with strings.

Different: A *banjo* has a round body and rarely is used in rock bands, which often feature guitars.

24.   novel   biography

Alike: Both are types of stories.

Different: A *biography* is about one particular person and is usually considered nonfiction.

25.   wastebasket   garbage can

Alike: Both hold trash.

Different: A *wastebasket* usually is smaller, is for paper, and is kept inside a building. A *garbage can* holds all types of rubbish and usually is emptied by city or town employees.

To demonstrate the importance of the differences in the alike-but-very-different words, have each student write a short piece that uses five to ten of the words above. They should use only one word from a pair. Have them read their pieces to the others and then reread them but substitute the other word in each pair (e.g., *cockroach* for *cricket*). Discuss the awkwardness, strangeness, or inaccuracy of the second version of each piece.

Activity

Ask your group to make lists of things in their everyday surroundings that are alike in at least one way but very different in other ways. Here are some examples:

1. canisters, mugs, vanilla extract (from the kitchen cupboard)
2. card, postmark, flier (from the mailbox)
3. cities, highways, symbols (from the atlas or from the map)
4. gasket, washer, hinge (from the toolbox)
5. castle, tropical, shell (from the aquarium)

You may want to ask your students to prepare posters of their alike-but-very-different lists to be displayed in the classroom.

Activity

The following game can be a challenge. Read the words and ask your group to "find the link." How many links are named before consensus is reached?

1. olives   green peppers

The link is _____.

   olives   green peppers   onions

The link is _____.

   olives   green peppers   onions   mushrooms

The link is _____.

   olives   green peppers   onions   mushrooms   sausage

The link is (*pizza*).

2. heads   tails

The link is _____.

   heads   tails   water

The link is _____.

Alike and Different

heads   tails   water   scales

The link is _____.

heads   tails   water   scales   gills

The link is (*fish*).

3. back   center

The link is _____.

back   center   end

The link is _____.

back   center   end   guard

The link is _____.

back   center   end   guard   tackle

The link is (*football players*).

4. match   light

The link is _____.

match   light   log

The link is _____.

match   light   log   fire

The link is _____.

match   light   log   fire   suit

The link is (*multiple-meaning words*).

5. lilac   rose

The link is _____.

lilac   rose   violet

The link is _____.

lilac   rose   violet   peach

The link is _____.

lilac   rose   violet   peach   red

The link is (*colors*).

This activity helps students look at words in new ways. They realize that words, because of their likenesses and differences, can fit into many categories. Give students time to think of other examples for this activity. Then have volunteers lead the class through their links. Each should begin by giving two words, then three, and so on. Topics might include "things in a backpack," "things in a grocery cart," "places with unusual names," "stories or characters by a certain author," "sports teams," or "musical groups."

Activity

How are the following things alike but very different?

1. a mouse and a lemon
2. a turtle and a melon
3. a hummingbird and a red pepper
4. a brussels sprout and a goldfish

You and your class can find out when you look at the photographs in *Play with Your Food* (Elffers 1997). With some clever additions of natural products such as gingerroots, black-eyed peas, and bean stems, Elffers turns a coconut into a moose, a cucumber into a frog, and okra into a grasshopper. The book is a visual feast, and you'll never again look at an artichoke in quite the same way. Have students give suggestions and, if economically feasible, create their own creatures from the produce aisle.

Science and social studies topics are especially conducive to exploring the notion of alike but different. Students may want to look for similarities and differences within topics such as rocks, machines, animal tracks, trees, types of maps, bodies of water, and ancient civilizations. *Do You Know the Difference? Wild Animals* by Andrea and Michael Bischhoff-Miersch (1995) is a model for how students can compare content-area terms that are alike but different. The book points out similarities and differences between familiar wild animals that often are confused. Examples include Indian and African elephants, dromedary and Bactrian camels, jaguars and leopards, and alligators and crocodiles.

Optical illusions are alike in that they fool the eye. Yet each is different in its constituent parts. *Picture Puzzler* by Kathleen Westray (1994) is a book for younger students. Westray points out that many objects within an optical illusion are the same size or color, but they appear different within a visual context because they are optical illusions. Older readers will have fun with Robert Gardner's *Experimenting with Illusions* (1990). The book includes a chapter on illusions in the natural world and reveals the secrets of several "magic" tricks.

The National Wildlife Federation's *Patterns in the Wild* (1992) is a spectacular book that I have used with learners of all ages to point out similarities and differences on our planet and beyond. The book includes photographs of naturally occurring spirals (e.g., sunflower seeds on a mature sunflower head, shells, ferns, sea horses' tails, rams' horns, the Milky Way), circles (e.g., lily pads, patterns on butterfly wings, starfish, and ladybugs), branches (e.g., deer antlers, eroded mountains, coral, lightning, leaf veins), rays (e.g., mushroom gills, pine needles, flower petals), stripes (e.g., rainbows, tree bark, clouds, sandstone cliffs), and more. The photographs are exquisite, and the book makes one more visually aware of the wonders of the universe. It also would be a useful addition to any geometry library.

Old House New House by Michael Gaughenbaugh and Herbert Camburn (1993) is about a family who purchases a Victorian home and begins to restore it. Through research and the help of an architect, the family succeeds in the restoration, but it is the content between the beginning and the happy ending that is the real story. The young man in the book, David Houston, reflects on the variety of homes he has seen. Architectural styles are illustrated and discussed in an easy-to-undertand manner. Included are brownstones, ranch style, Queen Anne (a Victorian style), Dutch Colonial Revival, Greek Revival, and so on. This book would be a helpful guide for a walking tour of your city or town; use it to help explore how the architectural styles your group sees are alike but different.

Activity

Divide your group into pairs. Show them the following activity by using an overhead or the chalkboard, or by printing it as a separate sheet. Each pair will read each set of words and then discuss how the words are related. Remind the group that (1) synonyms are words with similar meanings, (2) antonyms are words with opposite or nearly opposite meanings, (3) superordinate-subordinate words are categories and their members, and (4) alike-but-very different words are words that share at least one aspect of meaning. Add any content-area words that you might be studying. Dictionaries or other reference books might be needed for some of the word sets. A possible answer for each pair is given, but there might be more than one correct answer.

vehicle-motorcycle (3)	jubilant-joyous (1)
trumpet-tuba (4)	stingy-spendthrift (2)
hickory-spruce (4)	fabric-cotton (3)
microscopic-vast (2)	dispute-fight (1)
mist-deluge (2)	operations-division (3)
real-authentic (1)	gusto-apathy (2)
constellations-Pisces (3)	island-peninsula (4)
boats-canoe (3)	rare-exceptional (1)
fine-exquisite (1)	obscure-famous (2)
establish-uproot (2)	candle-flashlight (4)

A Final Word

The world of words is a labyrinth of links.

A synonym for *easy* is *simple*. A synonym for *hard* is *difficult*.

Easy and *hard* are antonyms.

Under the superordinate *Degrees of Difficulty*, *easy* and *hard* are subordinates.

Easy and *hard* are alike because they are used in figurative language: Take it easy with Pat. He's been between a rock and a hard place. His hard-nosed neighbor took him for an easy mark. Gave Pat the hard sell to make some easy money. Really came down hard on him—played hardball. Hard to swallow, huh? Pat was hard up for a while, but he has no hard feelings. Just said, "Easy come, easy go."

Did pioneers traveling to Easy Creek, British Columbia, eat hardtack made with hard water?

An easy chair might contain wood from a hardwood tree.

Did you hear that hard hat order her eggs over easy?

Easy, wheezy, breezy, hard, card, lard.

The links are numerous.

How are the words *flu* and *zoo* alike? They are rhyming words, but they also are clipped words. *Flu* is the clipped form for *influenza,* and *zoo* is the clipped form for *zoological garden.* The next chapter discusses clipped words and other forms of abbreviation and word building.

References

Aitchison, J. *Words in the Mind.* 2nd ed. Oxford, England: Blackwell Publishers, 1994.

Berent, I. M., and R. L. Evans. *The Dictionary of Highly Unusual Words.* New York: Berkley Books, 1997.

Carter, R. *Vocabulary: Applied Linguistic Perspectives.* London: Routledge, 1987.

Cook, V. *Inside Language.* London: Arnold, 1997.

Johnson, D. D. "Just the Right Word: Vocabulary and Writing," in *Theoretical Models and Processes of Writing,* edited by R. Indrisano and J. R. Squire. Newark, Del.: International Reading Association, in press.

———. *Vocabulary in the Elementary and Middle School Classroom,* manuscript in prep.

Johnson, D. D., and B. v. H. Johnson. *Comprehension and Reasoning, Level 4.* Logan, Iowa: The Perfection Form Company, 1989.

Johnson, D. D., and P. D. Pearson. *Teaching Reading Vocabulary.* 2nd ed. Fort Worth, Tex.: Holt, Rinehart and Winston, 1984.

Panati, C. *Panati's Extraordinary Origins of Everyday Things.* New York: Harper & Row, 1987.

Pearson, P. D., and D. D. Johnson. *Teaching Reading Comprehension.* New York: Holt, Rinehart and Winston, 1978.

Rodale, J. I. *The Synonym Finder.* New York: Warner Books, 1978.

Room, A. *NTC's Dictionary of Changes in Meanings.* Lincolnwood, Ill.: National Textbook Company, 1986.

Wallechinsky, D., and A. Wallace. *The Book of Lists: The '90s Edition.* Boston: Little, Brown and Company, 1993.

Young, S. *The New Comprehensive American Rhyming Dictionary.* New York: Avon Books, 1991.

References:
Children's Books

Bischhoff-Miersch, A., and M. Bischhoff-Miersch. *Do You Know the Difference? Wild Animals.* New York: North-South Books, 1994 (trans. copyright, Michael Neugebauer Verlag AG), 1995.

Elffers, J. *Play with Your Food.* New York: Stewart, Tabori & Chang, 1997.

Gardner, R. *Experimenting with Illusions.* New York: Franklin Watts, 1990.

Gaughenbaugh, M., and H. Camburn. *Old House New House.* Washington, D.C.: The Preservation Press, National Trust for Historic Preservation, 1993.

Jones, C. F. *Mistakes That Worked: 40 Familiar Inventions and How They Came to Be.* New York: A Doubleday Book for Young Readers, 1991.

Macaulay, D. *Cathedral: The Story of Its Construction.* Boston: Houghton Mifflin, 1973.

National Wildlife Federation. *Patterns in the Wild.* Washington, D.C.: 1992.

Scott Foresman and Company. *Roget's Children's Thesaurus* (rev. ed.). New York: HarperCollins Publishers, 1994.

———. *Roget's Student Thesaurus* (rev. ed.). New York: HarperCollins Publishers, 1994.

Westray, K. *Picture Puzzler.* New York: Ticknor & Fields Books for Young Readers, 1994.

CHAPTER 8

Word Formation

FYI, I'm a fan of fish sticks.
She watched a prerecorded infomercial about the fruitmatic.
The help in this bldg. got a COLA.

The three sentences above contain the four categories of word formation: affixation, conversion, compounding, and abbreviations. Aitchison (1994) used the expression "lexical tool kit" to refer to the mechanisms that enable us to create new words. We use these lexical tool kits to form words within the four categories. Actually, most of the two million or more words that compose the English language have been formed by adding affixes to existing words (*prerecorded*, fruit*matic*), by changing the word's grammatical function (the *help* is new; please *help*), by combining existing words to form compounds (*fish sticks*), or by abbreviating a word or words (*bldg., COLA*).

From Antipasto to Yuplet:
Affixes

Affixes include both prefixes (*de*code) and suffixes (kitchen*ette*). Crystal (1995, p. 128) identified "57 varieties of prefix." In the same way that some words have multiple meanings, many common prefixes have more than one meaning. For example, *under* can mean below (*under*ground) or less than (*under*cooked). There also is synonymity among prefixes. That is, some meanings have more than one prefix. The prefixes *in, il, im,* and *ir* in *in*accurate, *il*legal, *im*material, and *ir*relevant mean "not."

Crystal presented nine categories of prefixes and explained their impact on base words. Five of the most common categories:

negation—*a*typical, *dis*honest, *in*active, *non*writer, *un*happy

reversal—*de*ice, *dis*assemble, *un*tie

size or degree—*arch*rival, *mini*basket, *mega*store, *out*do, *over*do, *sub*standard, *super*sleuth, *ultra*clean, *under*rate

time or order—*ex*-friend, *fore*gone, *pre*test, *post*test, *re*write

number—*bi*focal, *di*cotyledon, *mono*syllable, *multi*cultural, *semi*annual, *tri*angle, *uni*directional

Three prefixes are particularly intriguing: *anti, de,* and *non. Anti* usually means against. Yet the word *antipasto* doesn't mean against the meal (i.e., against the pasto). The *anti* is a variant of *ante,* which means first or before as in the word *antebellum* (in the United States, before the Civil War). *Antipasto,* then, means before the meal. The prefix *de* is fairly new in U.S.-coined words. Mencken (1977) noted that prior to 1900, only five words with this prefix existed: defoliage, dehorn, demoralize, demote, and detassel. Now, of course, words with the *de* prefix are common: debrief, debug, declassify, and so on. The prefix *non* is more popular than ever: "Marvin talks nonstop about his nonstick cookware for nonfattening meals." (The prefix *non* is not to be confused with the 1990s slang term *non,* a noun for nerd.)

Adding suffixes to base words is the most frequent method of forming new English words. Suffixes may alter the meaning of the base word and often change the word's grammatical function. English has two types of suffixes: derivational and inflectional. Derivational suffixes change the meaning of the base word (*laugh, laughable*). Inflectional suffixes have no effect on meaning; they play only a grammatical role. They are limited in number and include verb tense (*jump, jumps, jumped, jumping*), plurality (*boys, dishes*), degree (*easy, easier, easiest*), and possession (*Jill's, girls'*).

The derivational suffix *ness* is added mainly to adjectives to create nouns (*goodness, slenderness*), and *ish* and *al* convert nouns to adjectives (*snobbish, recreational*). The suffixes *ify* and *ize* are used to change nouns to verbs (*beautify, modernize*), and *able* and *ive* convert verbs into adjectives (*drinkable, attractive*). The *ly, ward,* and *wise* suffixes are used to form adverbs (*quickly, upward, clockwise*). Although English has more than 100 suffixes, the following list of 20 includes some of the most common.

Noun Suffixes		**Adjective Suffixes**	
ance	annoyance	est	fastest
ation	inspiration	less	ageless
hood	statehood	ful	helpful
ness	kindness	able	changeable
dom	wisdom	like	apelike
ery	forgery	ive	instructive
ship	ownership	ous	virtuous
ism	truism	ish	piggish
ty	honesty	al	functional
er	buyer	y	chubby

More than one suffix can be added to a word (contempt*uously*, department*alization*), but prefixes are rarely combined even though it is permissible.

Some suffixes seem to reflect certain eras in our country. Bryson (1994) pointed out that "products ... ending in *-master* (*Mixmaster, Toastmaster*) generally betray a late-1930s or early-1940s genesis. ... The late 1940s saw a birth of a brief vogue for endings in *-matic*, so that car manufacturers offered vehicles with *Seat-O-Matic* levers and *Cruise-O-Matic* transmissions, and even fitted sheets came with *Ezy-Matic* corners" (p. 241).

Although the use of the suffix *ville* in established slang can be traced to the late 1800s, this suffix did not rear its irksome head in a serious way until the 1950s, when *ville*s became ubiquitous. Dalzell (1996) lists over 90 formerly "hip" words with this suffix. Here are just a few: drabsville, capital gainsville, ho-humsville, lootsville, slicksville, weirdsville, quitsville, yawnsville. Dazell noted that "thankfully, *-ville* faded back to Suffixville in the 1960s" (p. 84).

Phobia is a popular contemporary suffix. Soukhanov (1995) said that "phobia resembles—but surpasses—yet another suffix, this one *ism*, in two ways: like *ism*, *phobia* has emerged as a free-standing noun, and, like *-ism*, the suffix *-phobia* is extraordinarily productive in the formation of other terms" (p. 82). According to Jacobs (1998), *phobia* means morbid fear, and was coined by "Celsus, a Roman medical authority of the first century A.D." (p. C5). Today there are phobiologists (foe-bee-AH-loe-jists) who study phobias. The study is called phobiology (foe-bee-AH-loe-jee). Scaryville! Although such phobias as claustrophobia (fear of small, closed spaces) and acrophobia (fear of heights) are common, here are some that are not: geniophobia (fear of chins), redactophobia (fear of editors), aulophobia (fear of flutes), porphyrophobia (fear of purple), and arachibutyrophobia (fear of peanut butter sticking to the roof of one's mouth). Somehow I found the lengthy lists of unusual phobias somewhat comforting.

The suffix *o* seems to come and go in popularity. *Daddy-o* originated in the 1920s and reemerged in the 1950s. *Kiddo* and *bucko* also occasionally reappear. There are *righto* and *wrongo*; the nasty *weirdo, sicko, wacko,* and *creepo*; and the British *cheerio*. Two less well known coinages are *blendo* and *garmento*. According to Soukhanov (1995), *blendo* is a term used by interior decorators for a style that "mixes high-tech, Eurostyle, and antique furnishings into an integrated individualistic whole" (p. 378). A *garmento* is someone who works in the clothing industry.

The suffix *y* attached itself to many descriptive adjectives in the 1960s. There were *grubby, draggy, scuzzy,* and *yucky* (yuksville in the 1950s). The more uptown *pricey* became popular in the 1980s. It probably reached its pinnacle when yuppies were most visible. The word *yuppie* itself has become the base for creative word formation. Dickson (1990) illustrated the utility of suffixes in referring to words coined from *yuppie*. Some are "yuppification, yuppyesque, yupguilt, yuppieback (book aimed at the yuppie reader), yupsters (yuppie gangsters), ... yuptopia, yuppyish ... yuplet (a child yuppie)" (p. 259).

No discussion of prefixes and suffixes would be complete without the familiar antidisestablishmentarianism. What does the word mean? Morris and Morris (1988) said that work by British prime minister William Gladstone (1809–1898) "to effect the *disestablishment* of the Church of Ireland (that is, to separate it from the Church of England) led to the coinage of the word. Gladstone referred to opponents of his measure as believers in *antidisestablishmentarianism*" (p. 20).

Activity

Nonsense words can be created and given meaning with the addition of affixes. The following "words" were taken from an anonymous source on the Internet.

accordionated—*adj.* able to drive and refold a map simultaneously

elecelleration—*n.* the mistaken notion that the more you press an elevator button, the faster the elevator will arrive

phonesia—*n.* the phenomenon of dialing a telephone number and forgetting whom you were calling just as someone answers

Have your group try to form new words by adding prefixes and suffixes to root words. To get started, they can locate and list three nouns, three verbs, and three adjectives from a book that they are now reading. You might want to supply them with some of the prefixes and suffixes discussed in this section. Groups can compare lists and discuss the plausible meanings of nonsense words that have been created.

Activity..

The suffix *ness* usually is referred to as the most common suffix in the English language. It is used to make a noun out of an adjective (happ*iness*, mean*ness*). As a full group, think of a list of words that include the suffix *ness*. The list undoubtedly will be a long one, and it can be used as a specialized word source for a creative writing activity (e.g., "A Tale from Planet *Ness*").

Activity..

Share *The Phantom Tollbooth* by Norton Juster (1961) with your group. This classic is about young Milo who, with his sidekicks Tock and the Humbug, bravely scales the Mountains of Ignorance to rescue the princesses Rhyme and Reason. The entire book is a megalesson on language play. It contains idioms, multiple-meaning words, imaginative word formations (e.g., Lethargarians, Dictionopolis), and more. The writing has an engaging enough plot for younger learners and a witty, sophisticated use of language that older learners will grasp and savor.

She Strawberried the Eats:
Conversion

A second mechanism in our "lexical tool kits" is conversion. Conversion means to change the grammatical part of speech of a word without adding an affix. For example, the word *bottle* means glass container, and it is a noun. *Bottle* is converted to a verb in the sentence "First we'll make the apple cider, and then we'll *bottle* it." *Paper* is a noun, but it is a verb when we *paper* a room. We frequently create new words by changing nouns into verbs. We *oil* the pedals and then *bicycle* to the park to *sandwich* in a quick picnic. Here are some other common conversions:

verbs to nouns	The villain is a *cheat*.
adjectives to verbs	I always *dry* the dishes.
adjectives to nouns	Did you pass the *final*?
nouns to adjectives	The robber held a *plastic* gun.

Aitchison (1994) cited E. V. Clark's 1982 research demonstrating that young children, as well as adults, create words through conversion: "'He's keying the door,' commented a three-year-old, watching someone unlock a door. 'Is it all needled?' queried another three-year-old as a pair of pants were mended. 'I'm shirting my man,' said a five-year-old dressing a doll. 'Will you nut these?' requested a six-year-old when she wanted some walnuts cracked" (pp. 160–161).

Conversion is clearly a useful part of our "lexical tool kits" that we use to form words. On an historical note and much to the horror of the British, the Americans converted two frequently used words. One is *help*, used as a noun to refer to servants as early as 1630. The other is *loan,* used as a verb only by Americans (Flexner and Soukhanov 1997).

Conversions are not rare occurrences, so we probably shouldn't *table* our discussion of them with students. If we were to *catalog* all of the conversions we use in a single day, the list would be lengthy.

..........**Activity**

Have your group create words by converting the names of known individuals, places, or objects to either verbs, nouns, or adjectives. Have them also provide parts of speech, definitions, and sample sentences. The new word must reflect something for which the person, place, or object is well known. Here are some examples:

Edison—n. an inventor of many useful things. "People say that Jakeem is a real *Edison.* He just got another patent last month."

Ellis Island—adj. to be multicultural, diverse, and friendly to new immigrants. "Even today Boston and San Francisco are *Ellis Island* cities."

motorcycled—v. to travel on a motorcycle. "They *motorcycled* their way to the rally."

..........**Activity**

Have your students analyze articles in available magazines and newspapers to compile lists of word conversions. Then discuss whether they occur more frequently in one type of writing or another (e.g., satire), with different topics, or in articles by certain writers.

Homemade Applesauce:
Compounding

The third major element in our tool kits for creating new words is compounding. Simply stated, a compound word is a word made up of two or more other words. As is true of so many other aspects of language, compounding can be complex. Some compounds appear as a single word (*seashell*), and others appear as two words (*flying fish*). Still other words are hyphenated (*bridge-builder*). Johnson and Pearson (1984) provided a means of determining when two separate words (*elevator operator, diesel truck*) should be considered compounds. The authors said: "Linguistically, it would be inaccurate to regard *elevator* or *diesel* as adjectives modifying nouns, because they simply are not adjectives. A true adjective can appear as a relative clause. Hence *the black coat* can be paraphrased as *the coat that is black.* However, *the diesel locomotive* cannot be paraphrased as *the locomotive that is diesel.* Linguistically, entities like *diesel truck* and *elevator operator* are best regarded as compound nouns similar to *steamboat* or *truckdriver*" (p. 132).

Most compound words can be analyzed by paraphrasing them in some way to show the relationship between the two words within the compound. A *seashell* is a shell from the sea, and a *flying fish* is a fish that seems to fly. A *log jam* is a jam of logs, *starlight* is the light from stars, a *tearoom* is a room for tea, a *cat burglar* is a burglar similar to a cat, a *bluebird* is a bird that is blue, a *racehorse* is a horse that races, and a *bank teller* is a teller in a bank.

Compound words, then, vary in their underlying structures. Most can be analyzed by using a simple shorthand for paraphrasing as recommended by Johnson and Pearson (1984). *A* refers to the first word in the compound, and *B* refers to the second word in the compound. The following underlying structures will account for many compound words.

B is in A.	A *kitchen sink* is a sink in a kitchen.
B is of A.	A *storyteller* is a teller of stories.
B is from A.	*Horsehair* is hair from a horse.
B is for A.	*Bubblegum* is gum for blowing bubbles.
B is similar to A.	A *jellyfish* is a fish similar to jelly.
B is A.	A *longhorn* is a horn that is long.
B does A.	A *jumping bean* is a bean that jumps.

Some compound words, however, cannot be analyzed because the two component words contribute little or nothing to the meaning of the compound word. For example, *mushroom* is not a room in, of, from, for, or similar to mush. Mush is not a room, and it doesn't do room. McArthur (1996) calls such compounds "holisms." The two words in holisms may best be thought of as simply separate syllables. Examples of such holisms or "compound-lookalikes" include *cutoffs, goodbye, network, awesome, padlock, inside, dugout, playoffs, another, nightmare*, and *runaway. Butterfly* and *limelight* seem to be holisms. Yet their etymologies reveal analyzable forms. Louis (1983) stated that *flutterby* was the original word for *butterfly* (p. 81). Room (1986) discounted this notion, but suggested that "the name could refer to the pale or even dark yellow colour of the wings of many butterflies, including the brimstone and all the 'whites,' or it could derive from the old belief that butterflies stole butter and milk" (p. 31). *Limelight* originally was light from lime. Asimov (1979) stated: "The American chemist Robert Hare discovered that a blowpipe flame acting upon a block of calcium oxide—which is lime—produces a brilliant white light that could be used to illuminate theater stages" (p. 431).

Teaching students about the underlying structures of compounds is not essential. I do recommend, however, separating true compounds (*grasshopper*) from holisms (*anywhere*) when working with compounds.

Word Formation

Older students might enjoy being introduced to the structures that underly compounds. This activity deals with five of these structures.

1. B is A.	A *darkroom* is a room that is dark.
2. B is similar to A.	A *sunflower* is a flower that is similar to the sun.
3. B is for A.	A *fireplace* is a place for a fire.
4. B is from A.	*Applesauce* is a sauce made from apples.
5. B does A.	*Popcorn* is corn that does pop.

Have your students discuss the following compound words to determine which pattern each fits. Some compounds can fit more than one pattern (e.g., a *houseboat* is a boat both for a house and similar to a house, and for some people, it is a boat that is a house). As always, discuss the meanings of the words and have students use them in context.

blackboard (1)	kettledrum (2)	fingernail (4)
toothpaste (3)	wildcat (1)	sunlight (4)
bedspread (3)	bricklayer (5)	starfish (2)
earmuff (3)	blueberry (1)	bridegroom (3)
driftwood (5)	footprint (4)	handcuffs (3)
catfish (2)	boxcar (2)	whirlpool (5)
carsick (4)	flagpole (3)	barefoot (1)
flowerpot (3)	sailboat (5)	superwoman (1)
crybaby (5)	bulldog (2)	blueprint (1)
seaplane (3)	deerskin (4)	tow truck (5)

Formula puzzles help students to think about compound words that are built from stimulus synonyms and definitions. Tell your group that the answer to each puzzle will be a compound word. Each puzzle contains two synonyms or definitions, one for each of the base words in the compound word. For example: a novel + a place to put things = bookshelf. Here are more:

1. to pull or jerk + a vessel = tugboat
2. a plank + a saunter = boardwalk
3. where a person lives + ill = homesick
4. sleep furniture + a cover = bedspread
5. moving air + protection = windshield
6. H_2O + drop = waterfall
7. medications + shop = drugstore
8. move on wheels + piece of wood = skateboard

9. engine + bike = motorcycle
10. ice + nip = frostbite
11. footwear + string = shoelace
12. on top of + parka = overcoat
13. top of body + pain = headache
14. scarlet + lumber = redwood
15. animal home + one who tends = zookeeper
16. swimmer + curved metal = fishhook
17. not tame + blossom = wildflower
18. look + human = watchperson
19. entryway + buzzer = doorbell
20. seven days + no farther = weekend

Have your group create compound-word puzzles and see if they can stump their classmates, family members, or students in other classrooms.

Activity

This activity will prove more challenging to your students than the one above. This time they will make compounds from the antonyms for the words in the puzzle. When the puzzles are completed, challenge students to create their own.

1. over + sky = underground
2. bald + all = hairpiece
3. night + dark = daylight
4. long + mend = shortcut
5. death + night = birthday
6. empty + front = fullback
7. beneath + waken = oversleep
8. fix + slow = breakfast
9. leg + work = armrest
10. go + dark = stoplight

Short and Sweet:
Abbreviations

Abbreviations are short forms of words and phrases. Some might think that abbreviations first developed in the U.S. because of our "hurry-up" lifestyle, which leaves little time for R&R, but this theory is N/A. A no. of other societies used abbreviations, too. According to McArthur (1996), the ancient Egyptians abbreviated some of their pictorial writing, and the ancient Greeks and Romans frequently used short forms of words. Those who were literate during the Middle Ages used abbreviations to save time and costly materials.

A vol. could be written on the no. of abbrev. in English, and one has been: *Acronyms, Initialisms & Abbreviations Dictionary,* which contains more than 470,000 entries and is updated every year. Some abbreviations are so familiar that we take them at face value without thinking about their origins. "Zip code," for example, stands for Zone Improvement Plan. It was instituted in 1963 by J. Edward Day, postmaster gen. of the P.O. Dept. Abbreviations can be categorized as initialisms, acronyms, clipped words, blends, and FWOs (For Writing Only).

The ABCs of Initialisms

Initialisms are abbreviations that can be said aloud only as letters—not as words. Although the proliferation of initialisms seems to have gotten out of hand, imagine the media having to say or print "deoxyribonucleic acid" every time they use the initialism DNA. Here more examples of initialisms:

ACT (American College Test)

AFL-CIO (American Federation of Labor–Congress of Industrial Organizations)

AI (artificial intelligence)

A.M. (from the Latin *ante meridiem*, before noon)

AP (Associated Press)

APB (all points bulletin)

APO (Army Post Office)

APR (annual percentage rate)

ATM (automated teller machine)

ATV (all-terrain vehicle)

B&B (bed and breakfast)

BTO (big time operator)

BYO (bring your own)

CB (citizens band)

CC (closed-captioned)

COD (cash on delivery)

CPA (certified public accountant)

CPI (consumer price index)

CPR (cardiopulmonary resuscitation)

CPU (central processing unit)

D.V.M. (doctor of veterinary medicine)

DA (district attorney)

DOD (Department of Defense)

DOE (Department of Energy)

DOT (Department of Transportation)

e.g. (from the Latin *exempli gratia*,

EKG (electrocardiogram)

EMT (emergency medical technician)

EPA (Environmental Protection Agency)

ER (emergency room)

ESL (English as a Second Language)

ESP (extrasensory perception)

ETA (estimated time of arrival)

FAA (Federal Aviation Administration)

FBI (Federal Bureau of Investigation)

FCC (Federal Communications Commission)

FDA (Food and Drug Administration)

FDIC (Federal Deposit Insurance Corporation)

FHA (Federal Housing Administration)

FTC (Federal Trade Commission)

GAO (General Accounting Office)

GI (government issue)

GNP (gross national product)

GP (general practitioner)

GPA (grade point average)	POW (prisoner of war)
HMO (health maintenance organization)	R&B (rhythm and blues)
HQ (headquarters)	R&D (research and development)
I- (Interstate)	RDA (recommended daily allowance)
i.e. (from the Latin *id est*, that is)	REM (rapid eye movement)
ICU (intensive care unit)	RN (registered nurse)
ID (identification)	RR (railroad)
IOU (I owe you)	S&L (savings and loan)
IQ (intelligence quotient)	SAT (Scholastic Aptitude Test)
IRS (Internal Revenue Service)	SEC (Securities and Exchange Commission)
ISBN (International Standard Book Number)	SRO (standing room only)
IV (intravenous)	TB (tuberculosis)
LA (Los Angeles)	TBA (to be announced)
LPN (licensed practical nurse)	TLC (tender loving care)
LWV (League of Women Voters)	UAW (United Auto Workers)
M.A. (master of arts)	UFO (unidentified flying object)
M.D. (doctor of medicine)	UK (United Kingdom)
MIA (missing in action)	UN (United Nations)
MO (from the Latin *modus operandi*, mode of operation)	UPI (United Press International)
	USDA (United States Department of Agriculture)
NPR (National Public Radio)	
NSF (National Science Foundation)	USO (United Service Organization)
OD (overdose)	USS (United States Ship)
OR (operating room)	UV (ultraviolet)
P.M. (from the Latin *post meridiem*, afternoon)	VA (Veterans Administration)
	VCR (videocassette recorder)
PC (personal computer)	VHF (very high frequency)
Ph.D. (doctor of philosophy)	WP (word processing)
pj's (pajamas)	YTD (year to date)

Initialisms can cause confusion because some are multiple meaning; they can stand for more than one thing. APA is an initialism for the American Psychological Association, the American Paddleball Association, the American Philosophical Association, the American Psychiatric Association, the American Physicists Association, the American Pilots' Association, and more. LC can refer to the Library of Congress, line of communication, law courts, lance corporal, level crossing, lightly canceled, liquid chromatography, and so on. Note that LC differs from L/C (letter of credit), L.C. (lord chancellor), and l.c. (lowercase or, from the Latin *loco citato*, in the place cited).

Three U.S. presidents often are referred to by their initials: FDR, JFK, and LBJ. Dickson (1996) pointed out that President Hiram Ulysses Grant and Senator Robert A. Taft (son of President William Howard Taft) avoided initialisms—a wise decision. Harry

S Truman, our thirty-third president, didn't use a period after the "S" in his name because the "S" was not an abbreviation; it *was* his middle name.

Newman (1974) found that not only were many university presidents' first, middle, and last names interchangeable (e.g., Willis Bruce Duncan, Willis Duncan Bruce, Bruce Willis Duncan, Bruce Duncan Willis, Duncan Bruce Willis, Duncan Willis Bruce), but several also used an initial at the beginning of their names: R. Dudley Boyce, T. Felton Harrison, J. Renwick Jackson, W. Ardell Haines, J. Wade Gilley, D. Bank Wilburn, and others.

- **...Activity**

Have your group write poems that contain as many initialisms as they can incorporate. Here is an example:

> Al Miller was voted MVP.
> I saw him last night on my TV.
> Mable said he's driving a new RV.
> I guess now he's a VIP.

- -

- **...Activity**

Have your group collect initialisms from the world of sports (e.g., PGA, NHL, NFC), television networks (e.g., PBS), and food packages (e.g., MSG). Which of the three categories uses the most initialisms? Are the words from which the initialisms are derived ever revealed to the readers or listeners?

- -

Four initialisms deserve special mention: SOS, OK, EZ, and U. SOS is a multiple-meaning initialism. It is an abbreviation for Save Our Schools, Save Our Shore, Stamp Out Smog, and others. It is best known, of course, as a signal for help. Although many references state that SOS stands for Save Our Ship, Morris and Morris (1988) have set the record straight. They reported: "The first distress call used by the early Marconi Company was CQD—*CQ* being the general call to alert other ships that a message is coming and *D* standing for 'danger' or 'distress.' For various technical reasons this proved unsatisfactory and in 1908, by international agreement, a signal made up of three dits, three dahs, and three dits was adopted as the one most easily transmitted and understood. By coincidence, this signal is translatable as SOS" (p. 539).

H. L. Mencken (1977) referred to "OK" as "the most successful abbreviation ever coined" (p. 504). Bryson (1990) commented on the versatility of this initialism. He said that OK is "able to serve as an adjective ('Lunch was OK'), verb ('Can you OK this for me?'), noun ('I need your OK on this.'), interjection ('OK, I hear you.'), and adverb ('We did OK'). It can carry shades of meaning that range from casual assent ('Shall we go?'

'OK'), to great enthusiasm ('OK!'), to lukewarm endorsement ('The party was OK'), to a more or less meaningless filler of space ('OK, can I have your attention, please?')" (p. 164).

Okeydokey. But what is the origin of OK? Theories abound. Some scholars have dedicated years of research trying to determine the etymology of OK. President Woodrow Wilson, among others, thought that OK was Choctaw (*okeh*) in origin. Others think that it comes from the initials of Old Kinderhook (President Van Buren's nickname), or Orrins-Kendall (a cracker popular in the 1800s), or Old Keokuk (a Native American chief's name). Still others think that Andrew Jackson used it as an initialism for "Oll Korrect" or "Orl Kerrect"—except Jackson would have known the correct spelling of the words. Another theory is that it came from the Haitian port Aux Cayes, known for its high-quality rum, and some believe that it is based on a form of language play with intentional misspellings (e.g., "Oll Korrect"). The initialism A-OK is fairly recent (1961), and its origin is clear. NASA's PR officer, Colonel "Shorty" Power, first used it. He thought that Alan Shepard had said "A-OK" from his space capsule when Shepard actually said just "OK."

EZ is an initialism that substitutes for the word *easy.* EZ falls into the "intentional misspelling" category of words. We see *kwik* for quick, *freez* for freeze, *git* for get, *xpress* for express, and *valu* for value. It seems as if some ad writers are seeking revenge on their elementary school teachers, who held one too many spelling bees.

U is another noteworthy initialism. It can refer to university (e.g., BU, Boston University), uranium, unsatisfactory, and more. Most often it is used as an intentional misspelling for *you.* It is common to see businesses that offer "While-U-Wait" services.

Activity ....

Point out to students that some businesses use EZ and U in their names or as part of their product names. Have students find examples of these businesses in their neighborhood, in the Yellow Pages, or on products in supermarkets or discount department stores. Ask students to think about the types of businesses and products that use these initialisms. Why aren't schools named EZ-for-U Middle School or EZ University? Would they go to a physician who advertised EZ surgery? Why did the IRS name a tax form EZ? What types of goods or services would they consider purchasing if the goods or services had a U in their names? Are there disadvantages (such as cost or frustration) of using "While-U-Wait" services or "U-Assemble-It" goods?

ACORN:
Acronyms

Acronyms are abbreviations that are pronounceable words. They are composed of the first letter or letters of a group of words. Unlike some initialisms (e.g., Ph.D., a.k.a.), acronyms do not contain periods after the letters. ACORN is an actual acronym. It stands for (Ac)ronym-(Or)iented (N)ut. PAC (political action committee), COLA (cost-of-living adjustment), and MOMA (MOH-ma, New York's Museum of Modern Art) are acronyms, too. The sheer number of acronyms (not to mention initialisms) has caused us to communicate in a written and spoken language that comes close to being indecipherable to those not somewhat familiar with the words designated by the letters in these abbreviations.

> The HUD official saw a SWAT team near the NATO building.
> The MASH unit used a PET procedure.
> TESOL was discussed at a UNESCO meeting.

It probably makes you want to join my new group: MAGGOT ((M)any (A)cronyms (G)enerate (G)oof-ups (o)ver (T)ime).

It's getting worse. Computer devotees have gone overboard with acronyms: GIGO (GUY-go or GEE-go; garbage in, garbage out), BASIC (Beginner's All-purpose Symbolic Instruction Code), OOPS (Object-Oriented Programming System), CLASSMATE (Computerized Language to Aid and Stimulate Scientific Mathematical and Technical Education), GUI (GOO-ee, graphical user interface)—the list is extensive.

How did the propensity for acronym creation begin? Dickson (1982) noted that acronyms were in our language prior to World War II, but their use mushroomed from 1940 to the present day. "Even the name for them is modern, having been coined under federal auspices during the war. The term acronym (from *akros*, meaning tip, plus *onym*, name) was first introduced to scholars in a 1943 issue of *American Notes and Queries*, which traced it to Bell Telephone Laboratories, which had created the word as a title for a pamphlet to be used to keep workers abreast of the latest initialized titles for weapons systems and agencies" (p. 5).

Some acronyms are masquerading as ordinary words. These include laser (light amplification by stimulated emission of radiation), radar (radio detecting and ranging), scuba (self-contained underwater breathing apparatus), and Teflon (tetrafluoroethylene resin). Louis (1983) wrote that the word "tip" (i.e., money) stands for "to insure promptness"; however, etymologists disagree on its origin. "NIMBY" actually is an acronym (not in my back yard) that refers to a person who does not want a certain type of business or facility (e.g., a landfill, jail, a chemical plant) in his or her neighborhood.

Activity..

Have your group create clever headlines that incorporate acronyms. Here are some examples:

Which DOS Is Boss? (Which computer disk operating system is better or more successful?)

From Ham to RAM (technology from radio to computers)

HOPE Helps (The organization Health Opportunities for People Everywhere, often called Project HOPE, assists medical personnel in other countries.)

Groups of people who have a particular socioeconomic status, geographic location, pastime, or chronological age in common often have acronym-based words that refer to them. Historically, there are the 1960s yippies (from the Youth International Party) and the 1980s yuppies (from young urban professional). Acronym-based words that refer to specific groups have exploded since the use of "yuppies" became popularized. Prior to that, group terms such as "flippers" (male flappers), "greasers," and "eggheads" were not acronym derived. Here are just a few of the more recent acronym-derived words for people with common characteristics (the terms are from Soukhanov 1995; and Dickson 1990).

sippies (senior independent pioneers)

yuffies (young urban failures)

woopies (well-off older people)

yeepies (youthful, energetic elderly people)

rubbies (rich urban bikers)

skippies (school kids with income and purchasing power)

woofies (well-off, over fifty)

maffies (middle-aged affluent folks)

droppies (disillusioned relatively ordinary professionals preferring independent employment situations)

rumpies (rural, upwardly mobile professionals)

Activity..

Have group members devise acronym-based names for groups that are familiar to them. For example:

skitties (school kids interested in technology)

woshies (writers of the sixth-grade homeroom)

limmies (learners interested in mathematics)

Here are some common acronyms that your students might encounter in their content-area reading.

AFTRA (American Federation of Television and Radio Artists)

Amex (American Stock Exchange)

ARM (adjustable rate mortgage)

ASCII (AS-key, computer term for American Standard Code for Information Interchange)

CARE (Cooperative for American Relief to Everywhere)

ELF (extremely low frequency)

EPCOT (Disney's experimental prototype community of tomorrow)

Eurail (European railway)

FEMA (Federal Emergency Management Agency)

Fiat (Fabbrica Italiana Automobile Torino)

FICA (FIE-kah, Federal Insurance Contributions Act)

FORTRAN (Formula Translation, a computer language)

GATT (General Agreement on Tariffs and Trade)

INTELSAT (International Telecommunications Satellite)

MADD (Mothers Against Drunk Driving)

NASDAQ (NAS-dak; National Association of Securities Dealers Automated Quotations)

NATO (North Atlantic Treaty Organization)

NORAD (North American Air Defense Command)

NOW (National Organization for Women)

OPEC (Organization of Petroleum Exporting Countries)

OSHA (Occupational Safety and Health Administration)

Oxfam (Oxford Committee for Famine Relief)

PERT (computer term for program evaluation and review technique)

PIN (personal identification number)

RAM (random access memory)

SAC (Strategic Air Command)

sonar (sound navigation and ranging)

telex (Teletype Exchange)

TESOL (TEH-sull, Teachers of English to Speakers of Other Languages)

TOEFL (TOH-full, Testing of English as a Foreign Language)

UNESCO (United Nations Educational, Scientific, and Cultural Organization)

UNICEF (United Nations International Children's Emergency Fund)

VISTA (Volunteers in Service to America)

WIC (women, infants, and children; usually refers to the Department of Agriculture's food program)

One familiar abbreviation, CD-ROM (compact disc, read-only memory), is part initialism and part acronym. A few abbreviations can be initialisms or acronyms: ASAP (AY-sap, as soon as possible), AWOL (AY-wall, absent without leave), SASE (SAY-zee, self-addressed stamped envelope), and AARP (ARP, American Association of Retired Persons).

Activity..

Some acronyms go to great lengths to stand out from the others and to be remembered. For example, there is ABRACADABRA (Abbreviations and Related Acronyms Associated with Defense, Astronautics, Business, and Radio-electronics). Challenge your group to see who can devise the longest acronym. Remind them that it must be a pronounceable word.

Is My Lunch in the Fridge?
Clipped Words

A clipped word, or clipping, is an abbreviation in which part of a word stands for the whole word. Clipped words are not a contemporary contribution to word formation. The clipped form "gent" for gentleman can be traced to 1564 (McArthur 1996). "Mob," from the Latin *mobile vulgus* (a temperamental, fickle crowd), dates from the early 1700s (Mencken 1977; McArthur 1996). Words can be clipped from the back (e.g., "ad" from advertisement), the front (e.g., "copter" from helicopter), or the back and the front (e.g., "flu" from influenza).

Students have become adept at clipping. There are the clipped words prof (professor), econ (economics), alum (alumni, alumna, alumnus, alumnae), phys ed (physical education), co-ed (co-educational), anthro (anthropology), lit (literature), math (mathematics), gym (gymnasium), dorm (dormitory), poli sci (political science), grad (graduate), psych (psychology), el ed (elementary education), and soc (sociology).

Some first names are clipped words: Stan (Stanley), Jan (Janet), Will (William), Jen (Jennifer), Beth and Liz (Elizabeth), Alex (Alexander), Irv (Irving). Some are adaptations of clipping: Vicky (Victoria), Winnie (Winifred), Danny (Daniel), Benny (Benjamin), Jessie (Jessica).

Here are some common clipped words and the whole words from which they are derived.

amp (ampere)	comp (compensation, complimentary)
auto (automobile)	con (confidence, convict)
bike (adaptation of bicycle)	co-op (cooperative, used as a noun)
bio (biography)	croc (crocodile)
burbs (suburbs)	cuke (adaptation of cucumber)
burger (hamburger)	curio (curiosity)
bus (omnibus)	deli (delicatessen)
champ (champion)	demo (demonstration)
chemo (chemotherapy)	diff (difference, as in *same diff* meaning difference)
chimp (chimpanzee)	
celebs (celebrities)	doc (doctor)
combo (adaptation of combination)	exam (examination)

fax (adaptation of facsimile)

feds (federal government)

fries (French fried potatoes)

gas (gasoline)

gator (alligator)

hippo (hippopotamus)

hood (neighborhood, hoodlum)

info (information)

intro (introduction)

lab (laboratory)

legit (legitimate)

limo (limousine)

lube (adaptation of lubricate)

lunch (luncheon)

margarine (oleomargarine)

max (maximum)

med (medical)

meds (medications)

memo (memorandum)

metro (metropolitan)

morph (metamorphosis)

movie (adaptation of moving picture)

mums (chrysanthemums)

perm (permanent, meaning a treatment for hair)

phone (telephone)

photo (photograph, photography)

plane (airplane)

pol (politician)

prep (preparatory)

pro (professional)

prop (property, such as a "stage prop")

rattler (adaptation of rattlesnake)

ref (referee)

rep (repertory, representative)

retro (retroactive, retrospective)

rhino (rhinoceros)

robot (from *robota*, a Czech word for drudgery or work; Garrison, 1992)

sci fi (science fiction)

semi (semitrailer)

specs (specifications and spectacles)

squash (from the vegetable askutasquash)

stats (statistics)

sub (substitute, submarine)

super (superintendent)

taxi (taxicab, itself from taximeter cabriolet)

tech (technical, technology)

teen (teenager)

temp (temperature, temporary)

tie (necktie)

tux (tuxedo)

typo (typographical error)

ump (umpire)

van (caravan)

vet (veteran, veterinarian)

wig (periwig)

Activity

Have your group compile a list of clipped words (or adaptations of clipped words) for vehicles. Examples include Vette, Olds, Chevy, Caddy, Rolls, and Harley. Are there more clippings for expensive vehicles? Why or why not?

Some clippings deserve special mention. One is 'n for "and". Edwin Newman, in *A Civil Tongue* (1976), stated, "Actually, 'n is a concept. One letter and one apostrophe, taken together, suggest friendliness, informality, and no high prices" (p. 317). Examples include fish 'n chips, pork 'n beans, cheese 'n crackers, wash, dry, 'n fold.

Activity..

Ask students to describe what type of establishment would use 'n in its name. Do the students know of actual examples? Which foods could be connected by an 'n? Does "bread 'n butter" seem appropriate? How about "caviar 'n lobster"? Can they find examples in the supermarket?

"Dis" is a rather new clipped word, first appearing in the *New York Times* in 1987. It comes from the verb "disrespect", which first appeared in 1614 (Soukhanov 1995). "Mag" has been a popular clipping of "magazine." More recently, however, "zine" has replaced "mag," especially for magazines that cater to esoteric tastes.

Wordsational!
Blends

Blends are words that are formed from abbreviated forms of two or more other words. Blends also are called portmanteau (port-man-TOE) words. A portmanteau is a traveling bag with two compartments. Lewis Carroll is credited with first calling blends portmanteau words.

The word "brunch" is a familiar blend (from *br*eakfast and l*unch*). Morris and Morris (1988) wrote that "brunch" first appeared in England circa 1900. The word was at one point so widely used that all blends were referred to as brunch words. Crystal (1995) noted that often it is the second part of the blend that dictates the meaning of the entire word. For example, "motel" (*mo*tor + ho*tel*) is a type of hotel—not a type of motor.

Here are some common blends.

Amtrak (American + track)
beefalo (beef + buffalo)
bit (binary + digit)
blotch (blot + botch)
broasted (broiled + roasted)
caplet (capsule + tablet)
chortle (chuckle + snort)
Chunnel (Channel + tunnel)
clash (clap + crash)
clump (chunk + lump)
dumbfound (dumb + confound)
Eurasia (Europe + Asia)
farewell (fare + ye + well)
flare (flame + glare)

flurry (flutter + hurry)
glimmer (gleam + shimmer)
guesstimate (guess + estimate)
heliport (helicopter + airport)
infomercial (information + commercial)
Medicaid (medical + aid)
Medicare (medical + care)
meld (melt + weld)
moped (motor + pedal)
motorcade (motor + cavalcade)
paratroops (parachute + troops)
pixel (picture + element)
quasar (quasi + stellar)
slanguage (slang + language)

slosh (slop + slush)

smash (smack + mash)

splatter (splash + spatter)

splotch (spot + blotch)

squiggle (squirm + wriggle)

telecast (television + broadcast)

travelogue (travel + monologue)

twirl (twist + whirl)

The origins of some blends are particularly engaging. "Smog" (smoke + fog) would seem to be a relatively recent coinage; however, it first was used in 1905 by a Mr. Des Voeux in England. Des Voeux represented the Coal Smoke Abatement Society. More recent blends, according to Soukhanov (1995), include "agrimation," "compunications," and "vog." "Agrimation" is a blend of "agriculture" and "automation." It refers to the trend of having more farm work done by machines and less done by hand. Soukhanov pointed out, for example, that as a part of agrimation, "cowbots" would work with dairy cows. "Compunications" (computing + communications) is defined as "a coupling of the technologies for transmission and manipulation of information; the data and other information in such a system; the system itself or a network of such systems" (Soukhanov, 1995, p. 293). "Vog" is a blend of "volcanic" and "smog" or "fog." Soukhanov defines it as "the humid, polluted haze resulting from continuous volcanic eruptions and the venting of lava and noxious gases" (p. 316).

Activity

Have students create blends that reflect a combination of cuisines, such as TexMex (Texas + Mexico). Then have them create dishes that would reflect the blend. For example, a CalWis (California + Wisconsin) dish might be artichokes in cheddar cheese sauce.

FWO:
For Writing Only

Some abbreviations are not used in speaking; they are only for written communication. Here are just a few common examples:

acct. (account)

adj. (adjective)

adv. (adverb)

amt. (amount)

anon. (anonymous)

approx. (approximately)

assoc., assn. (association)

attn. (attention)

bldg. (building)

blvd. (boulevard)

co. (company)

dept. (department)

dir. (director)

doz. (dozen)

ed. (editor, edition)

encl. (enclosed, enclosure)

est. (estimate)

etc. (et cetera, and so forth)

ex. (example)	mo. (month)
ft. (foot)	no. (number)
gal. (gallon)	oz. (ounce)
govt. (government)	pl. (plural)
hr. (hour)	qt. (quart)
in. (inch)	ret. (retired)
instr. (instructor)	sq. (square)
ital. (italics)	tbsp. (tablespoon)
lb. (pound)	tel. (telephone)
mfg. (manufacturing)	usu. (usually)
mgr. (manager)	yd. (yard)
misc. (miscellaneous)	yr. (year)

Activity

Have your group compile a list of abbreviations that are used only in writing. Which field of study (e.g., mathematics, English), business (e.g., publishing), or governmental agency (e.g., the Postal Service) seems to use the most written abbreviations?

Activity

Your beginning language scholars will want to read two books that discuss the nature and history of the English language: Christina Ashton's *Words Can Tell: A Book About Our Language* (1988), and Janet Klausner's *Talk About English: How Words Travel and Change* (1990). Ashton's book includes information on prefixes and suffixes, compound words, and portmanteau words, and Klausner's book has several useful sections on various forms of abbreviations (e.g., clipped words).

A Final Word

We have a penchant for opening our lexical tool kits to tack affixes onto words, to remodel their parts of speech, and to solder words together. We also have a tool belt that holds hundreds of thousands of abbreviations. Etymology is the field of study that brings historical understanding to word formation. For example, the initialism "M.C." (Master or Mistress of Ceremonies) originally referred to a person hired by England's King James I (1566–1625). The M.C. was responsible for ensuring that proper etiquette was followed at royal social gatherings. In the next chapter, we will investigate the stories behind what some lexical handypeople have built.

References

Aitchison, J. *Words in the Mind.* 2nd ed. Oxford: Blackwell Publishers, 1994.

Ammer, C. *Have a Nice Day—No Problem! A Dictionary of Clichés.* New York: Plume, 1992.

Asimov, I. *Isaac Asimov's Book of Facts.* New York: Wings Books, 1979.

Bonk, M. R., ed. *Acronyms, Initialisms and Abbreviations Dictionary.* 25th ed. Detroit, Mich.: Gale Research, 1999.

Bryson, B. *The Mother Tongue: English and How It Got that Way.* New York: Avon Books, 1990.

————. *Made in America: An Informal History of the English Language in the United States.* New York: William Morrow, 1994.

Burke, D. *Street Talk-1: How to Speak and Understand American Slang.* Los Angeles: Optima Books, 1992.

————. *Street Talk-2: Slang Used by Teens, Rappers, Surfers, & Popular American Television Shows.* Los Angeles: Optima Books, 1992.

Carothers, G., and J. Lacey. *Dictionary of Colorful Phrases.* New York: Sterling Publishing, 1979.

Carver, C. M. *A History of English in Its Own Words.* New York: HarperCollins, 1991.

Crystal, D. *The Cambridge Encyclopedia of the English Language.* Cambridge: Cambridge University Press, 1995.

Dalzell, T. *Flappers 2 Rappers: American Youth Slang.* Springfield, Mass.: Merriam-Webster, 1996.

Dickson, P. *Words: A Connoisseur's Collection of Old and New, Weird and Wonderful, Useful and Outlandish.* New York: Dell, 1982.

————. *Slang! Topic-by-Topic Dictionary of Contemporary American Lingoes.* New York: Pocket Books, 1990.

————. *What's in a Name? Reflections of an Irrepressible Name Collector.* Springfield, Mass.: Merriam-Webster, 1996.

Elster, C. H. *There's a Word for It!* New York: Scribner, 1996.

Flexner, S. B., and A. H. Soukhanov. *Speaking Freely: A Guided Tour of American English from Plymouth Rock to Silicon Valley.* New York: Oxford University Press, 1997.

Fry, E. B., J. E. Kress, and D. L. Fountoukidis. *The Reading Teacher's Book of Lists.* 3rd ed. Englewood Cliffs, N.J.: Prentice Hall, 1993.

Garrison, W. *Why You Say It: The Fascinating Stories Behind Over 600 Everyday Words and Phrases.* Nashville, Tenn.: Rutledge Hill Press, 1992.

Jacobs, J. "Dreading Water." *Waterloo–Cedar Falls (Iowa) Courier,* 28 January 1998, p. 1.

Johnson, D. D., and P. D. Pearson. *Teaching Reading Vocabulary.* 2nd ed. Fort Worth, Tex.: Holt, Rinehart and Winston, 1984.

Kleinedler, S. R., comp., and R. A. Spears, ed. *NTC's Dictionary of Acronyms and Abbreviations.* Lincolnwood, Ill.: NTC Publishing Group, 1993.

Louis, D. *2201 Fascinating Facts.* New York: Wings Books, 1983.

McArthur, T. *The Concise Oxford Companion to the English Language.* Oxford, England: Oxford University Press, 1996.

Mencken, H. L. *The American Language.* New York: Alfred A. Knopf, 1977.

Morris, W., and M. Morris. *Morris Dictionary of Word and Phrase Origins.* 2d ed. New York: HarperCollins, 1988.

The New York Public Library Writer's Guide to Style and Usage. New York: New York Public Library and Stonesong Press, 1994.

Newman, E. *Strictly Speaking.* New York: Galahad Books, 1974.

———. *A Civil Tongue.* New York: Galahad Books, 1976.

The Princeton Language Institute, ed., and D. Ajjan, comp. *21st Century Dictionary of Acronyms and Abbreviations.* New York: Laurel, 1993.

Room, A. *NTC's Dictionary of Word Origins.* Lincolnwood, Ill.: National Textbook Company, 1986.

Soukhanov, A. H. *Word Watch: The Stories Behind the Words of Our Lives.* New York: Henry Holt, 1995.

References:
Children's Books

Ashton, C. *Words Can Tell: A Book About Our Language.* Englewood Cliffs, N.J.: Julian Messner, 1988.

Juster, N. *The Phantom Tollbooth.* New York: Bullseye Books, 1961.

Klausner, J. *Talk About English: How Words Travel and Change.* New York: Thomas Y. Crowell, 1990.

CHAPTER 9

Etymology:
Word Origins and Borrowings

Happy as a Lark

A baby Sardine saw her first submarine,
She was scared and watched through the peephole,
"O come, come, come, come," said the Sardine's mum,
"It's only a tin full of people."

(Milligan 1968; cited in Ammer 1992)

The witty lines above bring to mind the saying "packed in like sardines." The expression could not have been used before 1839, because food was not preserved in "tins," or cans, prior to that time. The word "sardine," however, is much older; it can be traced to 1393. Word historians believe that it is a toponym from Sardinia, an island in the Mediterranean Sea where the fish were plentiful. Although "packed in like sardines" is a rather recent addition to English, the other words in the expression are not. "Packed" dates from the 1370s, "in" was recorded in the 700s. Its use in the expression "the in crowd" did not appear until the early 1900s, though, and the American phrase "to have an in with someone" was not used before 1929. "Like" as a preposition can be traced to around 1200.

In this chapter, the origins of phrases now relegated to cliché status are discussed. Then borrowed words are examined. Finally, an alphabetized collection of familiar words and their engaging stories is presented.

As Old as the Hills:
Stale Similes?

Many similes (comparisons, often between two unlike things, using "like" or "as") have become moth-eaten—worn out. They usually signal inexperienced or unimaginative speaking and writing. Yet there is history even in the hackneyed. The origins of some similes are as plain as the nose on one's face (from the 1500s). Comparisons are obvious if something is "as cold as ice" or "as hard as a rock." Other comparisons are as clear as mud, and we must delve into the similes' origins for explanations.

The American saying "as happy as a clam" (from the 1800s) makes no sense unless one knows the entire simile and knows something about tides. The complete expression is "happy as a clam at high tide." Clams probably aren't so happy at low tide because that's when clam diggers can see them and gather them. At high tide, however, clams are safe from hungry humans and presumably are as happy as a lark.

According to Carothers and Lacey (1979), the simile "as happy as a lark" originated in the great state of Nebraska in the 1920s. The songbirds were thought to be happy because all they did was eat and sleep—and they were free as birds to fly where they wished.

Activity..........

The simile "to eat like a bird" means "to eat very little." Some birds, however, eat a great deal each day. Have pairs of your students choose a bird, and ask them to consult bird guides or other sources to determine how much and what the bird eats. Share findings with the group.

Elephants have a reputation for having good memories. As a group research activity, find out if the simile "a memory like an elephant" is an accurate one. Here are other similes whose factuality you might want your students to check: "as sly as a fox," "as stubborn as a mule," "works like a dog."

The pioneers of this country were a tough lot. How does cornmeal fried in bear grease sound for a snack? This less-than-enticing mixture was the basis for frontier hotcakes. The more genteel folks fried them in pork grease. In the early 1800s, fried hotcakes were so wildly popular that "to sell like hotcakes" was to sell something briskly (Garrison, 1992).

To "know someone or something like a book" also dates from pioneer days. Books were rare on the frontier; sometimes there were only a few for an entire community. Adults had to memorize these books if they wanted to teach their children reading skills.

The simile "neat as a pin" was recorded in the late 1700s as "neat as a new pin." Originally pins rusted quickly because they were made from iron wire. Only new pins were free of corrosion.

There are varying accounts of how "fit as a fiddle" originated. The simile can be traced to the early 1600s. Funk (1955) stated, "Although 'fiddles' were known in England back at least in the early thirteenth century, it was some four hundred years later, evidently, before their shape, form, tone, and other qualities became so pleasing as to invite complimentary applications to humans. ... 'To play first fiddle' was to occupy a leading position, and one 'fit as a fiddle' was beyond further need of improvement in health or condition" (p. 56).

Garrison (1992) reported that audiences listening to early fiddles knew when the instruments were warped and out of tune. Only an undamaged and well-tuned fiddle was "fit" for performances. Carothers and Lacey (1979) attributed the expression to Irish fiddlers who had to play throughout the night and therefore had to be in top physical form.

Before whistles were made from metal or plastic, they were whittled from wood. For their tone to be pure, the interior of the whistles had to be free of foreign matter and moisture. "To be clean as a whistle" is still used today even though wooden whistles are rare.

One might think that "as easy as falling off a log" comes from the short distance from log top to ground. A person could fall off a log and probably not be injured. This American simile, however, is thought to have come from logrolling. Although remaining upright on a log while rolling it in water might appear simple, it is much easier to fall off that log.

Another "easy" simile, "as easy as pie," was originally "as easy as eating pie." This American expression from the early 1900s implies that eating a pie is much simpler than preparing one.

"Like a bull in a china shop" does not refer to the huge animal in a store that sells table service. It is a play on words. The 1800s simile, according to Funk (1948), refers to British trading policies with China. During this period, John Bull was a cartoon character who represented England. Some scholars surmise that the cartoonist based his "Bull in a China shop" on an Aesop's fable in which an ungraceful donkey breaks dishes in a pottery shop.

To "drop someone or something like a hot potato" was in use in the early 1800s. But why a potato and not a turnip or a cabbage? Ammer (1992) said that the simile uses "potato" because "potatoes, which hold a fair amount of water, retain heat very well" (p. 96). Potatoes also are a fairly common vegetable; they are "the fourth most important crop in the world after wheat, rice, and corn" (Chalmers 1994, p. 292). More people probably have felt a hot potato than a hot artichoke.

The simile "as cool as a cucumber" means that one is calm and not easily upset. A cucumber, though, really is cool. Chalmers (1994) noted that a cucumber "literally maintains its insides at a temperature several degrees cooler than the surrounding atmosphere" (p. 124). Ammer (1992) reported there is "evidence that the inside of a field cucumber on a warm day is 20 degrees cooler than the air" (p. 70). Although the word "cucumber" entered English around 1384, the vegetable itself was eaten by the ancient Romans.

Eggs, Toast, Yogurt:
Borrowed Words

Some languages strive to keep their vocabularies free of foreign influences, but English is an unabashed borrower of words from other languages. Crystal (1995) wrote that loan words from more than 120 languages have entered the English vocabulary. McArthur (1996) stated, "English has borrowed massively from French, Latin, and Greek, significantly from Italian, Spanish, German, Danish, and Dutch, and to varying degrees from every other language with which it has come in contact" (p. 137). The terms "borrowings," "borrowed words," and "loan words," however, are not accurate. English doesn't return the words, and the words remain with the source language as well as become part of English.

Why do some languages borrow from one another? A multicultural mix of people within a country ensures that words from other lands frequently will be used and will be absorbed by the most commonly used language. Another reason for borrowing is that sometimes there simply isn't an equivalent word in one's own language to describe a particular food, tree, computer part, ceremony, or the like. A distant third reason for borrowing words is to show that one is "learned," well traveled, or well off. If you want to join a club, and a member tells you that a monthly appointment with one's couturier is de rigueur among club members, you might reconsider joining.

Many borrowed words passed in various forms through more than one language before entering English. Unfortunately, compilers of some lists of borrowed words do not thoroughly investigate the history of the words. The word "mosquito," for example, frequently appears on borrowed-word lists as Spanish in origin. It appeared in English in the 1580s as the Spanish word for little fly or little gnat. The Spanish word *mosca* (i.e., fly), however, comes from *musca*, which is Latin for fly. The words "rodeo," "armadillo," and "vamoose" also are often attributed to Spanish, but they too can be traced further to Latin. Words such as "fiasco," "bandit," and "replica" can be found on Italian borrowed-word lists, but they also had their origins in Latin before entering the Italian language.

Etymology: Word Origins and Borrowings

Form teams whose purpose is to locate words that came into American English from other languages and countries. You may want to group students according to their own ancestral backgrounds. Team members might interview relatives and community members or write to embassies, cultural organizations, and ethnic clubs to ask about words that contributed to English. Each team can prepare a poster display of the words (and their stories) they have located.

The following list of words borrowed by English gives their languages of origin and the approximate years when they entered the English language. You may want to share some of them with your students. They might enjoy guessing the languages of origin and the approximate years.

admiral (1297 Arabic)

algebra (1551 Arabic)

alias (1432 (adverb), 1605 (noun) Latin)

alphabet (1425 Greek)

ancient (1390 Latin)

assassin (1531 Arabic)

avocado (1763 Nahuatl (an Indian language of Mexico and Central America))

axis (1398 Latin)

bandage (1599 (noun), 1774 (verb) French)

banjo (1774 a Bantu language (West Africa))

bazaar (1588 Persian)

bleak (1300 Scandinavian)

bloom (noun and verb) (1200 Scandinavian)

bungalow (1676 Hindi (India))

cafe (1802 French)

camel (950, Hebrew)

campus (1774 Latin)

caravan (1588 Persian)

cashew (1703 Tupi-Guarani (an Indian language of South America))

charisma (1875 Greek)

chef (1826 French)

chimpanzee (1738 West Africa, Angola)

chocolate (1604 Nahuatl)

chow mein (1903 Chinese)

cinnamon (1390 Hebrew)

circus (1380 (a Roman circus), 1791 (a traveling circus) Latin)

cliché (1832 French)

coach (meaning carriage) (1556 Hungarian)

coffee (1601 Turkish or Arabic)

cookie (1703 Dutch)

cougar (1774 Tupi (an Indian language of the Amazon Valley))

coyote (1759 Nahuatl)

criterion (1661 Greek)

critic (1588 Greek)

dachshund (1881 German)

dessert (1600 French)

dinner (1300 French)

drum (1427 Dutch)

egg (before 1200 Scandinavian)

extra (adjective) (1654 Latin)

fellow (1250 Scandinavian)

flat (adjective) (1300 Scandinavian)

formula (1638 Latin)

forum (1464 Latin)

frankfurter (1894 German)

gap (1325 Scandinavian)

gazelle (1600 Arabic)

genius (1393 Latin)

geyser (1780 Icelandic)

giraffe (1594 Arabic)

granola (1970 Italian)

gumbo (1805 probably a Bantu language (West Africa))

gung ho (1942 Chinese)

hamburger (1889 German)

hammock (1657 Haitian)

horde (a group) (1555 Turkish)

impala (1875 Zulu (South Africa))

jazz (1913 West Africa)

jubilee (1450 Hebrew)

kangaroo (1770 Aboriginal language of Australia)

kayak (1757 Inuit (Greenland))

kindergarten (1852 German)

kiwi (fruit) (1835 Maori (New Zealand))

koala (1808 Aboriginal language of Australia)

landscape (1603 Dutch)

lilac (color) (1625 Persian)

llama (1600 Quechua (an Indian language of South America))

loafer (unambitious person) (1830 German)

magazine (publication) (1583 Arabic)

muggy (1731 Scandinavian)

noodle (pasta) (1779 German)

oaf (1625 Scandinavian)

okra (1679 West Africa)

opera (1644 Latin)

orangutan (1699 Malay (Indonesia))

pajamas (1800 Persian)

passport (1500 French)

pastime (1489 French)

peach (1400 Persian)

peninsula (1538 Latin)

petunia (1825 Guarani (an Indian language of South America, especially Paraguay))

phenomenon (1625 Greek)

pizza (1935 Italian)

polo (1872 Tibetan)

poodle (1825 German)

putty (1663 French)

ratio (1660 Latin)

rhinoceros (1300 Greek)

saga (1709 Icelandic)

sauerkraut (1617 German)

sauna (1881 Finnish)

scarlet (1250 Arabic)

schwa (1818 Hebrew)

scowl (1340 (verb), 1500 (noun) Scandinavian)

shawl (1662 Persian)

similar (1611 Latin)

simile (1387 Latin)

sofa (1625 Arabic)

spaghetti (1849 Italian)

spinach (1399 Persian)

status (1671 Latin)

suite (1673 French)

syrup (1398 Arabic)

tapioca (1648 Tupi)

tariff (1591 Arabic)

tea (1655 Chinese)

toast (bread) (1398 (verb), 1400 (noun) Latin)

tomato (1753 Nahuatl)

tote (verb) (1677 West Africa)

trivia (1902 Latin)

tundra (1841 Lappish (northern parts of Finland, Russia, Norway, and Sweden))

turquoise (1567 Turkish)

tycoon (1857 Chinese)

waffle (noun) (1744 Dutch)

waltz (1781 German)

yak (1795 Tibetan)

yam (1697 West Africa)

yoga (1820 Sanskrit (India))

yogurt (1625 Turkish)

American English borrowed heavily from Native American groups, especially from the Algonquians, who were living in the areas where colonists settled. Words such as "hickory," "chipmunk," "toboggan," and "woodchuck" are from Algonquian dialects. As with most borrowed words in the English language, the Algonquian words did not just drop into our language unchanged. Mencken (1977) and Barnhart and Metcalf (1997) noted that the words "rahaughcums" and "raugroughcuns" were used by Captain John Smith in his work *True Relation* (1607–1608). Barnhart and Metcalf stated: "Captain John Smith was brought before Powhatan, the 'emperor' of the Indians, who was lying on a high bed 'covered with a great Covering of the *Rahaughcums*.' ... Later in the *True Relation* he mentions Powhatan sending him 'many presents of Deare, bread, *Raugroughcuns*'" (pp. 8–9).

Mencken reported that in various later works, the words became "aracoune" (1612), "rarowcun" (1624), and finally, in 1672, "raccoon." "Moose" (1672) had been "mose" (1637), "moos" (1616), and "mus" (1613). The Native American *mus* referred to the animals that eat leaves and bark from tree branches.

The Plot Thickens:
Etymology or Word Origins?

Although "etymology" and "word origins" often are used interchangeably, language scholars differentiate between the terms. McArthur (1996) pointed out, "Whereas scholarly dictionaries of etymology describe the histories of many thousands of words in dense entries with often formidable arrays of abbreviations and parentheses, books and articles on word origins tend to discuss a more limited range of words whose unusual 'stories' are often described in an expansive and relaxed style" (p. 1032).

McArthur hit the nail on the head. Dictionaries of etymology can be intimidating to amateur word sleuths. Here is a *partial* entry for the word "hill" in *The Barnhart Concise Dictionary of Etymology: The Origins of American English Words* (1995, p. 353): "**hill** *n.* Probably about 1175 *hulle*, in dialect of Southwest and Middle England; later *hil* (probably about 1200); found in Old English *hyll* (about 1000), from Proto-Germanic* *Hulnis*; cognate with Old Frisian *holla* head, Frisian *hel* hill, Middle Dutch *hille*, Low German *hull* hill, and Old Saxon *holm*, Old Icelandic *holmr* island (Danish *holm* and Swedish *holme* islet)."

Such entries, although impressive, probably would not appeal to many beginners in the study of etymology. Word origins, which McArthur refered to as "informal" and "nontechnical" (p. 1032), are capable of capturing the novice etymologist's attention, though. The remainder of this chapter explains the origins of some English words with just a dash of etymology included where appropriate. You may want to share these tales with your students.

From "Ampersand" to "Zany":
Stories of Word Origins

ampersand—The word for the "and" character (&) entered English in 1837. The character evolved from frequent use of the Latin word for "and," et. Years ago, children had to recite the difference between the letter "a" and the word "a," between the letter "i" and the word "I." To do so, they would say "a per se a," "i per se I." The *per se* is Latin for "by itself." At the end of their recitation, they would see the "&" and would say "and per se and." This became corrupted to "ampersand."

bunk (foolishness or nonsense)—Sometimes it pays to be a long-winded speaker. In 1820, General Felix Walker was a North Carolina congressional representative whose territory included Buncombe County. Walker's speeches were so lengthy that other congressmen left the room. "Buncombe" became synonymous with unimportant chatter. It was later spelled "Bunkum" and then clipped to "bunk."

curfew—This borrowing is from the French *couvre-feu* or "cover the fire." In the Middle Ages, bells were rung prior to darkness to alert people that it was time to extinguish all flames. Any unintentional fire quickly would spread to medieval wooden structures. Although the word entered English in 1330, it did not mean "to get off the streets and go home" until the 1800s.

dismal—The ancient Romans believed that there were twenty-four unlucky days in each year. "Dismal" came from the Latin *dies mali* or "bad days." The belief in "dismal days" lasted through the Middle Ages. The current meaning of "dismal" (i.e., cheerless, grim) entered English in 1593.

eavesdrop—Before there were gutters and spouts on buildings, eaves (i.e., the overhangs on roofs) extended far enough from the dwellings' foundations to keep rainwater from flooding the premises. The dry space under the eaves allowed one to overhear conversations in a house—even during a gentle rain. The word for the actual roof structure, "eavesdrop," was recorded in the mid-1400s. The verb "eavesdrop" entered English in 1606.

figurehead—This word is from seafaring language. It refers to the head or bust on the bow of a ship. According to Isil (1996), the figurehead reflected characteristics of the ships' owners or of the ships themselves. Of course, the figurehead had little to do with the functioning of the vessel. In 1883, the word "figurehead" also began to be used for a person who might be at the forefront of a group but had little to do with the group's progress or success.

gunk—In 1932 a patent was given for a dense liquid soap that had the trademark name Gunk. By 1949, gunk had come to mean sticky or greasy sludge.

hazard—Hazard was originally a dice game of chance. The origin of the word is from the Arabic *az-zahr* (i.e., the die). In 1548, "hazard" took on the meaning of "danger, threat, or risk."

italic—The slanted type style, meaning "from Italy," was developed by Teobaldo Mannucci in 1501. Mannucci was from Venice, Italy, and ran a print shop that was well known for its high-quality work. Prior to Mannucci's introduction of italics, all type was strictly vertical.

junk (garbage)—This word for "trash" or "something of small value" came from sailors in the 1300s. The word referred to pieces of rope or cable that no longer were useful. The more broad definition of "any items that are no longer wanted" appeared in 1880. In 1946, the word "junky," meaning "trashy," entered American English.

khaki—This word, which means "dust" in Persian, refers to the cloth and to its olive-brown color. It came to English in 1857 via the British Guide Corps stationed in India. They adopted khaki uniforms because they were not as easily seen as their older white uniforms.

loophole—Originating in the architecture of medieval castles, this word meant a hole in a wall that was small on the outside but wider on the inside of the wall. Clearly, a person on the inside would have an advantage over an attacker trying to aim an arrow into a loophole. In 1663 the word was first used to mean "a way out of something."

mammoth (adjective)—This synonym for "gigantic" came, of course, from the enormous extinct animal that looked like an elephant. The word's use as an adjective, however, is attributed to Thomas Jefferson. He described a room in the soon-to-be White House as so huge it could accommodate a mammoth. Jefferson kept a gift of a large cheese in the mammoth room, and soon everything in the country, from big loaves of bread to important legislation, was being described as mammoth.

nest egg—This term is based on the power of suggestion. People who raised chickens would never remove all the eggs from a nest. They would leave behind one egg or even a phony egg to encourage hens to lay more. As strange as this seems, it apparently works with birds other than hens too. Almond (1985) reported, "An experiment on one songbird, in which each day all but one egg was removed from the nest, led to the production of seventy-two eggs—though the usual clutch was less than a half-dozen" (p. 174). Today a nest egg is an amount of money that can come in handy on rainy days.

outlandish—This word probably originated from some narrow-minded word coiner. It came from an Old English word that meant "foreign place." During the 1300s, people from unfamiliar lands (or "outlanders") often were viewed with suspicion or ridicule. "Outlander" became "outlandish," but now the word refers to anything unconventional.

phony—This word comes from the fawney ring, which was used by con artists in the 1700s. They would leave a worthless but expensive-looking fawney in an obvious place. When a less-than-honest person picked up the ring, the con artist would demand a payment for his or her silence. The con artist got the money, the dupe got the fawney ring, and we got the word "phony."

quarantine—This word comes from the Latin *quadraginta*, which means "forty." Medieval sailing vessels could harbor all sorts of ailments. Venice, Italy, required any ship thought to carry disease to stay away from the town for forty days.

rostrum—Many ancient shipbuilders put a rostrum on each warship—and not because sailors were orators. A rostrum, which originally meant "beak," was a protruding structure used to ram other warships. The Romans placed seized enemy rostra as prized spoils of war in the speakers' areas of the Roman Forum. Eventually, the platform on which a speaker stood came to be called a rostrum.

sloppy—This adjective comes from the word "slop," which meant "baggy clothing." In the early 1600s, as part of an effort to improve the ragged appearance of its sailors, the British Royal Navy ordered slops for the men. The clothing probably was akin to our jumpsuits, but of course, they were not tailored. The word "sloppy" was first used as an English adjective in its present sense in 1825.

turnpike—Toll roads are not an exclusively modern annoyance. As early as the 1400s, access to roads was controlled via spiked poles, or pikes. When an amount was paid to the gatekeeper, the pike was turned so the traveler could proceed.

ukulele—This word entered English in 1896. Although the instrument was introduced to the Hawaiians by Portuguese settlers, it was a British officer, Edward Purvis, who inspired the Hawaiians to give their own name to the instrument. Apparently, Purvis was quite the performer, because the descriptive Hawaiians called him *ukulele* or "leaping flea." The name eventually was transferred to the instrument.

volume (a book in a set of books)—This meaning of volume (1382) came from the Latin *volvere*, meaning "to roll or turn." Ancient "books" were written on parchment, which had to be rolled from one stick to another as the books were read. The parchment was referred to as the *volumen.*

windfall—This word has meant an "unexpected stroke of good luck" since 1542. The word entered English in 1464, when trees in certain areas of England could not be chopped down because the timber was critical for shipbuilding. The only time one could use any of this wood was when the trees were blown down by gusty winds.

xylophone—This musical instrument comes from the Greek *xylon* and the English *phone*. It literally means "the sound of wood." Today in America, wooden xylophones aren't as common as they were in 1866, when the word entered English.

yarn—The word "yarn," meaning the twisted threads used for weaving, knitting, or rope making, is an old-timer. It comes from the Old English *gearn,* which dates to around 1000. To make yarn out of fine threads was tedious work, so many a story, or yarn, was told while spinning.

zany—This adjective was once a noun. It referred to a familiar character in Italian plays, Zanni, who was a clown or a buffoon. "Zanni" was a Venetian form of "Giovanni," Italian for "John." In 1616, the noun became an adjective meaning comical, ridiculous, or playful.

Tell your group that the American humorist Gelett Burgess (1866–1951) coined the word "blurb." Burgess designed a satirical book jacket for a booksellers' convention that he attended in 1907. On the back of the jacket was gushing praise for the phony book by an equally fictitious "Miss Belinda Blurb." Eventually, a blurb became a short promo for any product.

Have group members write their own blurbs for their favorite fiction or nonfiction work, movie, television show, or computer program. Remind them that a blurb is succinct and usually glowing.

Here are some "word origin" children's books that you might want to share with your students.

Naming Colors by Ariane Dewey (1995) gives the histories of color words (e.g., black, white, red, green). The author also discusses "colors from the garden" (e.g., pumpkin, apricot), "colors from spices" (e.g., mustard, sage), "colors named after places" (e.g., indigo, which is Greek for "a substance from the Indus River"), "colors from everyday things" (e.g., fire-engine red), and "new colors" (e.g., bubblegum pink).

The word "bleachers" comes from baseball. In the early days of the sport, fans sat on benches that were directly in the sun and therefore always "bleached out." This is just one word origin from Jane Sarnoff and Reynold Ruffins's *Words: A Book About the Origins of Everyday Words and Phrases* (1981). The authors have grouped the stories of the words and phrases under headings such as "Clothes" (e.g., denim, galoshes, corduroy), "Money" (e.g., nickel, bank, dollar), "Reading and Writing" (e.g., ink, book, paragraph), "Mystery" (e.g., clue, private eye, jury), and more.

Although it is not a recent title, Isaac Asimov's *Words from Myths* (1961) is timeless. The author tells the tale of Atlas, for example, whose name means "to support." Asimov then describes how early map makers put a picture of Atlas supporting the earth on the top page of their packets of maps, and points out that Gerhardus Mercator in the 1500s was the first to use the word "atlas" for his book of maps. Students will be surprised to learn that even a common word such as "cereal" comes from a myth (from the Roman goddess Ceres).

Lynda Graham-Barber's *Gobble! The Complete Book of Thanksgiving Words* (1991) contains word origins of "corn," "turkey," "feast," "stuffing," and several other words associated with the November holiday. The book also includes some history about the Pilgrims' celebration and even includes a *Mayflower* passenger list with the most popular first names tallied (there were fifteen Johns and five Marys) and the most unusual names listed (e.g., Remember, Wrestling, Peregrine). Graham-Barber's *Mushy! The Complete Book of Valentine Words* (1991) gives the word origins of Valentine-related words such as "February," "card," "chocolate," "verse," "heart," and more.

Patricia Gordon and Reed C. Snow's *Kids Learn America! Bringing Geography to Life with People, Places, & History* (1992) has many word origins tucked among its reader-friendly pages. For example, people from Oklahoma are sometimes called Sooners. That's because early settlers of the Oklahoma Territory claimed land too soon—before the official opening date to do so. There is a tale from Iowa on how Delicious apples got their name, and a tale about how "Penn" became "Pennsylvania." There are craft activities, recipes, maps, trivia, and a lot more to interest students in each of our states.

Activity..

Divide your groups into teams of three. Pass out a slip of paper to each team. Tell the teams to write a brief, convincing word origin for the word "album" (as in "photo album"). The origin should include the approximate year the word entered the English language. Collect the slips of paper and read each one. At some point, slyly include and read the correct word origin for "album" (below). Have team members guess which origin for the word is the correct one. Repeat the procedure with the following authentic word origins. The dates in which the words entered English are in parentheses.

album (1651)—This word is a direct borrowing from Latin. Ancient Romans recorded news items for the masses on an album (a white tablet), which was put in public places.

alibi (1743)—This Latin word (actually *alibi,* too) meant "elsewhere." In ancient Roman times, if a person declared that he or she was *alibi* when a crime was committed, it meant that the person was not at the scene of the crime. Today's usage is close to the original.

ambitious (1382)—This word comes from ancient Rome. Politicians during that time would travel far and wide to butter up voters. The Romans called these attempts to get votes *ambitiosus*—"ambitious" in our language.

apron (1307)—Someone goofed along the way on this word because he or she didn't speak clearly. The word originally was *naperon* from French via Latin, and became "napron" in English. After 1450, this protective piece of cloth was no longer "a napron" but was slurred into "an apron."

asterisk (before 1382)—This word comes from the Greek word *askeriskos,* which means "little star." The character * is now used most frequently to signal a footnote.

backlog (1684, 1883)—In the 1600s, this American English word referred to a huge log that was placed in the back of a fireplace. The backlog was supposed to be essential for a properly made fire. By 1883 "backlog" had come to mean "a supply or heap."

bug (computer problem, 1945)—Grace Murray Hopper, a pioneer computer programmer, said that her team coined this term when a large moth got caught in their computer and caused trouble with the machine.

candidate (1600)—In ancient Rome, politicians went out to meet the people just as they do today. Of course, the politicians wanted to make a good, lasting impression on the voters. The Latin word *candidatus* meant "to be dressed in white." The Roman politicians made sure they were *candidatus,* and met the voters in clean, white togas.

chop suey (1888)—Americans took the name for this food from the Chinese *tsap sui,* which means "mixed fragments" or "odds and ends."

clink (jail, 1515)—This slang term for a jail comes from the Clink, a real prison in London.

coconut (1613)—This word is based on the Portuguese *coco,* which meant "a scowling face." If one looks at one end of a coconut, one can see indentations that resemble a face.

comma (1599)—The word for this familiar punctuation mark comes from the Greek word *komma,* which meant "a piece cut off." In a sentence, a comma indicates that a part of the sentence is cut off or separated from the rest of the sentence.

kowtow (1804)—The Chinese word *k'o-t'ou* means "to hit the head." Long ago it was a Chinese custom for those visiting an important person to touch their foreheads to the ground as a sign of respect.

magazine (1583)—In Arabic, a *makhzan* was a storehouse where harvests and perhaps tools were kept. In the 1730s the word was first used for a periodical, which can be thought of as a storehouse of information.

muscle (noun, 1392)—The Latin *musculus* meant "little mouse," but *musculus* also was used to refer to a muscle. Word historians think that "little mouse" described the rippling, or quick, mouselike motion, of a muscle when it is flexed.

nausea (1425)—The Greek word *naus*, meaning "ship," forms the base of "nausea." This root makes sense when one thinks of being on a ship that is tossed about by rough water and wind. The Latin *nausea* actually meant "seasickness."

panic (noun, 1627)—The ancient Greeks thought that the god Pan was responsible for spreading fear among people and animals. The word became an English verb in 1827.

papier-mâché (1753)—This term for shreds of paper and glue comes from Old French and Latin. It literally means "chewed paper."

poll (1625)—In the 1300s, the word *polle* meant "the hair on the top of the head." Votes often were tallied by counting the tops of heads in large gatherings. By 1625, the word meant "the recording of votes."

quack (impostor, 1638)—This is a clipped form of *quacksalver*, which meant a person who sold ointments that were supposed to heal.

salary (around 1280)—In the days of ancient Rome, salt was a precious commodity—so much so that Roman soldiers were given a *salarium*, or "salt money," to purchase *sal* (salt). From *salarium* comes the modern word "salary."

seedy (1749)—This synonym for "run-down" or "shabby" came from the appearance of a plant that has gone to seed.

sideburns (1887)—This word is a flip-flop of "Burnside." General Ambrose Burnside was a Union officer in the American Civil War who wore whiskers along the sides of his face.

spud (1440)—This synonym for "potato" originally meant "a spade or digging device." New Zealanders were the first to use the word "spud" for a potato in 1845, probably because it referred to the tool used to dig up the vegetable.

tabloid (1884)—Originally a trademark for a compressed, small pill, this word is made up of "tablet" plus "oid." Eventually the word came to be used for a compact version of anything—especially newspapers.

tulip (1578)—The name of this springtime flower comes from a Persian word that means "turban." If you examine a tulip, its overlapping petals and the shape of the flower resemble a turban.

As a twist on the game, you may want to include the words below. Although etymologists have theories about the origins of these words, none have been proven. We do know, however, when the words entered the English language.

banter (to engage in playful or teasing talk), 1935
botch (to flub, bungle, mess up), 1530
gavel (small hammer), 1805
gull (water bird), 1450

hubbub (noise, loud confusion), 1555

penguin (flightless bird), 1587

pooch (a dog), 1924

pump (shoe), 1555

shenanigans (mischief), 1855

snooze (to sleep), 1789

tizzy (nervousness, animated confusion), 1935

zip (zero), 1900

Activity

Have students suggest words whose origins they would like to know. Then take your class on a research excursion to the school media center, the computer lab, or the public library to locate and share the histories of these words. Dictionaries, thesauri, and specialized books such as those mentioned in this chapter will be helpful.

A Final Word

Joseph T. Shipley (1945) said, "Word history traces the path of human fellowship, the bridges from mind to mind, from nation to nation" (p. viii). He noted that people from all abilities, occupations, and socioeconomic strata have had a hand in shaping our language. Shipley also pointed out that fewer than 2 percent of our words are of English origin. From puzzled schoolchildren came "ampersand," sailors donated "figurehead," and petty criminals gave us "phony." We "borrowed" the word "tote" from West Africa, "yogurt" from Turkey, and "gung ho" from China. To study etymology or word origins is to study the story of humankind.

In the next chapter, a potpourri of language devices will be discussed. "Potpourri" entered English in 1611, when it referred to a stew containing a variety of meats. The word can be traced to a Latin word that meant "to grow rotten." A rotten pot of meat is not hard to imagine in the 1600s when there was no refrigeration. Some etymologists, however, believe that the "rottenness" referred to was actually just the mixture of odors that might come from a combination of meats. It wasn't until 1749 that the word came to refer to a mixture of spices and flower parts.

References

Almond, J. *Dictionary of Word Origins.* New York: Citadel Press, 1985.

Ammer, C. *Have a Nice Day—No Problem! A Dictionary of Clichés.* New York: Plume, 1992.

Ayto, J. *Dictionary of Word Origins: The Histories of More than 8,000 English-Language Words.* New York: Arcade Publishing, 1990.

Barnette, M. *Ladyfingers and Nun's Tummies: A Lighthearted Look at How Foods Got Their Names.* New York: Times Books, 1997.

Barnhart, D. K., and A. A. Metcalf. *America in So Many Words: Words That Have Shaped America.* Boston: Houghton Mifflin, 1997.

Barnhart, R. K., ed. *The Barnhart Concise Dictionary of Etymology: The Origins of American English Words.* New York: HarperCollins, 1995.

Carothers, G., and J. Lacey. *Dictionary of Colorful Phrases.* New York: Sterling Publishing, 1979.

Carver, C. M. *A History of English in Its Own Words.* New York: HarperCollins, 1991.

Chalmers, I. *The Great Food Almanac: A Feast of Facts from A to Z.* San Francisco: Collins Publishers, 1994.

Crystal, D. *The Cambridge Encyclopedia of the English Language.* Cambridge: Cambridge University Press, 1995.

Freeman, M. S. *The Story Behind the Word.* Philadelphia: ISI Press, 1985.

Funk, C. E. *A Hog on Ice and Other Curious Expressions.* New York: Harper & Row, 1948.

———. *Thereby Hangs a Tale: Stories of Curious Word Origins.* New York: Harper & Row, 1950.

———. *Heavens to Betsy!* New York: Harper & Row, 1955.

Funk, W. *Word Origins and Their Romantic Stories.* New York: Grosset & Dunlap, 1950.

Garrison, W. *Why You Say It: The Fascinating Stories Behind Over 600 Everyday Words and Phrases.* Nashville, Tenn.: Rutledge Hill Press, 1992.

Isil, O. A. *When a Loose Cannon Flogs a Dead Horse There's the Devil to Pay.* Camden, Maine: International Marine, 1996.

McArthur, T. *The Concise Oxford Companion to the English Language.* Oxford: Oxford University Press, 1996.

Mencken, H. L. *The American Language.* New York: Alfred A. Knopf, 1977.

Morris, W., and M. Morris. *Morris Dictionary of Word and Phrase Origins.* 2nd ed. New York: HarperCollins, 1988.

Room, A. *NTC's Dictionary of Word Origins.* Lincolnwood, Ill.: National Textbook Company, 1986.

Shipley, J. T. *Dictionary of Word Origins.* New York: Dorset Press, 1945.

References:
Children's Books

Asimov, I. *Words from Myths.* Boston: Houghton Mifflin, 1961.

Dewey, A. *Naming Colors.* New York: HarperCollins, 1995.

Gordon, P., and R. C. Snow. *Kids Learn America! Bringing Geography to Life with People, Places, & History.* Charlotte, Vt.: Williamson Publishing, 1992.

Graham-Barber, L. *Gobble! The Complete Book of Thanksgiving Words.* New York: Bradbury Press, 1991.

———. *Mushy! The Complete Book of Valentine Words.* New York: Bradbury Press, 1991.

Sarnoff, J., and R. Ruffins. *Words: A Book About the Origins of Everyday Words and Phrases.* New York: Charles Scribner's Sons, 1981.

CHAPTER 10

A Potpourri of Language Play

Drumsticks and Technicians:
Euphemisms

Euphemisms (YOU-fah-miz-ims) are polite, inoffensive, or comforting words that are used in place of words thought of as too direct, demeaning, or upsetting. The word "euphemism" entered English in the 1600s. It comes from a Greek word that meant to speak well about a person or a thing. "Cash advance" is a euphemism for a loan. Somehow a cash advance seems less painful or threatening than a loan on which one usually must pay interest.

Hugh Rawson, in *A Dictionary of Euphemisms & Other Doubletalk* (1981), pointed out that euphemisms "are embedded so deeply in our language that few of us, even those who pride themselves on being plainspoken, ever get through a day without using them" (p. 1).

Some euphemisms seem harmless, but others are insidious. Job titles periodically are revised with euphemistic labels. A clerk or a salesperson is now an "associate," "representative," or "vendor." A garbage collector and a gardener have become a "sanitation engineer" and a "landscape artist" respectively. A temp, or temporary worker, is now a "contingent worker." "Janitor" is a second-order euphemism. "Janitor" became "custodian" and then "building maintenance specialist."

"Technician" occasionally is used as a euphemistic job title. I have heard of "technicians" going to homes and businesses to deliver customized "treatments." Are these technicians relaxation experts? Are they providing personalized skin care? No, they're exterminators spraying homes for "pests" (i.e., cockroaches, silverfish, carpenter ants, etc.). Technicians speak of periods of "heightened activity" among their targets. That means a place is overrun with pests.

Using euphemisms for job titles seems innocuous. All work has dignity, but if some workers feel better about being called by a euphemistic title, little harm is done. The only potential problems are the seeming insensitivity or confusion that could result if one isn't familiar with the "upgraded" job title, is applying for a job, or needs a service.

Activity.................................

Have students look in "Help Wanted" sections of old newspapers in your local library to find and share job titles and services that were once known by names different from those currently in use.

Some topics, such as illness and death, can be touchy. It does no harm to express one's sympathies to grieving relatives or friends about their "loss." The use of euphemisms such as "long illness" for "cancer" and "pass away" for "die" shows respect for "surviving members" of a family and for the "departed."

Other harmless uses of euphemisms include updated names of places and things. Andrew D. Blechman, in a *Des Moines Register* column, quoted the executive director of the local Metro Waste Authority. "We call sludge biosolids. ... And we call our landfill Metro Park East, which sounds like an office park. But people who live around it still call it the dump" (April 12, 1997). In the same column the superintendent of Altoona, Iowa's Wastewater Treatment Facility remarked, "People are always looking for ways to make things look more esthetically pleasing than they really are." Altoona's facility doesn't "process sewage," it "reclaims water."

Activity.................................

Tell your group that some words and phrases associated with schools have become euphemistic. In some locales, school districts are called "learning communities" and the administrative offices where superintendents work have become the "learning resource centers." Course names have been updated, too. Home economics now is "consumer science," and some physical education classes have become "leisure" or "wellness" classes.

Have group members locate old class schedules, yearbooks, handbooks, and report cards from their other schools. Then have them compare words and phrases for classes, schoolrooms, rules, and behavior standards. Are the older terms or the recent terms more euphemistic? Why? Do group members agree with the use of the updated terms?

The word "zoo" offends some of those who think that animals should roam freely. Some zoos are now euphemistically called "wildlife preservation centers" or "nature parks." The hunting and killing of wild animals now often is referred to as "game management" or "harvesting."

Euphemisms abound when referring to prisons. The facility itself may be called a "re-education camp," a "correctional institution," a "secure facility," or a "state farm." Guards are "correctional officers," and prisoners sometimes are called "residents." A particularly unaccommodating resident is no longer ushered into "solitary confinement" but guided into "seclusion."

There are euphemisms for some foods. "Drumstick" is a euphemism for "poultry leg," created because in the 1700s, any reference to legs was considered impolite. Other than causing confusion on a menu, euphemisms for foods are not objectionable. Examples include "rock lobster" (crayfish), "variety meats" (organs such as kidneys), and "caviar" (a second-order euphemism for "roe" and "fish eggs"). French names for foods lend a euphemistic flavor to their English translations. Familiar examples include "escargot" (edible snails), "foie gras" (fat liver from a goose), and "vichyssoise" (cold potato soup). One euphemism for a food came about because of World War I and World War II. During both world wars, the use of hamburger (whose name means "from Hamburg, Germany") was considered by some to be unpatriotic. The euphemism "Salisbury steak," therefore, frequently was substituted for "hamburger" on menus. This eponym comes from the name of physician James H. Salisbury (1823–1905), who believed that if one ate well-cooked hamburger at least three times a day, one could be cured of a variety of maladies. Today, Salisbury steak usually is served with gravy (now referred to as "sauce" in certain restaurants).

Some names for dishes are outright dysphemisms (DISS-fah-miz-ims); they intentionally have names that sound disagreeable. Examples include "monkey bread" (no monkeys in the ingredients) and "doggie biscuits" (biscuits for humans—no Rover in the ingredients).

Activity

Have your group gather recipes that have euphemistic names (e.g., "Calamari Canapés") and dysphemistic names (e.g., "Mississippi Mud"). Put them into a class cookbook or on your school's website.

There sometimes is a fine line between savvy marketing and deception in advertising, and the use of euphemisms can cross this line. Writers of real estate ads may use euphemisms such as "quaint," "rustic," "cozy," and "imaginatively decorated" for "strange," "run-down," "cramped," and "outlandish decor." Ads for automobiles often use the euphemisms "sharp" and "mint" for "loaded" used cars.

Activity ....

Kathlyn Gay's *Caution! This May Be an Advertisement: A Teen Guide to Advertising* (1992) can supplement your work with euphemisms. Although the vocabulary level and requisite prior knowledge of some topics (e.g., ancient Rome) are more appropriate for older students, the material can be adapted to lower grade levels. After all, most students are seasoned observers of advertisements. Gay's Chapter 8, "On Guard," includes sections called "Tricky Words," "Phony Markdowns," "Fine Print," "Scams, Swindles, and Hoaxes," and "Corporate Deceptions."

Activity ....

Have your group look through real estate ads in a newspaper's Sunday edition. Widely circulated big-city newspapers have the largest number of real estate ads. Tell them to list euphemisms from the ads (e.g., "luxury," "spectacular," "oversized"). Point out that often there are no definitions of terms such as these anywhere in the ads. Reading real estate ads in newspapers also becomes an exercise in deciphering abbreviations. The writer of the ad usually is charged per word, so abbreviations are common. Have students list abbreviations that they find such as furn (furnished), renov (renovated), flrs (floors), and fplc (fireplace).

Some television stations broadcast weekend real estate shows. Students can listen for euphemisms used in describing properties and can jot them down to share with the class.

Activity ....

Tell students that occasionally there are reports in the media about people who have been swindled out of money because they were influenced by print ads or phone sales that use euphemisms for less-than-desirable vacation spots. Divide your class into teams of three or four and have them write a sales or rental brochure for a ramshackle resort. Tell students that such resorts usually are "near water." Remind students that unless they see something in person, they can be duped by the use of euphemisms.

Food packages contain euphemisms. Are companies being deceptive or just creative when they refer to a package as "king size" or "super size"? What are they comparing the "jumbo" sizes to when one rarely sees "medium size" or "small size" packages of the same product? The word "mini" seems to account for any size that is not "extra large." "Mini" sounds cuter and less stingy than "small."

There are quite a few euphemisms for firing people. Employers use such terms as "reduction in force," "repositioning," "streamlining," "right-sizing," "workforce adjustment," "redeployment," and "release of resources." Corporations use these euphemisms so they don't appear cruel or greedy to the public. No matter what it's called, if one involuntarily is a part of a "career change opportunity," one begins to worry about how to pay the bills.

Military units around the world use euphemisms to avoid startling their own citizens or to show respect for families of those who "fell." Some wars are called "conflicts." To be "combat ineffective" is to be wounded or dead. If a soldier "accounts for someone," that someone is killed. A "surgical strike" or "preventive strike" is accomplished by "air support" (i.e., a target is bombed).

Here are some euphemisms and their "translations" that you might want to share with your group.

action figures (boys' dolls)

action pictures, action shows (television shows or movies with violence)

affordable, budget, economical (cheap)

to apprehend a person (to arrest a person)

authentic reproduction, faux (not the real thing)

to bend the rules (to cheat)

cash-flow problem (no money)

coach class or tourist class (not first class or business class; coach or tourist class usually means cramped seats, no beverage before takeoff, and so on)

costume jewelry (jewelry that contains no precious gems or precious metals)

creative, disingenuous (dishonest, e.g., "creative financing")

direct mail (advertisements, junk mail)

discomfort (pain)

disorder (an illness)

embroider the truth, erroneous report, fabrication, fib, prevaricate, stretch the truth, terminological inexactitude (lie)

erratum (a mistake)

filler (cheap ingredients used to increase the size of a food product)

gratuity (a tip left for good service at a restaurant)

to have heated words (to argue angrily)

intrusion detector (a burglar alarm [to signal "surreptitious entry," or a burglary])

inventory leakage, inventory shrinkage (theft)

live demonstration (an in-person sales pitch)

lived-in (untidy, unclean)

message from our sponsor (a commercial from an advertiser)

to monitor (to watch or listen to people without their knowing it)

motion discomfort (sickness from movement in a car, ship, plane, or the like)

negative saver (someone with no money)

no-pops (popcorn kernels that don't pop—formerly called "old maids")

overqualified (too smart for the employer)

personal flotation device (a life vest for passengers on an airplane)

procedure (an operation, surgery)

sensitive information (secret information)

suggested donation (an entrance fee)

water landing (a plane crash in water)

Rawson (1981) said, "it almost always takes more words to evade an idea than to state it directly and honestly" (p. 10). In a tongue-in-cheek manner, Rawson introduced the FOP ("Fog or Pomposity") Index to determine just how roundabout, pretentious, or sneaky some euphemisms are. The higher the FOP Index, the more evasive or effusive the euphemism. Here's how the FOP Index works.

1. Select a word that has a euphemism, and write the word and the euphemism next to one another. For example:

   used   previously owned

2. Count the number of letters and syllables in the noneuphemism. "Used" has 4 letters and 1 syllable.

3. Count the number of letters and syllables in the euphemism. "Previously owned" has 15 letters and 5 syllables.

4. Give one point for each letter in the noneuphemism and euphemism.
   "used" = 4 letters = 4 points
   "previously owned" = 15 letters = 15 points

5. Give one point for each additional syllable the euphemism contains. "Previously owned" has 4 more syllables than "used," or 4 more points. Here is our total number of points so far:
   "used": 4 points (4 letters)
   "previously owned": 15 points (15 letters) + 4 points (4 more syllables than "used") = 19 points

6. Now add one more point for each additional word the euphemism contains. "Previously owned" has one more word than "used," so that brings the total to 20 points.

7. Finally, divide the euphemism's total number of points by the number of letters in the noneuphemism. This gives us the FOP Index. For "previously owned," the FOP Index is 5.0 (20 divided by 4).

Here are some more words, their euphemisms, and their FOP Indexes.

   free   complimentary
   "free" = 4 letters + 1 syllable (4 points)
   "complimentary" = 13 letters + 5 syllables (17 points)
   no additional words in the euphemism
   17 divided by 4 = FOP Index of 4.25

job   capacity

"job" = 3 letters + 1 syllable (3 points)

"capacity" = 8 letters + 4 syllables (11 points)

11 divided by 3 = FOP Index of 3.67

The FOP Index does have exceptions. For example, the real estate term "studio" is a euphemism for "an apartment with no separate bedroom."

. . . . .Activity

Your group might enjoy determining the FOP Index for euphemisms presented in this section.

Smug Mugs:
Anagrams

David Crystal, in *The Cambridge Encyclopedia of the English Language* (1995), said that word games "provide the clearest example of the lengths to which people are prepared to go to indulge in strange linguistic behavior. We take considerable enjoyment from pulling words apart and reconstituting them in some novel guise, arranging them into clever patterns, finding hidden meanings in them, and trying to use them according to specially invented rules" (p. 396). Anagrams are a type of word game that can spawn this peculiar linguistic behavior.

An anagram is the rearrangement of letters in a word or words to form another word or words. Sometimes the rearranged word or words are a synonym or a fitting commentary on the original word or words. For example, "enraged" can be rearranged to form "angered." The word "committees" can be rearranged to "cost me time."

According to Bergerson (1973), anagrams were all the rage in the 1600s among the literary set. Yet anagrams are an ancient form of language play; Bergerson stated that "they were invented by the Greek poet Lycophron in 260 B.C." (p. 40). Here are some anagrams listed by Bergerson.

Toboggan slide	Got on a big sled
The sleigh ride	Here is delight
Grover Cleveland	Govern, clever lad
Fragile	E.g., frail
The detectives	Detect thieves
Brush	Shrub

Activity..

Here is a helpful way to introduce anagrams to your group.

1. Write the original word.
2. Draw a blank line underneath it.
3. Below the blank, write a clue—a synonym or a word related to the original word.
4. Have students rearrange the letters of the original word to form an anagram to match the clue.

For your convenience, here are several examples. The answers are in parentheses.

1. hint
   (<u>thin</u>)
   trim

2. tool
   (<u>loot</u>)
   cash

3. rate
   (<u>tear</u>)
   cry

4. much
   (<u>chum</u>)
   friend

5. warts
   (<u>straw</u>)
   wheat

6. stone
   (<u>notes</u>)
   music

7. meat
   (<u>team</u>)
   squad

8. untie
   (<u>unite</u>)
   bring together

9. master
   (<u>stream</u>)
   river

10. react
    (<u>trace</u>)
    follow

11. stake
    (<u>takes</u>)
    seizes

12. stale
    (<u>least</u>)
    smallest

13. rested
    (<u>desert</u>)
    sand

14. later
    (<u>alert</u>)
    sharp

15. softer
    (<u>forest</u>)
    trees

16. plate
    (<u>petal</u>)
    flower

17. hatred
    (<u>thread</u>)
    sew

18. slime
    (<u>smile</u>)
    happy

19. marsh
    (<u>harms</u>)
    injures

20. talks
    (<u>stalk</u>)
    celery

21. plums
    (<u>slump</u>)
    slouch

22. maple
    (<u>ample</u>)
    more than enough

23. waters
    (<u>rawest</u>)
    least fried

24. aside
    (<u>ideas</u>)
    plans

25. chase
    (<u>aches</u>)
    smarts

26. strap
    (<u>parts</u>)
    components

27. shape
    (<u>heaps</u>)
    stacks

28. pears
    (<u>spare</u>)
    surplus

29. trout
    (<u>tutor</u>)
    teach

30. reins
    (<u>siren</u>)
    warning

31. stores
    (<u>sorest</u>)
    hurts the most

32. staple
    (<u>pleats</u>)
    folds

33. times
    (<u>items</u>)
    objects

34. garden
    (<u>danger</u>)
    risk

35. ocean
    (<u>canoe</u>)
    paddles

36. sauce
    (<u>cause</u>)
    reason

37. listen
    (<u>enlist</u>)
    sign up

38. swath
    (<u>thaws</u>)
    softens

39. shades
    (<u>dashes</u>)
    runs

40. stored
    (<u>sorted</u>)
    grouped

41. caters
    (<u>reacts</u>)
    replies

42. staple
    (<u>pastel</u>)
    light shade

43. stare
    (<u>rates</u>)
    prices

44. depot
    (<u>opted</u>)
    chose

45. result
    (<u>rustle</u>)
    flutter

46. slide
    (<u>delis</u>)
    eateries

47. signal
    (<u>aligns</u>)
    matches up

48. drapes
    (<u>spread</u>)
    widen

49. danger
    (<u>gander</u>)
    male bird

50. artist
    (<u>traits</u>)
    qualities

A Flight of Stairs:
Collective Nouns

Collective nouns are words that refer to groups of people, animals, or things. We talk about an *academy* of scholars, a *litter* of puppies, and a *deck* of cards. The use of collective nouns can be traced in English to the 1400s when collective terms were deemed necessary to refer to particular groups of hunted animals. Word enthusiasts took a cue from the hunt and coined collective nouns for groups of humans and groups of things. In *An Exaltation of Larks* (1977), Lipton wrote that collective nouns "are prime examples both of the infinite subtlety of our language and the wild imagination and verbal skill of our forebears" (p. 7). He categorized collective nouns according to six types (p. 9): appearance ("a *bouquet* of pheasants"), characteristic ("a *leap* of leopards"), comment ("a *plague* of locusts"), habitat ("a *nest* of rabbits"), onomatopoeia (i.e., a word that sounds like its referent, such as "a *gaggle* of geese"), and error ("a *school* of fish," which was a mistake made by a long-ago writer who meant "a *shoal* of fish").

Here are some collective nouns for people, animals, and things.

People

a slate of candidates

a company of soldiers

a congregation of religious people

a corps of engineers, a corps of drum and bugle players

a faculty of educators

a band of musicians, a band of criminals

a colony of artists

a troupe of dancers

a cast of characters

a crew of sailors

a gang of outlaws

a party of restaurant patrons

a force of police officers

a board of examiners, a board of regents

Animals

a colony of ants, penguins, badgers

a herd of elephants

a flock of sheep, a flock of birds

a swarm of bees

a pride of lions

a string of ponies

a kindle of kittens

a pod of seals, a pod of whales

a gang of elk

a company of parrots

a skulk of foxes

a crash of rhinoceroses

a knot of toads

a troop of kangaroos, a troop of monkeys

a smack of jellyfish

a clowder of cats

a sloth of bears

a parliament of owls

a pack of dogs

Things

a set of dishes

a clutch of eggs

a bunch of bananas, a bunch of grapes

a bundle of sticks, a bundle of money

a stack of pancakes, a stack of bills

a batch of cupcakes, a batch of cookies

a bed of flowers, a bed of herbs

a fleet of ships

a portfolio of work, a portfolio of investments

a bouquet of flowers

a bank of computers

a palette of colors

Activity

Ruth Heller's *A Cache of Jewels and Other Collective Nouns* (1987) is an attractive introductory book on collective nouns to share with younger readers. Among her examples are a *muster* of peacocks, a *clump* of reeds, and a *drift* of swans.

Activity

Have group members create their own collective nouns for people in particular occupations. The collective nouns must be related in some way to the occupations. Here are some examples: a *register* of nurses, an *atlas* of geographers, a *range* of cooks, a *click* of photographers.

Phooey on Dewey;
Forward; Don't Call Us, We'll Call You:
Slogans, Mottoes, and Catchphrases

A slogan is a word, phrase, or sentence that is intended to influence people to think a certain way or buy something. The word "slogorne" entered English in 1513. At that time, it referred to an Irish or Scottish clan's battle cry. By 1680, the word was spelled "slogan," and by 1704 it had its present meaning.

According to Crystal (1995), slogans are similar to proverbs in that they are short with obvious rhythmic elements. "Phooey on Dewey" was a campaign slogan created by Harry S Truman's supporters in the presidential election of 1948. Supporters of Republican candidate Thomas E. Dewey also had to counter the Democrats' "Don't Tarry—Vote Harry." The Dewey campaign's "Save What's Left" paled in comparison.

Crystal pointed out that if slogans are somewhat long, their structure must be balanced. An example is the slogan "In Hoover We Trusted, Now We Are Busted" from Franklin Delano Roosevelt's 1932 campaign. Herbert Hoover was taking the blame for the Great Depression, and one of the Republican's lackluster campaign slogans, "It Might Have Been Worse," did little to rally the voters.

Alliteration is a characteristic of some slogans. In the presidential campaign of 1860, one of several slogans from Abraham Lincoln's Republican platform was "Land for the Landless." The slogan referred to Lincoln's support for the sale of inexpensive public land to prospective homesteaders. Another slogan from the campaign was "The United States Is Rich Enough to Give Us All a Farm." The format for this rallying cry follows what Crystal refers to as the "conversational style" of some slogans.

Bailey (1976) said, "Slogans are comforting shorthand for thinking, which is usually avoided as hard work, and for this reason are open to criticism. Even so, they are an essential part of the nation's history. They serve to highlight the main issues, provide colorful pegs on which to hang facts, and add life to what all too often is made unnecessarily dull" (p. viii).

As any writer knows, it is more difficult to express an idea succinctly than to have free range on word count. The notion of "comforting shorthand for thinking," therefore, is contrary to what slogan developers must go through to select and combine a few words that could contribute to or detract from their ultimate goal. The business of persuasion is a serious enterprise. Slogans can be more than "colorful pegs"; they can be downright indecorous. One of Barry Goldwater's campaign slogans in 1964 was "In Your Heart You Know He's Right." Lyndon Johnson's campaign countered with "Bury Barry" and the memorable "In Your Guts You Know He's Nuts."

Have your students compile lists of slogans for products and services. Do some of the slogans rhyme? Do they use alliteration? Are they conversational in tone? A resource that will be helpful to you in getting students started is Urdang and Braunstein's *Every Bite a Delight and Other Slogans* (1992), which contains 5,000 slogans. Although many companies and public service agencies periodically update their slogans, Urdang and Braunstein's book is invaluable for its breakdown of slogans into categories: automobiles, broadcasting, cereals, clothing, computer equipment and software, detergents, fitness, fruit drinks, hotels and motels, lawn and garden products, medications, newspapers, office equipment and supplies, pet food and products, restaurants, shipping, toys and games, watches and clocks, and many more. Students might also want to create their own slogans for objects in their classroom or in their desks. Depending on the condition of these items, the slogans might be facetious or satirical.

Mottoes are more moving and inspirational than slogans. Their intent is less commercial, although they strive to be persuasive. Burrell (1997) stated, "A motto can be a form of encouragement, or something to reflect upon in times of trouble. It can serve as advice, as a practical rule for deciding the proper thing to do, or as a reminder of duty" (p. 161). There are personal mottoes, group mottoes, and geographic mottoes. A personal motto of U.S. Representative and frontiersman David "Davy" Crockett (1786–1836) was "Be sure you're right, then go ahead." The Girl Scouts' motto is "Do a good turn daily." A national motto is "E Pluribus Unum" (One from Many). All fifty states have mottoes. Some are one word (e.g., Wisconsin—"Forward"), and others are lengthy (e.g., Iowa—"Our liberties we prize and our rights we will maintain").

Most people think that the U.S. Postal Service has a motto: "Neither snow nor rain nor heat nor gloom of night stays these couriers from the swift completion of their appointed rounds." These stirring words are inscribed on the New York City Post Office, which was completed in 1912. Actually, this is not the motto of the Postal Service. As Burrell noted, the inscription "is merely what one inspired architect thought would be a fitting inscription for the building" (p. 3). No more razzing recitation of these words when the mail carrier's delivery is late.

Have your group find mottoes of organizations in your community (e.g., Rotary International). Who created the mottoes? How long ago? Your local Chamber of Commerce can help you identify groups and "contact people." Then have individuals in your group write a motto for your class, school, and community. Display these on your school's website or in the school newspaper.

A catchphrase, according to Rees (1995) is "a phrase that has 'caught on' with the public and is, or has been, in frequent use" (p. vi). "Just what the doctor ordered," "meanwhile, back at the ranch," and "the greatest thing since sliced bread" are catchphrases. Bumper stickers often carry catchphrases of the day. This medium of rolling commentary is a diversion when one is stuck in gridlock or looking for one's "lost" car in a crowded parking lot. Bumper stickers are not new, though. Dickson (1991) noted, "As best as can be determined, one of the first, if not the very first, true bumper stickers came out of the Gill Studios of Shawnee Mission, Kansas. The firm's founder, Forest Gill, had been working with fluorescent inks and with self-sticking labels. As World War II ended, he was getting orders for cardboard bumper signs, and he began experimenting with self-sticking signs with colorful ink" (p. 9).

Popular bumper stickers have included "I'm in no hurry, I'm on my way to work," "If you can read this, thank a teacher," and "Be alert: This country needs more lerts."

Activity

Have your group design a bumper sticker for your school. Then have a local printing company or a mail-order company produce the stickers. Have students sell them at a school festival and use the profits to purchase a gift for your school.

Burrell (1997) said, "On his visit to the United States in 1831, Alexis de Tocqueville noticed that the Americans he encountered tended to exhibit two opposing tendencies: they did not want to be told what to do or think, and yet their collective will could easily be rallied behind certain carefully chosen words" (p. 4). Tocqueville was correct, and here is a sprinkling of slogans, mottoes, and catchphrases, beginning with the rumblings for liberty within the thirteen colonies and continuing through many a presidential campaign, that have spurred us on, comforted us, or caused us to chuckle.

1750s—"What are the damages?" (catchphrase for "How much does it cost?")

1754—"Join or Die" (a slogan that originally was a cartoon caption by Ben Franklin under a drawing of separated pieces of a snake; each piece had the initials of one of the thirteen colonies)

1760s—"Taxation without representation is tyranny" (statement by James Otis, colonist from Massachusetts, that became a Revolutionary War slogan)

"Give me liberty or give me death" (statement by Patrick Henry, American patriot, (a.k.a. "The Forest Born Demosthenes") that became a Revolutionary War slogan)

"Don't Tread on Me" (slogan on Virginia colonists' banners and on John Paul Jones's warship flag)

1779—"I have not yet begun to fight" (John Paul Jones's answer to British commander Pearson's demand for Jones's surrender; it eventually became a catchphrase)

1800s—"Chalk that up to experience" (catchphrase)

1816—"Buy American" (post–War of 1812 slogan)

1832—"To the victor belong the spoils of the enemy" (statement by William Marcy, senator from New York, referring to a politician's "right" to make political appointments; it eventually became a catchphrase)

1836—"Remember the Alamo" (a reference to the defeat of Texans by Mexican general Santa Anna; it became a Texas slogan at the battle of San Jacinto)

1840—"Tippecanoe and Tyler Too" (campaign slogan for presidential candidate William Henry Harrison, who fought as a general in the Battle of Tippecanoe against Native Americans in the Indiana Territory; John Tyler was Harrison's running mate)
"Henry Clay Will Carry the Day" (campaign slogan for the Whig candidate from Kentucky)
"A Pig in a Polk" (campaign slogan opposing Democrat James Polk)

1845—"Manifest Destiny" (catchphrase used by editor John O'Sullivan in the *United States Magazine and Democratic Review;* it became a slogan for American expansion, especially in the Oregon Territory)

1846—"Fifty-four Forty or Fight" (slogan originated by Ohio Senator William "Foghorn" Allen, referring to American expansion in the Oregon Territory to the 54 degree 40th parallel. Eventually a compromise on the 49th parallel was reached with England. Bailey (1976) noted that the slogan became so popular, newborns were named Fifty-Four Forty)

1848—"The true Republic: men their rights and nothing more; women their rights and nothing less" (statement by Susan B. Anthony at the Women's Rights Convention in Seneca Falls, New York, that later become the motto of *The Revolution,* a suffragette newspaper)

1850s—"Not a dry eye in the house" (catchphrase)

1850—"Go West young man and grow up with the country" (statement by Horace Greeley, well-known newspaperman, that became a slogan for westward expansion)

1852—"We Polked 'Em in '44; We'll Pierce 'Em in '52" (campaign slogan for Democrat Franklin Pierce)

1858—"A house divided against itself cannot stand" (statement by Abraham Lincoln, an Illinois Republican nominee for the U.S. Senate, that became a slogan during the Civil War)

1859—"Pikes Peak or Bust" (slogan used by gold seekers in the Colorado gold rush)

1866—"Forty Acres and a Mule" (slogan and false promise repeated to newly freed slaves by the Reconstructionists)

1868–1876—"The Era of Good Stealings" (slogan referring to the graft during the terms of President Ulysses S. Grant)

1871—"No King, No Clown to Rule This Town" (slogan in the *New York Sun* in reference to the corruption perpetrated by William Marcy "Boss" Tweed and his Tammany Hall organization)
"Throw the Rascals Out" (slogan used by voters who were fed up with government scandal)
"There is no substitute for hard work" (motto attributed to Thomas A. Edison)

1880s—"Ballots for Both," "I Wish Ma Could Vote" (slogans used in the women's suffrage movement)

"Time flies when you're having fun" (catchphrase)

1880—"I don't mind if I do" (catchphrase)

1888—"As Maine Goes, So Goes the Nation" (slogan used by the Republican Party because Maine, a Republican stronghold during this time, held state elections before the national election was held)

1892—"Grover, Grover, All is Over" (campaign slogan used by opponents of Democrat Grover Cleveland)

1898—"Remember the Maine" (slogan referring to the explosion that killed over 250 crew members of the battleship *Maine* while it was near Havana, Cuba; it was used to incite anger against Spain)

1900s—"That's a hard act to follow" "Don't do anything I wouldn't do" (catchphrases)

1900—"It's all done with mirrors" (catchphrase)

1901—"Speak softly and carry a big stick; you will go far" (motto attributed to Teddy Roosevelt, but he said that it was an African proverb)

1907—"Join the Navy and See the World" (slogan used to recruit personnel)

1914—"All dressed up and nowhere to go" (catchphrase)

"He Kept Us Out of War" (campaign slogan of the Democrats referring to Woodrow Wilson; America soon entered World War I)

"He Kept Us Out of Suffrage" (slogan used by the suffragettes because Wilson opposed giving women the vote)

1917—"Make the World Safe for Democracy," "The War to End War," "Are You Idle Today? The Boys in the Trenches Are Not," "A Woman's Place Is in the War" (slogans during World War I; the fourth slogan was meant to encourage women to work outside the home)

1920s—"Last of the big spenders," "We aim to please," "And I don't mean maybe" (catchphrases)

1920—"Back to Normalcy" (campaign slogan for Republican Warren G. Harding)

"Do the day's work" (one of Calvin Coolidge's mottoes)

"Remember Teapot Dome" (slogan referring to the scandal of 1922, during the Harding administration, when government lands in Teapot Dome, Wyoming, were leased "under the table" to wealthy oil company owners)

"Al Smith: Up from the Street" (campaign slogan for self-made Democratic candidate Alfred Smith)

"A Chicken in Every Pot," "Hoo but Hoover?" (campaign slogans for Republican Herbert Hoover)

1930s—"Famous last words," "Now you see it, now you don't" (catchphrases)

"He Saved America" (campaign slogan referring to Democratic incumbent Franklin D. Roosevelt)

"Let's Make It a Landon-slide" (campaign slogan for Republican Alfred "Alf" Landon)

1940s—"Back to the drawing board," "I just work here," "Now I've seen everything," "I kid you not," "You can't win 'em all" (catchphrases)

1940—"We Want Willkie," "Willkie for the Millionaires—Roosevelt for the Millions" (campaign slogans for Republican Wendell Willkie and incumbent FDR)

1941—"Remember Pearl Harbor" (slogan referring to the surprise attack on Pearl Harbor by the Japanese)

1942—"Loose Lips Sink Ships," "Be Smart—Act Dumb" (slogans encouraging Americans to not divulge any information that might hurt the country's war efforts)

1944—"Dewey or Don't We?," "Three Good Terms Deserve Another" (campaign slogans for Republican Thomas A. Dewey and incumbent FDR)

1950s—"(That's the) story of my life," "hint hint," "Have I got news for you!," "That's the way the cookie crumbles," "Be my guest" (catchphrases)

1950—"Is it bigger than a breadbox?" (catchphrase)

1952—"I Like Ike," "We're Madly for Adlai" (campaign slogans for Republican Dwight D. Eisenhower and Democrat Adlai Stevenson)

1956—"The Mighty Tower—Eisenhower," "Vote Gladly for Adlai" (different slogans, same candidates)

1960s—"All systems go" (catchphrase)

"On the Right Track with Jack," "Nix on Nixon" (campaign slogans for Democrat JFK)

"Stick with Dick" (campaign slogans for Republican Richard Nixon)

1961—"Don't call us, we'll call you" (catchphrase)

1964—"USA for LBJ," "Go-go Goldwater in '64" (campaign slogans for Democrat Lyndon B. Johnson and Republican Barry Goldwater)

1968—"Who but Hubert?," "Nixon + Spiro = Zero" (campaign slogans for Democrat Hubert Humphrey)

"Nixon's the One" (campaign slogan for Republican Richard Nixon)

"Alive and well and living in ..." (catchphrase)

1970s—"Laugh (or cry) all the way to the bank," "On a scale of one to ten," "Not a pretty sight" (catchphrases)

1972—"Nixon Is Through in '72," "The Nation Needs Fixin' with Nixon" (campaign slogans for Democrat George McGovern and Republican incumbent Richard Nixon; after the Watergate scandal, Democratic voters' bumper stickers proclaimed, "Don't blame me, I voted for McGovern")

1974—"Have you thanked a green plant today?" (popular bumper sticker that was one of many completions of the catchphrase "Have you ... today?")

1976—"Happy birthday, America!" (congratulatory catchphrase seen on buttons, bumper stickers, and banners in celebration of America's Bicentennial)

1977—"May the force be with you" (catchphrase from the film *Star Wars*)

1980s—"Been there, done that," "Decisions, decisions" (catchphrases)

1980—"Anyone but Reagan" "Jimmy Carter Does the Work of Two Men—Laurel and Hardy" (campaign slogans for Democrat Jimmy Carter and Republican Ronald Reagan)

1983—"We're spending our kids' inheritance," "Live long enough to be a burden to your kids" (popular bumper stickers displayed by older Americans)

1984—"Are we having fun yet?" (catchphrase seen on bumper stickers and heard in informal conversation)

"Just Say No" (slogan used by First Lady Nancy Reagan to combat drug use)

"Read my lips—no new taxes" (catchphrase created by Republican presidential candidate George Bush)

Activity.....

Have your group locate slogans, mottoes, and catchphrases from the decade of the 1990s. Local and state political parties and historical societies are resources students can use. Then have students create an "America Speaks" mural composed of slogans, mottoes, and catchphrases from one period of time in our history to another. This mural can be displayed in your town hall, city hall, or local mall.

A Final Word

The use of euphemisms spans the gamut of intent—from compassion to diplomacy to wiliness to fraudulence. Anagrams can turn "danger" into "garden" and "slime" into "smile." Collective nouns have taken us from a *pack* of dogs in the Middle Ages to today's *pack* of gum. Slogans, mottoes, and catchphrases such as "All the Way with JFK," "The buck stops here," and "The rest is history" reflect who we are as a nation.

Our visit to the remarkable realm of language play is finished—for this trip. We began with names—from Mush and Sons, purveyors of produce, to What Cheer, Iowa. The hink pink family introduced "a skunk bunk" and "a peewee kiwi." We got a handle on idioms and learned that even Shakespeare used slang. An examination of multiple-meaning words gave us over ninety meanings of *down* and ambiguous headlines such as "Drought Causes Small Ears." Proverbs reminded us that "Haste is slow" and "A day is lost if one has not laughed." A study of how words are alike and different took us to a restaurant where we learned that one critic's *moist* is another critic's *soggy*. Word formation presented capital gainsville, ho-humsville, AP, ID, sippies, and skippies. "Neat as a pin" and "cool as a cucumber" made sense when their origins were revealed. Americanisms such as "no-pops," "Loose Lips Sink Ships," and "hint hint" have shaped our history. I am filled with wonder and am humbled by the rich but often neglected topic of language play. I take language play seriously.

References

Bailey, T. A. *Voices of America.* New York: Free Press, 1976.

Barnhart, R. K., ed. *The Barnhart Concise Dictionary of Etymology: The Origins of American English Words.* New York: HarperCollins, 1995.

Bergerson, H. W. *Palindromes and Anagrams.* New York: Dover Publications, 1973.

Bertram, A. *NTC's Dictionary of Euphemisms.* Lincolnwood, Ill.: NTC Publishing Group, 1998.

Blechman, A. "The Name's the Thing." *The Des Moines Register,* 12 April 1997, sec. T, pp. 1–2.

Burrell, B. *The Words We Live By.* New York: Free Press, 1997.

Carruth, G. *What Happened When: A Chronology of Life & Events in America.* New York: A Signet Book, 1989.

Crystal, D. *The Cambridge Encyclopedia of the English Language.* Cambridge: Cambridge University Press, 1995.

Dickson, P. *Timelines.* Reading, Mass.: Addison-Wesley, 1991.

Fry, E. B., J. E. Kress, and D. L. Fountoukidis. *The Reading Teacher's Book of Lists.* 3rd ed. Englewood Cliffs, N.J.: Prentice Hall, 1993.

Lipton, J. *An Exaltation of Larks.* New York: Penguin Books, 1977.

Rawson, H. *A Dictionary of Euphemisms & Other Doubletalk.* New York: Crown Publishers, 1981.

Rees, N. *Dictionary of Catchphrases.* New York: Cassell, 1995.

Urdang, L., and J. Braunstein. *Every Bite a Delight and Other Slogans.* Detroit: Visible Ink, 1992.

Wallace, A., D. Wallechinsky, and I. Wallace. *The Book of Lists #3.* New York: Bantam Books, 1983.

References:
Children's Books

Gay, K. *Caution! This May Be an Advertisement: A Teen Guide to Advertising.* New York: Franklin Watts, 1992.

Heller, R. *A Cache of Jewels and Other Collective Nouns.* New York: Grosset & Dunlap, 1987.

Glossary

abbreviation—A short form of a word or phrase. *Dept.* is an abbreviation for *department.*

acronym—An abbreviation that is a pronounceable word. *FEMA* (FEE-mah) is an acronym for *Federal Emergency Management Agency.*

affix—Letter or letters added to the beginning or end of a word to change its meaning or grammatical function.

anagram—The rearrangement of letters in a word or words to form another word or words. *Spare* is an anagram for *pears.*

analogy—An analogy shows the relationship among particular words. *"Add* is to *delete* as *refill* is to *deplete"* is an analogy.

antonym—Words with opposite meanings. *Cold* and *hot* are antonyms.

aptronym—A person's name that is well-suited to his or her occupation. Marvin Nickel, coin collector, is an aptronym.

blend—A word that is formed from abbreviated forms of two or more other words. *Glimmer* is a blend from *gleam + shimmer.*

borrowed word—A word from another language that becomes part of English. *Kindergarten* was borrowed from German.

catchphrase—A phrase that becomes popular with the public because it is colorful and succinct. *Famous last words* is a catchphrase.

clipped word—An abbreviation in which part of a word stands for the whole word. *Burger* is a clipped word for *hamburger.*

collective noun—A word that refers to a group of people, animals, or things. *School* is a collective noun that refers to a group of fish.

compound word—A word formed by combining two or more other words. *Seashell* is a compound word (i.e., *sea + shell*).

contradictory antonyms—Words that exclude one another. *Complete-incomplete* are contradictory antonyms.

contrary antonyms—Antonyms that differ in degrees. *Earsplitting* and *inaudible* are contrary antonyms. *Earsplitting* can be found on one end of the *Sound* continuum and *inaudible* on the other end. In between are degrees such as *blaring, loud, toned-down,* and *soft.*

conversion—A word whose grammatical function is changed without adding an affix. In the sentence "We'll bicycle to the park," *bicycle* is a conversion from a noun to a verb.

counterparts—Antonyms that show a reciprocal relationship. *Employer-employee* are counterparts.

derivational suffix—A suffix that changes the meaning of the base word. *Able* is a derivational suffix in *laughable.*

eponym—A word derived from a person's name. The word *watt* is an eponym, from British inventor James Watt.

established slang—Time-tested words or phrases that are synonyms for more standard words or phrases. A *big-ticket item* is established slang for something expensive.

etymology—The in-depth study of the history of words.

euphemism—A polite, inoffensive, or comforting word or phrase used in place of a word or phrase that is thought of as too direct, demeaning, or upsetting. *Negative saver* is a euphemism for someone with no money.

hink hink—One-syllable words that sound the same and are spelled the same but have different meanings and answer a question. Question: What is it called when a sauce for potato chips dives into a pool? Answer: a dip dip.

hinkety hinkety—Three-syllable words that have the same sound and spelling but different meanings and answer a question. Question: What might you call a round handbill? Answer: a circular circular.

hinkety pinkety—Three-syllable rhyming words that answer a question. Question: What might you call a yellow fruit's bright, large handkerchief? Answer: a banana bandanna.

hink pink—One-syllable rhyming words that answer a question. Question: What could you call a fast present? Answer: a swift gift.

hinky hinky—Two-syllable words that have the same sound and spelling but different meanings and answer a question. Question: What might you call it when a preserved cucumber is in a difficult situation? Answer: a pickle pickle.

hinky pinky—Two-syllable rhyming words that answer a question. Question: What could you call a tiny bird from New Zealand? Answer: a peewee kiwi.

idiom—A saying whose meaning is different from the usual meanings of the individual words. *To talk a blue streak* is an idiom that means to talk a lot and often quickly.

inflectional suffix—A suffix that has no effect on meaning; it plays only a grammatical role. Inflectional suffixes include verb tenses (*jumps, jumped, jumping*), plurality (*boys, dishes*), degree (*easier, easiest*), or possession (*Jill's, girls'*).

initialism—An abbreviation that can be said aloud only as letters—not as words. *GPA* is an initialism for *grade point average.*

jargon—Technical words or phrases that are specific to an occupation or hobby. *Constructivist orientation* is a part of an educator's jargon.

motto—A moving, often inspirational word or phrase devised by a person or group. "Be sure you're right, then go ahead" was the motto of U.S. Representative and frontiersman David "Davy" Crockett (1786–1836).

multiple-meaning word—A word that has more than one meaning. *Story* is a multiple-meaning word. It can mean a real or imaginary tale or a level of a building.

onomastics—The study of names.

pink pink—One-syllable words that have the same sound but different spellings and meanings and answer a question. Question: What is a peeping sound that costs very little money? Answer: a cheap cheep.

pinkety pinkety—Three-syllable words that have the same sound but different spellings and meanings and answer a question. Question: What might you call paper that doesn't move? Answer: stationary stationery.

pinky pinky—Two-syllable words that have the same sound but different spellings and meanings and answer a question. Question: What might you call a salesperson who works in a basement? Answer: a cellar seller.

polysemy—More than one meaning for a word or words; multiple meanings.

prefix—An affix added to the beginning of a word to form a new word. *In* is a prefix in *inaccurate*.

proverb—A saying that gives advice or offers an observation about life. *Beauty is in the eye of the beholder* is a proverb.

pseudonym—A name other than a person's given name. Frederick Austerlitz's pseudonym was Fred Astaire.

repeating slang—Slang in which a word is repeated in the expression. *Hush-hush* and *buddy-buddy* are repeating slang.

rhyming slang—Slang in which the words in the expression rhyme. *Fender bender* and *fuddy-duddy* are rhyming slang.

simile—A comparison, often between two unlike things, using *like* or *as*. *As happy as a clam* is a simile.

slogan—A word, phrase, or sentence that is intended to influence people to think a certain way or to buy something. "A Chicken in Every Pot" was a campaign slogan for Republican presidential candidate Herbert Hoover in 1928.

subordinate word—A word that is a member of a particular category. *Chair* is a subordinate word for the category *Furniture*.

suffix—An affix added to the end of a word to change its grammatical form or its meaning. *Ness* is a suffix in *goodness*.

superordinate word—A word that is a category label. *Flowers* is a superordinate word for the category members *zinnia, tulip,* and *rose*.

surname—A person's last name.

synonyms—Words that mean nearly the same thing. *Big* and *large* are synonyms.

toponym—A word derived from a place name. *Paisley* is a toponym, from Paisley, Scotland.

word origin—A history of a word that is less technical than the word's etymology.

Bibliography

Aitchison, J. *Words in the Mind.* 2d ed. Oxford, England: Blackwell Publishers, 1994.

Almond, J. *Dictionary of Word Origins: A History of the Words, Expressions, and Clichés We Use.* New York: Carol Publishing Group, 1985.

Ammer, C. *Have a Nice Day—No Problem! A Dictionary of Clichés.* New York: Plume Books, 1992.

Ayto, J. *Dictionary of Word Origins: The Histories of More than 8,000 English-Language Words.* New York: Arcade Publishing, 1990.

Bailey, T. A. *Voices of America.* New York: The Free Press, 1976.

Barnette, M. *Ladyfingers and Nun's Tummies: A Lighthearted Look at How Foods Got Their Names.* New York: Times Books, 1997.

Barnhart, D. K., and A. A. Metcalf. *America in So Many Words: Words That Have Shaped America.* Boston: Houghton Mifflin, 1997.

Barnhart, R. K., ed. *The Barnhart Concise Dictionary of Etymology: The Origins of American English Words.* New York: HarperCollins, 1995.

Baz, P. D. *A Dictionary of Proverbs.* New York: Philosophical Library, 1963.

Berent, I. M., and R. L. Evans. *The Dictionary of Highly Unusual Words.* New York: Berkley Books, 1997.

Bergerson, H. W. *Palindromes and Anagrams.* New York: Dover Publications, 1973.

Bertram, A. *NTC's Dictionary of Euphemisms.* Lincolnwood, Ill.: NTC Publishing Group, 1998.

Brock, S. *Idiom's Delight: Fascinating Phrases and Linguistic Eccentricities.* New York: Vintage Books, 1988.

Bryson, B. *The Mother Tongue: English and How It Got That Way.* New York: Avon Books, 1990.

———. *Made in America: An Informal History of the English Language in the United States.* New York: William Morrow, 1994.

Burke, D. *Street Talk-1: How to Speak and Understand American Slang.* Los Angeles: Optima Books, 1992.

———. *Street Talk-2: Slang Used by Teens, Rappers, Surfers, & Popular American Television Shows.* Los Angeles: Optima Books, 1992.

———. *Biz Talk-1: American Business Slang & Jargon.* Los Angeles: Optima Books, 1993.

———. *Street Talk-3: The Best of American Idioms.* Beverly Hills, Calif.: Optima Books, 1995.

Burrell, B. *The Words We Live By.* New York: The Free Press, 1997.

Carothers, G., and J. Lacey. *Dictionary of Colorful Phrases.* New York: Sterling Publishing, 1979.

Carruth, G. *What Happened When: A Chronology of Life & Events in America.* New York: A Signet Book, 1989.

Carter, R. *Vocabulary: Applied Linguistic Perspectives.* London: Routledge, 1987.

Carver, C. M. *A History of English in Its Own Words.* New York: HarperCollins, 1991.

Crystal, D. *The Cambridge Encyclopedia of the English Language.* Cambridge: Cambridge University Press, 1995.

Dalzell, T. *Flappers 2 Rappers: American Youth Slang.* Springfield, Mass.: Merriam-Webster, 1996.

Dickson, P. *Words: A Connoisseur's Collection of Old and New, Weird and Wonderful, Useful and Outlandish.* New York: Dell, 1982.

———. *Slang! Topic-by-topic Dictionary of Contemporary American Lingoes.* New York: Pocket Books, 1990.

———. *Timelines.* Reading, Mass.: Addison-Wesley, 1991.

———. *What's in a Name? Reflections of an Irrepressible Name Collector.* Springfield, Mass.: Merriam-Webster, 1996.

Dunn, J. *Idiom Savant: Slang as It Is Slung.* New York: Henry Holt, 1997.

Elster, C. H. *There's a Word for It!* New York: Scribner, 1996.

Fergusson, R. *The Penguin Dictionary of Proverbs.* New York: Penguin Books, 1983.

Flavell, L., and R. Flavell. *Dictionary of Proverbs and Their Origins.* New York: Barnes & Noble, 1993.

Flexner, S. B., and A. H. Soukhanov. *Speaking Freely: A Guided Tour of American English from Plymouth Rock to Silicon Valley.* New York: Oxford University Press, 1997.

Freeman, M. S. *The Story Behind the Word.* Philadelphia: ISI Press, 1985.

Fry, E. B., J. E. Kress, and D. L. Fountoukidis. *The Reading Teacher's Book of Lists.* 3rd ed. Englewood Cliffs, N.J.: Prentice Hall, 1993.

Funk, C. E. *A Hog on Ice and Other Curious Expressions.* New York: Harper & Row, 1948.

———. *Thereby Hangs a Tale: Stories of Curious Word Origins.* New York: Harper & Row, 1950.

———. *Heavens to Betsy! And Other Curious Sayings.* New York: Harper & Row, 1955.

Funk, W. *Word Origins and Their Romantic Stories.* New York: Grosset & Dunlap, 1950.

Garrison, W. *Why You Say It: The Fascinating Stories Behind Over 600 Everyday Words and Phrases.* Nashville, Tenn.: Rutledge Hill Press, 1992.

Geller, L. G. *Word Play and Language Learning for Children.* Urbana, Ill.: National Council of Teachers of English, 1985.

Gleason, N. *Proverbs from Around the World.* New York: Carol Publishing, 1992.

Golick, M. *Playing with Words.* Markham, Ontario: Pembroke Publishers, 1987.

Gulland, D. M., and D. G. Hinds-Howell. *The Penguin Dictionary of English Idioms.* New York: Viking Penguin, 1986.

Isil, O. A. *When a Loose Cannon Flogs a Dead Horse There's the Devil to Pay.* Camden, Maine: International Marine, 1996.

Johnson, D. D. "Just the Right Word: Vocabulary and Writing," in *Theoretical Models and Processes of Writing*, edited by R. Indrisano and J. R. Squire. Newark, Del.: International Reading Association, in press.

Johnson, D. D., and B. v. H. Johnson. *In So Many Words Series*. Logan, Iowa: Perfection Learning, 1990.

————. *The Brain Train*. Elizabethtown, Penn.: Continental Press, 1994.

Johnson, D. D., and P. D. Pearson. *Teaching Reading Vocabulary*. 2d ed. Fort Worth, Tex.: Holt, Rinehart and Winston, 1984.

Kleinedler, S. R., comp., and R. A. Spears, ed. *NTC's Dictionary of Acronyms and Abbreviations*. Lincolnwood, Ill.: NTC Publishing Group, 1993.

Lighter, J. E. *Random House Historical Dictionary of American Slang: Volume 1, A–G*. New York: Random House, 1994.

Lipton, J. *An Exaltation of Larks*. New York: Penguin Books, 1968, 1977.

Mansoor, M. *Wisdom from the Ancients: Proverbs, Maxims and Quotations*. Madison, Wisc.: Mayland Publishing, 1994.

McArthur, T. *The Concise Oxford Companion to the English Language*. Oxford: Oxford University Press, 1996.

Mencken, H. L. *The American Language*. New York: Alfred A. Knopf, 1977.

Mieder, W., S. A. Kingsbury, and K. B. Harder, eds. *A Dictionary of American Proverbs*. New York: Oxford University Press, 1992.

Morris, W., and M. Morris. *Morris Dictionary of Word and Phrase Origins*. 2nd ed. New York: HarperCollins, 1988.

Partin, R. L. *The Social Studies Teacher's Book of Lists*. Englewood Cliffs, N.J.: Prentice Hall, 1992.

Pinker, S. *The Language Instinct*. New York: HarperPerennial, 1994.

Princeton Language Institute, ed., and D. Ajjan, comp. *21st Century Dictionary of Acronyms and Abbreviations*. New York: Laurel, 1993.

Rawson, H. *A Dictionary of Euphemisms & Other Doubletalk*. New York: Crown Publishers, 1981.

Rees, N. *Dictionary of Catchphrases*. New York: Cassell, 1995.

Rogers, J. *The Dictionary of Clichés*. New York: Wings Books, 1985.

Room, A. *NTC's Dictionary of Changes in Meanings*. Lincolnwood, Ill.: National Textbook Company, 1986.

————. *NTC's Dictionary of Word Origins*. Lincolnwood, Ill.: National Textbook Company, 1994.

Shipley, J. T. *Dictionary of Word Origins*. New York: Dorset Press, 1945.

Shook, M. D. *By Any Other Name*. New York: Prentice Hall, 1994.

Smith, E. C. *American Surnames*. Baltimore: Genealogical Publishing, 1995.

Soukhanov, A. H. *Word Watch: The Stories Behind the Words of Our Lives*. New York: Henry Holt, 1995.

Spears, R. A. *NTC's American Idioms Dictionary*. Lincolnwood, Ill.: National Textbook Company, 1987.

————. *NTC's Dictionary of American Slang and Colloquial Expressions.* Lincolnwood, Ill.: National Textbook Company, 1989.

Sperling, S. K. *Tenderfeet and Ladyfingers: A Visceral Approach to Words and Their Origins.* New York: Penguin Books, 1981.

Strouf, J.L.H. *The Literature Teacher's Book of Lists.* West Nyack, N.Y.: Center for Applied Research in Education, 1993.

Titelman, G. Y. *Random House Dictionary of Popular Proverbs and Sayings.* New York: Random House, 1996.

Urdang, L., and J. Braunstein. *Every Bite a Delight and Other Slogans.* Detroit, Mich.: Visible Ink, 1992.

Urdang, L., W. W. Hunsinger, and N. LaRoche. *A Fine Kettle of Fish and Other Figurative Phrases.* Detroit, Mich.: Visible Ink Press, 1991.

Vanoni, M. *I've Got Goose Pimples: Our Great Expressions and How They Came to Be.* New York: Quill, 1989.

Index